Unzipped

HODDER &
STOUGHTON

First published in Great Britain in 2007 by Hodder & Stoughton
An Hachette Livre UK company

1

A CIP catalogue record for this title is available from the British Library

Hardback ISBN 978 0 340 93749 5
Trade Paperback ISBN 978 0 340 93750 1

Typeset in Sabon by Hewer Text UK Ltd, Edinburgh
Printed and bound by Mackays of Chatham Ltd, Chatham, Kent

Hodder Headline's policy is to use papers that are natural, renewable
and recyclable products and made from wood grown in sustainable
forests. The logging and manufacturing processes are expected to
conform to the environmental regulations of the country of origin.

Hodder & Stoughton Ltd
A division of Hodder Headline
338 Euston Road
London NW1 3BH

Picture acknowledgements

Unless otherwise stated, all photos are from the author's private collection. Hodder &
Stoughton has made every reasonable effort to contact copyright holders. If there have been
any inadvertent omissions, these can be corrected in future editions.

Section 1, page 3 top: EMI records; page 4 top: © Friedhelm Holleczek; page 5 top EMI
records, bottom: © Bob Gruen; page 6 top: © Bob Gruen; page 8: © Tony Timmington.
Second section, page 1: © Allan Ballard/Scope Features; page 2 top: © Paramount, bottom:
© Reg Wilson; page 4 top: © Allan Ballard/Scope Features; page 5 top: © Willie Rushton,
bottom: © Bob Gruen; page 6 top: © Gunta Andressen; page 7 bottom: © Juri Reetz;
page 8: © Vicki Tischler-Blue

This book is dedicated to my Mother's memory . . .
The only person in the world who knew me inside and out!

FOREWORD

....

I met Suzi when my late husband, Mickie Most, brought her to London from Detroit. Right from the first, I could see she had star quality. She was a one-off, and so determined. I knew she would definitely make it.

I called her parents, Helen and Art (remarkable people) to let them know that she was at my house and safe and sound. They asked me to look after her and of course I assured them I would. I've been doing so ever since and I always need to know she's ok.

Suzi set a trend and I know she will always be remembered as a forerunner.

Chris Most

ACKNOWLEDGEMENTS

....

Thank you to the following for being a part of my life and the journey so far and thank you to all my friends who contributed to this book. I found your words moving and humbling from A to Z. Here they are:

Diana Bailey, Ray Beavis, Jeff Beck, Vicki Tischler-Blue, Mike Chapman, Charles Dance, Pat Doonan, Andy Dowding, Colin Fry, Robbie Gladwell, Ronnie Hallin, Tom Hanks, Bob Harris, Noddy Holder, Ron Howard, Bill Kenwright, Andrew Lloyd Webber, Gary Marshal, Paul McCartney, Dave Neal, Tim Rice, Shirlie Roden, Farren Short, Henry Winkler, Reg Webb and Gudrun Wolter.

Thanks to Bill Ellis for all your help above and beyond the call of duty.

Thanks to Kevin Howlett, real radio magic.

Thanks to Cynthia Lennon who pointed me in the right direction. Thanks to Lynn and Skip and all the fans around the world, without you this book would have no reason to exist.

And most of all: my husband Rainer Haas (finally I met my match!); the Quatros from Italy and the Sanisleys from

Budapest who started it all; my mom, I still need you desperately; my dad, who taught me never to give more than 150% on stage; sister Arlene ('the devil made us do it'); Patti, ('you had a dream'); Nancy, ('my growing-up buddy, have you counted your fingers lately?') and brother Mickey, (you can still make me cry when you play the piano.

My two children, Laura (yes honey, I will 'walk through the fire with you') and Richard Tuckey, bitten by the same bug as me . . . don't ever give up!

Len Tuckey (for the good times).

Granddaughter Amy, attached at the hip.

Bill, Grandma and Granddad Tuckey. I miss you.

And special thanks to Chris and Mickie Most, Chris for writing the foreword and Mickie, who made it possible for me to live my dream.

Suzi Quatro

CONTENTS

....

INTRODUCTION

....

Knock knock knock.

'Who is it?'

'You've got five minutes!'

Shit. 'Okay.'

One last mirror check. Flick the hair. Throwing my towel around my neck I open the dressing room door, stride quickly down the hall, past the catering tent, past security, and finally into the very tunnel that a certain well-known fascist dictator walked through to make his speeches – a very spooky place to be, with echoes of *'Heil Hitler!'* bouncing off the walls. The venue the Waldbühne, the place Berlin, the date 3 June 2000, my fiftieth birthday.

I arrive backstage and greet the band. 'Hi, guys. All set?'

Honk honk. Tap tap. Ah ah ah ah ah ah ah. 'Testing one two three . . . testing one two three.'

'Right, everybody, pay attention! I want total concentration tonight. Keep the tempos up and watch me like a hawk – there's twenty-two thousand three hundred people out there and I don't want any fuck ups.'

I strap on my bass guitar, adjusting the tone and volume. *Boom boom boom*, pacing, waiting. *Please God, Let them like me tonight!* Now, let's see. First it's 'The Wild One', 'Tear Me Apart', 'She's in Love with You', *bang bang bang*, no stopping. Then 'Stumblin' in', segues into '48

1

Crash' and don't forget it starts with the bass drum only. Right. 'Glycerine Queen' into the bass solo, then the drum bit with Andy. For God's sake don't forget the new sequence! Then 'Can the Can', 'Devil Gate Drive'. False tabs. Straight into the guitar riff for 'If You Can't Give Me Love', with the acapella section. Okay, I think I've got it!

Tour manager: 'We're all set. You can announce her now.'

'Right, everybody. This is it. Have a good one!' *Please God, let them like me – especially tonight 'cos all my best friends are here!* I kiss my husband – 'Good luck, darling.'

'*Meine Damen und Herren . . . hier ist Suzi Quatro!*'

Screams. Applause. A shot of adrenalin. The intro tape begins. Guitar riff. 'Oh Suzi Q . . . oh Suzi Q . . . oh Suzi Q baby I love you my Suzi Q.' (Dale Hawkins.) The drummer, saxophonist, pianist, guitarist, trombonist and trumpet player walk out and take their places. Little Susie from Detroit takes a big breath and looks up to the heavens. Then . . .

Suzi Quatro strides to centre stage and the show begins.

23 October 2006, 12.23 p.m.

Can't believe I said yes. Ninety thousand words by the end of January – how the hell am I going to do that? But I've signed the contract, so there's no turning back.

Now, where am I gonna write? I need complete silence. . . . Hey, I got it – what could be better? Thank God I did all that grunt work and catalogued everything. Okay, let's get my ass up to the third floor. 'Ego Room. Mind your head' – I just love that sign. Jesus, look at all this stuff – videos, DVDs, scrapbooks, photos, awards, tour jackets, backstage passes, even my original leather jumpsuit hanging from the ceiling. Sometimes I can't believe I've been doing this job for forty-two years. Now, where the hell do I start?

I am little Susie from Detroit. I am Suzi Quatro. We are the same. We are different. Born Susan Kay Quatro, Detroit, Michigan, 3 June 1950, Gemini. 'Duality' is the keyword.

Are you ready? Then let's get unzipped! Little Susie first.

1
THE EARLY YEARS

....

Hi, little Susie here. I live in Grosse Pointe Woods, a very nice suburb of Detroit, alongside Eyties, Krauts, Polaks and Hunkies, second to last of five children born to Art Quatro (Italian) and Ilona Sanisley (Hungarian), known as Helen. Meet Arlene, born 24 November 1941, Mickey, the only boy, 12 June 1943, Patti, 10 March 1947, me, and baby Nancy, 29 August 1953. The first-born, half-sister Carol, Dad created 'out of wedlock' (shame on you!) just before seducing Mum by goosing her in the ass at the local Saturday night dance. Didn't mention his kid until she was hooked. Mom had unusual beauty – high Hungarian cheekbones, hazel eyes, perfect soft pale skin, rosy red cheeks and large white teeth (the last two of which I inherited), and a large ass – hence the goosing! They danced, then he drove her home and serenaded her on his little ukulele while gushing with love for his family. Little did she know what a stinker he was. The virginity that Mom saved until the age of twenty-five was soon to bite the dust. In her words, 'Garlic and paprika – boy, oh boy, what a mix!

Fast forward a few years. It's 1953, and I was three years old when new baby sister Nancy came home from hospital, delivered by caesarean. Both mother and child nearly died. We were all strict Catholics so the doctors were obliged to ask, 'Mr Quatro, there's a problem. Who should we save – mother or child?' To which he replied, 'Godammit – save them both!' This is my earliest memory.

I was watching from the porch as Mom slowly climbed out of the family station wagon, cradling the new addition. She put Nancy into her crib for a nap – then jealousy reared its head. Creeping quietly into the bedroom, I took my sister's tiny, perfect little hand into my mouth and bit her fingers.

I hid in the bathroom, giggling, as I heard the commotion. 'What on earth is the matter with this baby? Why is she crying so hard?'

Four years later, lying in bed, guilt came rushing in. 'I'm sorry, Nancy,' I shouted across the passage. 'God, I am so sorry.'

'What are you talking about?' Nancy shouted back.

'Well,' I sobbed, 'when you were a little baby I bit your fingers.' I really was crying hard – that gulping kind when you can't get any air into your lungs. '*Please* forgive me!'

And, on the subject of fingers, this was not an isolated incident. In kindergarten there was a bully named Billy, and one day when he was throwing his weight around I finally snapped. With all the strength a six-year-old could muster I slammed a door on his fingers and nearly severed them! Maybe I should apologise to Billy too. But you know what? I don't think I will! We Quatros are made of tough stuff.

My grandfather, Michael Quattrocchi, emigrated to New York from Italy at the tender age of nine, never to see his parents again. When he arrived, the authorities took one look at his name – unspellable, unpronounceable – and told him he was now Mike Quatro. So no, to all those people who ask – it may sound like a stage name but it isn't. He eventually married a fifteen-year-old fellow Italian, Laura Boscolli, and after being an itinerant miner for some time ended up in Detroit where the car industry was starting to boom.

Grandpa Quatro was the person I loved most in the whole world. He always had time for this affection-starved little girl from a big family, and there are many snapshots of me either sitting on his lap or standing by hanging on to his hand. In one treasured picture Grandpa is watching his favourite TV show on the black-and-white set in their living room, me perched on a chair in front, and to this day I can hear his voice: 'Susanna, shhhhht! *Bonanza*!' It was one of the only times I was ever quiet.

No matter which state or city you lived in in those days, nationalities stayed within their ethnic neighbourhoods. So Grandpa never got to grips with the English language and was very hard to understand. We all complained, but he strenuously denied there was any problem. 'Whadda you say to me? Idona unddastanda. I no atalka lika dat.' So cute! He was both a man's man and a ladies' man, a wonderful cook, and good-looking enough to have been a movie star. Tall, with wavy hair and dimples in his cheeks – my ideal man. The funny thing is that Rainer, my husband, bears an uncanny resemblance to him, and to make matters worse Rainer was born on 3 March, the same day as my dad (make something of that if you will!).

When Grandpa was ninety-seven, lying in a hospital bed with nothing wrong except old age, I spoke to him from England and will never forget his words to me. 'Susanna, I donna want you to worry. Everything she gonna be okay.

Ets'a my time. The quality ova my life, shesa over. I go now
. . .' And he did. Michael Quattrocchi lived like a man, and
died like a man. I love you, Grandpa!

Laura, Grandma Quatro, was way before her time – liber-
ated, outspoken and tough as nails. She was tiny, just about five
foot tall, and very pretty even in her old age. A strong dis-
ciplinarian, she spanked us many a time with her dreaded
wooden spoon. She had only just turned sixteen when my dad
was born, and really they were more like brother and sister.
Grandma was always over at our house, which caused jealousy
and resentment in my mother who always felt she took second
place and wasn't good enough in her mother-in-law's eyes. But
there was one incident for which Mom never forgave her.

Dad, a typical Italian, always had trouble keeping his
trousers zipped up. After getting one girl pregnant (Grandpa
insisted his son marry her so the child would not be a bastard,
although the couple never spent a single night together and an
annulment quickly followed) he went on to seduce and marry
Mom, producing two children in quick succession. But it didn't
stop there. Dad held down two jobs, General Motors in the
daytime and playing music at night. It was at one of these gigs
that he decided to dally with someone who can only be
described as a groupie. She showed up one day at my grandparents' house, where Mom and Dad were still living, and she
was pregnant and angry – not a good combination.

Mom shared this story with me on her final visit to England
before she died in 1991. 'There I was, Arlene and Mickey
holding my hands, as I answered the door to this pregnant
young woman who said, "Your husband is the father of my
child." I nearly died, Susan – very nearly died.'

'Wow, Mom! Why didn't you leave him?'

'Because . . . where would I go? I had no training for work, I had two children, and most importantly I loved your father.'

When Dad returned from his day job, the shit hit the fan. Mom recalled, 'He told me that if I left him he would become a tramp and travel on the trains.' Then Grandma stepped in big time and gave Dad the telling off of his life, reminding him that he had a family and this was where his loyalty must lie. Mom always felt it was Grandma's influence and not his love for her that kept them together, and consequently disliked Laura for evermore.

Dad wrote a song about this time of his life, called 'Slipping Out of My Arms'.

Slipping Out of My Arms

I've had a sweet dream broken, so now my heart I'll open
And tell you why I feel so blue, it's because I'm losing you

Not long ago we were in love
Just like a pair of turtle doves,
But now you're slipping, slipping out of my arms.

We used to have our share of fun, now I'm afraid that it's all done
Because you're slipping, slipping out of my arms.

I know you used to love me just as much as I loved you,
And our love was beautiful to see.
Suddenly you changed and now I don't know what to do
Because I know your love was never meant for me.

I dreamed of going on through life, with you beside me as my wife.
Instead you're slipping, slipping out of my arms.

(Art Quatro)

Many times we talked of this, my mother and me. She always said, 'You can forgive, but you can never forget.'

Compared with Dad's family, Mom's struggled. They lived on the poor side of town, and we used to make weekend trips with food and other essentials. I often commented on the 'smell' where they lived. Mom said it was the factories, but I know now it was poverty.

Mom's father, Jonos (Grandpa John Sanisley), I never knew – he died from lung cancer before I was born. He was a brilliant linguist, speaking five languages fluently. Mom always said he was not a happy man: a drinker, and physically abusive, he had never recovered from the death of his son Johnny, who was shot in the back by a crazy neighbour who thought he was stealing her chickens.

Marushka (Grandma Mary Sanisley) had met and married Jonos in Budapest, where she had daughter Isabella before emigrating to the States. When Mom was born they were living in Indiana. Grandma spoke very little English – she and Mum communicated in Hungarian – and because of a stroke, which had caused one of her eyes to go up into her head, she scared the shit out of me as a child. Whenever I heard, 'Sushi, Sushi, come give Grandma kiss', I used to run away.

Grandma died when I was six years old, and on the day of the funeral, I came down the stairs, collapsed and was put to bed with a very high fever. I guess I wasn't supposed to go to her burial. My mother's description of her end is quite beautiful. 'She was very ill, just hanging on. I finally arrived at the hospital, going immediately to her bed. She said in Hungarian, "Ilona, you made it. I waited for you." Then she passed away. On the way home I turned on the radio, and on came "Catch a falling star and put it in your pocket, never let it fade away". Maroushka watches me from heaven to this day. I can feel it.'

The neighbourhood I grew up in was great: doors were never locked, within a four-block radius everyone knew everyone, else (and we were all big families with lots of kids), so we were in and out of each other's houses all day long. My best friend, Linda, lived two doors away. The Theuerkorns were a German–Italian family, with one boy and four girls just like the Quatros, and of similar ages too. Linda and I met when we were five, and remain friends to this day – she made a wonderful surprise appearance on my *This Is Your Life* in 1999. Back when we were kids, if I wasn't sleeping over at Linda's she was sleeping at my house. God, we were so close! I remember kneeling down in front of the crucifix in Mom's bedroom praying that Linda would be allowed to spend the night. How sick is that? Praying should be for more important things. But I guess when you're that young sleepovers are essential.

One day when we were six we were really bored, and then I had an idea. 'Hey, Linda, why don't we get that huge bag of potato chips, spread them on the floor and slide across the kitchen like a big skating rink?' So we did. Those chips were great – *whoosh*, like magic from one end of the room to the other – until mid-slide Mrs Theuerkorn came in. 'What do you kids think you're doing? Susie Kay, I think you'd better go home right now,' she yelled as she roughly bundled me into my snowsuit. On another dull afternoon we were sitting in Linda's bedroom when I decided, for some unknown reason, to twist the hands off the alarm clock. On that occasion Noreen, Linda's scary older sister, came in and grabbed the clock, screaming, 'Go home, Susie Kay. Go break your own goddam clocks!'

In my defence can I just say that I was a highly energetic child, just this side of hyper. Our family doctor once said, 'Mrs Quatro, please don't ever give this child vitamins!' Shy but talkative, always anxious to please, raised to be a 'good' Catholic girl. When I'm good, I'm very very good. When I'm bad, I'm better!

I attended Catholic school for first grade only, the reason being Sister Inez (nasty little Sister Inez – sorry, God!). She had it in for me from day one and finally, in desperation, called Mum in to discuss my 'energy levels'. While she was explaining how nervous I made her I was running around in circles and somehow got my hands tangled up in her rosary beads. Saint and sinner tumbled to the floor in a heap. 'See what I mean,' she screamed. Mom immediately enrolled me in the regular school across the street – Amen, praise the Lord.

And, while I'm on the subject of prayers and all things holy, it's confession time. I always had this thing about being liked. (*Excuse me, little Susie from Detroit, even though you are telling the first part of this story I, Suzi Quatro, may cut in every now and again just in case there's something important you leave out. Is that okay? Okay, that's fine.*) So I decided that after school I would buy all my friends some ice cream. Problem was, where to get the money from. Idea! Sneaking into church after school, I went to the side of the altar where you can light a candle for your loved ones and – oh, my God, did I really do this? (*Yes, you did, and may your soul burn in hell. . . . Hey, just kidding – after all, you were only seven.*) But Catholics major in guilt. Next week, kneeling in the

confessional box – 'In the name of the Father, the Son and the
Holy Ghost . . . bless me, Father, for I have sinned' – 'Yes, my
child, and what is it you've done?' whispered Father Barton.
'Well, you know those collection boxes next to the altar—'
That's as far as I got. The light inside the box went off as the
priest jumped out of his seat. Robes swishing, rosary clicking,
he was coming to get me. Holy shit! I legged it out of there as
fast as I could.

Five kids means attention is divided five ways, and to do this
equally is impossible, even with the best of intentions. I felt
like the little orphan in the family, the one that just didn't fit
in, the horse nobody bet on, the voice no one heard. Consequently I grew up feeling insecure. At night I had regular
nightmares, and Mom said she could hear me pacing the floor
for hours. In my dreams 'entities' would take my hand and
lead me down a long tunnel. Curious to a fault, I would
follow. But once I nearly couldn't get back. As I struggled to
wake up I swear I saw two arms rising back to the ceiling –
two arms that had been holding me down. I finally broke
though the barrier, and woke screaming and crying.

   Once, Mom and Dad went for a rare evening out and were
late getting back. Time went on and my mind wandered into
'what if' land, as only a six-year-old imagination can do.
What if they don't come back? What if they've had a car
accident? What if I really am an orphan now? They did, of
course, return that evening, but this did nothing whatsoever
to allay my feeling of being alone.

   In 1958 we had the first big wedding in the Quatro family. I
was eight, and at seventeen my eldest sister Arlene was going
to marry her eighteen-year-old sweetheart Leo. (By the time

she was twenty-five I was an aunt three times over – Leo, Davey and actress Sherilynn Fenn of *Twin Peaks* fame.) So this first family wedding was a big deal – book the Grosse Pointe Yacht club, order the dress, the cake, the invitations, and afterwards frame the picture for the wall. Perhaps we should just pause there for a moment. Arlene's actually been married seven times ('Well, at least I always searched for the truth,' she says). By the time she was on number four Dad got so tired of framing and reframing the wedding photo that he simply cut out husband number three's head and pasted on the latest one.

Anyway, when her first wedding was being planned, everyone in the family seemed to have a part to play: Mom as the mother of the bride, Dad as the father of the bride, brother Mickey as an usher, sister Patti as a bridesmaid, and youngest sister Nancy, beautiful, perfect little Nancy, as a flower girl. But what about me? One evening I caught Mom and Dad discussing the forthcoming event, and I believe it was destiny that I overheard this conversation.

'What are we going to do about Susie?' asked Dad.

'Well, Art, I guess at the very least we better get her a new dress.'

And on the day there I was, in my new blue dress, holding the train of my sister's wedding gown as she walked out of the church, trying hard to look like I was at least part of the festivities. Later on, at the reception, I climbed into one of the ushers' laps and 'pretended' to fall asleep – I guess I needed to feel close to someone. I overheard my dad remark, 'Jesus, Helen, look at Susie – there's no need for that kind of behaviour!'

(*Well, in hindsight from where I am now in my life, I see it as a positive thing. Whether they did or didn't ignore you, you perceived it that way. So you became me because of this. In a way the family gave you your career and the absolute need to be heard and succeed against all odds. And that ain't a bad thing – you should really say thank you!)*

It was Dad's two jobs that enabled us to live in Grosse Pointe. Yeah, sure, we always had a nice car, food in our stomachs and clean clothes – but what we didn't have was all the latest fashions. Clothing five kids was expensive, and Mom was both frugal and practical. I remember feeling embarrassed that my clothes were 'copies' of the real thing. I even had a kilt that didn't open up at the side but was stitched together. And I got Patti's hand-me-downs – problem was, she's six feet tall and I'm five foot two. Somehow or other, I always felt not good enough.

Marylou Ball and her sister Nan were among my best friends and their dad had a better-paid job at Ford, which meant they got the best of everything. They were even given a brand-new Ford Mustang each when they turned sixteen. Jealous? Bet your sweet ass I was, but at least Marylou and I got to cruise the neighburhood in style.

During my early school years I wanted so badly to be in the popular crowd, but didn't feel I was good enough. So I offered to share my candy with the 'in' crowd, in exchange for membership. They took the candy – then they turned me down. So when I think of my schooldays it's with mixed feelings. Aptitude-wise I was in the top twenty-five per cent and always hung around with the smart kids, but grade-wise I was average except for the subjects I loved – music, sport and English. I also found my forte on the typewriter. I'm like lightning on a keyboard, and I even take shorthand. Even today I can key faster than my computer can process it – I always have to wait for it to catch up.

It's funny how you never remember yourself like your friends do. Not long ago I was in Miami walking along a beach with Marylou when she said, 'It's no wonder you made it – you were always so "focused".'

'I don't remember it that way, Lou Lou. . . . Hey, do you remember those granny dresses your parents bought us in New York? Yours was blue, mine was red. I wish I could find that picture – we looked so cute.'

'Yeah, I wish I could find that picture too – I've looked everywhere.' Long pause. 'Who was it that had on the wrong shoes?'

Of course, she knew perfectly well that it was me, because neither Marylou nor her sister Nan would be caught dead in the 'wrong' anything! Now, these kind of fashion faux pas can push you either way – fashion-mad or I don't give a damn. Since I am a blue jeans and T-shirt girl my direction is obvious, although it must be said they have to be *good* jeans and T-shirts and fit me skin-tight – don't forget I was rear of the year in 1982. (*Wouldn't it be great to win that again, the wrong side of 50! Remember what your sisters said – that you won 'asshole' of the year?*)

Pyjama parties were all the rage when I was growing up, and it was at one of these that I reckon I learned a valuable lesson. We had done the slow song crying over boys thing (I didn't join in because I thought it was really stupid) and the scary stories, and had had some popcorn and been raided by the boys, when I had a great idea. 'Why don't we play a game? All we have to do is say something truthful to the person next to us.' I thought it would be interesting. Wrong. What it turned into was insult after insult as each girl in turn unburdened herself. As much as I am a lover of truth it seems that diplomacy is a much safer bet. (*Don't pretend you learned that one, Susie – to this day your mouth gets your ass in trouble.*) Fair enough!

One night in 1962 I had my making out, necking, whatever you want to call it, debut. It was nearly Christmas and I had been invited for a sleepover at my friend Carol's house. I was absolutely amazed at all the gifts, not only under the tree but piled up in several rooms. Carol told me they were allowed to open one present each day for the ten days leading up to the 25th. Well, they *were* very rich – huge house, lots of cars, live-in home help – in fact typical Grosse Pointe on the street where the 'mansions' were.

Anyway, we did the usual – ate pizza, had popcorn with a movie – until it was time for bed, but I wasn't sleepy. Somehow I ended up in the basement where Carol's older brother Gregg was listening to some music, and I guess the timing must have been right. First we danced a little, and then he put on Gene Pitney's 'Half Heaven Half Heartache' and we began kissing – that's it, just kissing. After all, I was only twelve years old. This went on for four hours while Gene Pitney sang the same song over and over again. Isn't it amazing how long you can smooch when you're that young? I met up with Gregg again in 2001 in Florida, and now possess a snapshot of us doing just that – kissing! Back in 1962 I wore his silver identity bracelet for about six months, and then that particular 'romance' bit the dust.

Dad's routine – up at 5.30 a.m., off to the plant, back at 5 p.m., quick dinner, short nap, gig at 8p.m., home at 1a.m. –

meant we hardly ever saw him. How the hell he found time to get my mother pregnant a total of eight times (she miscarried three) I don't know. Mom used to warn us never to marry a musican – so what did I do? I became one. Always figured Dad got it right and Mom got the short end of the stick.

Her life was cooking, cleaning and raising five kids, while fostering a total of nine orphans over the years. She did all this unselfishly, with unconditional love. But I would love to have seen her truly smile just once. The lasting memory I carry with me of my mom is that she was unfullfilled. Had she had the chance she could have done so much more with her life, and my sisters are in agreement (*Mmmm, I'm beginning to see the picture now. Starting to understand you, little Susie. Why don't you put in that poem you wrote for your mom – I think it's important.*)

A Mother

A mother's face, one more cradle to rock
A mother's place, cold heart to unlock
Day after day, no pleasure in sight,
Is there no way to ease her plight?

A lonely smile sweeps her broom
Dust of emptiness fills the room
Pictures of children share the wall
Night after night shadows fall
On barren seeds within her womb

A mother's face so soft to touch
Was it my disgrace I needed so much

(S. Quatro, 1988)

16

(*You know, if I remember correctly she didn't like that poem at all. Didn't she actually throw it away?*) I presented it to her, framed with a picture of her holding me as a baby – I thought it was beautiful. But the next time I visited them I noticed one of my press pictures hanging there instead. 'It seemed such a waste of a pretty frame, Mom Susan,' said. (*Interesting analogy, don't you think? What a waste of a pretty frame.*) After her death in 1991, I found the poem perfectly preserved in a plastic cover in her bedroom drawer. Mom, I never meant to hurt you. It wasn't that you didn't give me enough. It's as the last line says – I needed too much!

While I was researching this book an amazing thing happened. One morning I was thinking about Mom's religious beliefs, which were strong throughout her life. I grabbed a large folder full of various items from my past – there must have been over a hundred pieces of paper and paraphernalia. As I was rifling through them an envelope fell out on to the floor, address side up: to Susan Kay Quatro, Atlantic Hotel, Cromwell Road . . . it was from my mother. Inside were several holy cards (she always sent these with the appropriate prayer on the back, depending on what kind of problems I was having), some stage reviews of my brother's concerts and a letter dated to me dated 15 September 1972. I just *know* I didn't find this by accident. So here's an open letter to Mom.

> To Helen (Ilona Ottila) Sanisley
> 'Pearly Gates'
> Angels corner
> Heaven

Dear Mom,

You were so religious – a strict Catholic right till the end. Thank you for your unconditional love, your unconditional

17

support, the valuable lessons you taught me and our shared belief in all things holy. I so loved attending mass with you in the States, in England, throughout our life together. If there is any justice you are an angel in heaven, because you were surely one on earth. I pray that I am living my life through your example. I am your daughter through and through. God bless you, Mom. Rest in peace. If I had one wish it would be to spend just one more day with you. I love you.

Your daughter Susan Kay Quatro

xxxxxxooooooxxxxxx

PS: I'm gonna start going to church again, as soon as this book is finished. That's a promise!

So Dad was a party animal and Mom a homemaker. And me? Well, I got Dad's zest for life and Mom's heart – I think like a man but with the emotions of a woman. In my quest to understand what made me tick, and why I couldn't just coast along like everyone else, I was either talking ten to the dozen or comatose, ridiculously happy or suicidal, and with a never-ending need to communicate. I would jump from topic to topic expecting everyone to follow me . . . Everything I did had a sense of urgency. So I must thank Dad for giving me my first astrology book when I was about ten years old. Flicking immediately to my own birth sign, Gemini, I began to read – and Eureka! So that's the reason I am like I am.

Now Dad was a bullshit artist of the highest degree. Once, back in 1970, Mom, Dad, Patti, Nancy and I boarded the double-decker El Capitane train for the ride three days and two nights to Las Vegas. We were planning to see Wayne Newton, an absolute legend in Vegas, live at Caesar's Palace –

but it was sold out. So what did my dad do? He marched up to the front of the queue and explained to the casino manager, 'I am a big director from General Motors and I *might* bring my entire company to your hotel on our next annual outing.' Snap your fingers, say abracadabra and 'Right this way, Mr Quatro. We have the best seats in the house for you and your family.' As we walked past the waiting stars and customers, with our noses in the air, I overheard someone remark, 'Who the hell is that?' Classic!

I too have always had more than my fair share of bravado. At ten years old, on our annual Easter break driving down to Florida, I remember writing to the huge American television comic Red Skelton: 'Dear Mr Skelton, I am very funny and would love to appear on your television show. I would appreciate it if you could give me a job. Please write back right away. Love, Susie Quatro, 1101 Torrey Road, Grosse Pointe Woods, Michigan.' He didn't reply.

Life in the Quatro household was very 'showbiz' – every family get-together, from birthdays and Easter to Thanksgiving and Christmas, was an excuse to put on some kind of performance. My particular party pieces were 'Hit the Road, Jack', with six-foot-tall sister Patti (I, of course, sang the male part) and 'Five Foot Two' with baby sister Nancy. (God, all these height references – do you think I have a Napoleon complex?) One particularly memorable rendition took place early one morning in 1959. Nancy and I noticed an ambulance pulling up across the street. Dad ran out to see if he could help and came back saying that Mr Mohe had just died of a heart attack. Light bulb over my head . . . 'Hey, Nancy, why don't we go over and sing Mrs Mohe a song, she could probably use some cheering up.' Yep, I know, but it seemed like a good idea at the time! Donning full finery, we pranced across the street ready to do our good deed for the day. Ding dong . . . break into song. 'Five foot two, eyes of blue, you know what those eyes . . .' Bang, the door slammed shut. Were we punished? You bet your ass – for a week!

Mom and Dad had their arguments, as all parents do. But Dad, being Dad, couldn't resist the opportunity to turn every event, good or bad, into a 'show'. So mid-argument, on the excuse of needing the toilet, he would sneak out to the kitchen and instruct us kids to 'get some Kleenex and the violin and wait for my cue'. Then, as Mom's crying and complaining reached its peak, Dad would motion us to begin crying into our hankies and playing the fiddle in a mock funeral dirge. I can't remember if Mom laughed. (*Don't think she did!*)

'You kids are talented and beautiful – every single one of you.' Oh, yes, Dad, your sacred loins could produce no less. (*Thank God he doesn't live in England, or it would be quite crowded up here in the Ego Room.*) Anyway, the talented part I believed, but the beautiful bit not really – it's one of my insecurities. I was cute, short and chubby (Dad used to call me his 'little fat sausage'). And now, as an adult, I realize that of course I am cute, short and . . . slim! Hooray!

In the Quatro house there were two pianos, one in the front room and one in the basement, two accordions, one with a French scale which is pitched slighter higher than a regular one and gives it its sound, a violin, a banjo, a ukulele, and . . . a bass.

We were all encouraged to play as many instruments as possible and given whatever lessons we asked for – on the condition that we practised daily. One bad report would result in the lessons being cancelled, which happened to me only once.

It's fair to say that we Quatros are a very musically talented family. Let's start with Dad. Art Quatro was a child prodigy on the violin and went on to teach himself keyboards of every kind, plus accordion and bass. And although he had to have a day job due to his huge family, he started up a booking agency and became the most popular bandleader in the area, playing for weddings, high society parties, dances – you name it. When we went out locally as a family everyone recognized him, and I was always proud of this. (*You were more than proud, Susie. You wanted to be a part of it, didn't you? Don't forget the Oakland Hills Country Club, his regular Sunday gig. You were paid twenty-five cents to sit in front of his jazz trio and play 'Mack the Knife' on your bongo drums. Mom never knew*.) So, over to Mom. She sang, as did her relatives in Hungary, particularly in the church. Arlene played harp when she was young (I think her halo slipped a bit, though!), also piano, and she too sings.

And now to my big brother Mickey, Michael Arlen Quatro, who deserves his own chapter and has sold many albums in his own right, the biggest being *Collaboration with the Gods*. He's just this side of genius, just a little crazy (these two traits often go hand in hand) and, oh, so gifted. I speak from my heart when I say he's the best piano player I've ever heard. It's unbelievable what he can do. It would take two normal pianists to play all the notes he manages with two hands – they move across the keys like lightning. I grew up listening to him playing Rachmaninov, Bach, Beethoven and his absolute masterpiece, the theme from *Dr Zhivago* – you would swear there was an entire orchestra playing. He can always reduce me to tears, because his playing is truly touched by God.

Mickey played gigs with my dad from a very young age,

dressed in his mini-adult suit and wowing the audiences. The adulation continued into his teenage years as he appeared nationwide on TV. In the seventies he started up a booking agency and put on many successful festivals, still playing a little piano on this side. Then, after witnessing the rock star phenomenon first hand (sex and drugs and rock and roll), he decided he would *be* one – which he is not. He is a classical pianist . . . a classical pianist . . . a classical pianist. God, the amount of times I tried to cram that into his brain! But after my success as a rock and roll musician/singer he was determined to do the same.

My brother married young, had two kids, then found himself a mistress and eventually divorced. His second wife, Lyn, was the love of his life. In the early seventies she shot herself in the head after an argument with him and died, after which he started to experiment with crack cocaine. The funny thing is he was a non-smoker and a non-drinker, but, typical of his character, he jumped in at the deep end and began frequently freebasing. My parents, especially Mom, went through hell – Dad was somehow able to switch off his emotions. Mom was always Mickey's great protector, loving him unconditionally and forgiving him everything. Her constant refrain throughout her life was 'Take care of your brother. He has a heart of gold but he's my lost little lamb. So never stop loving him.' We all sometimes wonder if Mickey's addiction played a part in triggering the cancer that took Mum's life.

In 2000 I threw a big New Year's Eve party at my home in Essex and flew him over as my guest. Imagine my son and his friends – eighteen-year-old heavy metal merchants – standing there, listening to Mickey play . . . and crying. He gets everyone that way and should have been a huge star. Mickey and I are both Geminis and have many similar traits, good and bad. The difference is that mine work for me but Mickey's definitely work against him.

Other things were not shared, though I didn't realize it for some time. For years I celebrated my birthday on 12 June, and it wasn't until I needed my birth certificate for school that Mom noticed the mistake. 'Goodness, Susie! *Mickey* was born on 12 June and *your* birthday is 3 June.' Mom had so many kids she was bound to get things confused sometimes. Hey, God, assuming I arrive at the golden gates after my older brother, he'd better be there in prime position, sitting at a white Steinway and playing 'Smile' (Mom's favourite song) to welcome me. Here is a poem my mother sent me during Mickey's darkest drug days. She wanted me to turn it into a song, but I couldn't do it because no melody seemed appropriate.

Blinded by the White

Cocaine the devil's game
Hits the brain, drives you insane,
Blinded by the white.

Takes you up to heaven, and throws you down to hell.
Cocaine you're under its spell.
Blinded by the white.

A life of pain, your time and money spent.
On cocaine trips you went.
Blinded by the white

God gave you a good body, not to be a zombie.
But to be somebody.
Blinded by the white

Curb your appetite before it's too late.
Get help fast, don't wait.
Till you are blinded by the white.

(Helen Quatro)

This poem was written in 1978, the same year that I received a frantic phone call from my father while in California. He said that if I wanted to see my brother alive again, I'd better come to Detroit immediately. Both my parents hoped that where they had failed to get through, I would succeed. 'He respects your success, Susie, and he just might hear you,' Dad explained. 'You are our last hope.' I flew back that very evening. At Mickey's house I slowly walked up the path to the front door, wanting to see – but also *not* wanting to see – inside. There were no carpets, no furniture, no curtains – just a few lightbulbs and one swinging chair hanging from the ceiling. Then I saw my brother, thin and white. He smiled an empty wide smile, trying desperately to convey to me that all was normal. Then he proceeded to tell me that his career was going wonderfully and he was selling lots of albums – just one minute away from huge success. But his darting eyes told a different story.

I listened as long as I could, till I could stand no more. 'Mickey, what are you doing to yourself? Look at this place – look how you're living. I have a question. Is the high you get from crack cocaine worth the low that follows?'

'Yes,' he replied.

I looked at him long and hard, my heart breaking. 'Mickey, if you don't stop what you're doing, you will die.' I gave him a hug, told him 'I love you', kissed his cheek and said goodbye.

My parents and I drove back home in silence. I flew back to California the next morning not knowing if I had done any good or if I would see my brother again.

And as for the musical talents of the rest of the family? Patti, has a strong voice, plays good guitar and piano, can score music and had a stint in California-based all-girl band Fanny. When all three sisters joined me for a TV special in England back in 1998, recorded live for ITV at the Minerva Theatre in Chichester, and the comment was made that 'She goes for it, Suzi – just like you.' Patti was the 'good' one of the family, a top-level student who never caused any trouble and was the apple of Dad's eye. Both Pisceans, they had a special understanding of each other.

As for me, I play piano, bass, guitar and percussion, for all of which I can read and write. I can sing and dance too, and did so at every opportunity. While everyone else did just one song at our family get-togethers, I would do three – a 'ham' from the start! And finally Nancy, the prettiest in the family without a doubt, plays violin and piano. Her voice was operatically trained and Mom used to call her 'my little nightingale'.

In 1958 there was a nationwide search for young musicians to form a junior band who would become a regular feature on the *Lawrence Welk Show*, a very popular TV variety programme which was filmed in California. My brother got the job of pianist and went to live with my dad's sister Aunty Dee in La Canada, a suburb of LA. After the first transmission, featuring Mike Quatro doing a solo spot, we made the front page of the Grosse Pointe newspaper. I went into school that day feeling so proud. A huge, scary, imposing woman called Dr Fenton taught music, and during class she suddenly reeled on me, saying, 'So, Miss Quatro . . . since your brother is so famous, and your family is so musical, you must be able to tell us what a quartet is.'

Well, of course I knew the answer, but could I get it out? 'Um . . . um . . . three?'

These things come back to haunt us. Years later I was on holiday in Miami when I took a phone call from record producer Mickie Most.

'Suzi, I'm in the middle of mixing your tracks and want to add a string quartet, but I didn't want to spend your money without asking you.'

'Great,' I said. 'Go ahead, do it. What a good idea. How many strings is that?'

Long pause. 'Four,' said a bemused Most.

It was at the age of five that something unforgettable happened in my musical world. I even know the exact date: 6 January 1957. Arlene and I were watching the *Ed Sullivan Show*, a Sunday night must for the majority of American families. 'Ladies and gentleman, here he is . . . Elvis Presley.' Pandemonium broke out and Elvis went into 'Don't Be Cruel'. This moment is forever burned into my psyche – Arlene was screaming, I was mesmerized, and when Elvis went 'Mmmmm' I felt my first sexual thrill, although I didn't know what it was at the time. I was hooked. Then in stormed our dad, who looked at us, looked at the screen and switched it off, saying, 'That's disgusting.' And in that moment Suzi Quatro was born. It never occurred to me that Elvis was a *man* – I just knew I was going to be like him. A little while later my dad came home from work and threw a disc on the hallway table. 'Okay, dammit – so the kid can sing!' It was a copy of 'Love Me Tender'. Before my mother died in 1991, she gave me a copy of a poem I had written a little while after seeing the 'king' for the first time.

Hey Rock and Roll Star

It didn't take much to make you believe again
Now that the depression is over
You're all shook up,
And the people are cheering
And the people want you
And the people love you
No, it didn't take much
To make you believe again.

(Susie Quatro, 1957)

After falling in love with Elvis I decided, at seven years old, that I wanted to be a beatnik, and began wearing a beret on my head, with a fake cigarette dangling from my mouth, beating on imaginary drums and reciting poetry. I begged my dad for a set of real bongos so I could perfect my act. Two weeks before Christmas I began my annual search around the house for presents and discovered, at the back of my dad's closet, a beautiful set of drums. Honest to a fault, when he came home from work I piped up, 'Hey, Dad, I found my Christmas present!'

'Susie, do you mean those bongos in my closet? Do you know how much they cost? Do you really think I would give a two hundred-dollar set of drums to a little girl like you!'

I was devastated . . . then, on Christmas Day, they *were* mine! I have slides of me sitting in front of the tree with the rest of the family, hands poised in bongo-playing action and happy as can be.

After I fell in love with Elvis music in general became my passion. Luckily, because I had older siblings I was able to listen to all those fantastic sounds from the fifties and sixties. I have vivid memories of Arlene, with a blonde DA (duck's ass) haircut, button-down shirt, bobby socks, loafers, and bermuda shorts, doing line dances to the latest hits in the basement with her girlfriends. Do-wop was fading into the beginning of rock and roll and it was so exciting. It's still my favourite era today, and it's the music I feature on the regular radio show I've done since 1999, *Rockin' with Suzi Q* on Rockin' Radio 2.

When Arlene married and moved on, Patti's record collection grabbed my interest – Neil Sedaka, Jimmy Gilmer and the Fireballs, the Jive Five and many more. But I didn't have my own record player, and Patti kept her records locked up in a box. Thank God I found the key and was able to satisfy my lust for music. These records were all the more important because they were somebody else's. I felt it was forbidden, and we all know how exciting that can be. I still remember getting my first transistor radio. I took it to bed, plugged in the earphone and stuck it under my pillow as the Beach Boys' 'Surfin' Safari' thrilled my ears.

So as the fifties turned into the sixties there I was going to school, fretting about my figure, squeezing blackheads, wondering if a certain boy liked me, listening to music, going to school dances, studying, playing in the orchestra, hanging out with my friends – waiting for my life to begin. I resided in Nowheresville, USA, and had no idea where my life was heading.

Mom once asked me, 'Susie, where are you always running to?'

'I don't know, Mom. To my future?' I was so anxious to get there.

2
DREAMS CAN COME TRUE

....

It's 1964, I'm fourteen years old, and again the Quatro family is watching the *Ed Sullivan Show*. 'Now for all you young-sters out there [screams!] sh . . . sh! . . . calm down now . . . Here they are, all the way from England. *The Beatles!*'

'Oh, my God!' I said. 'Patti, look at their hair. It's so long! Aren't they cute?'

It was a moment that changed our world of music for ever. The phone rang, and Patti and I raced to separate extensions. It was Marylou and Nan Ball (probably dressed perfectly), and they were as excited as we were. Then all of a sudden Patti said, 'Hey, why don't we form an all-girl band?'

Silence. We were stunned for a moment, then all four voices started talking at once.

'I'll play drums,' said Nan.

'I'll play rhythm guitar,' said Marylou.

'I'll take lead guitar,' said Patti, 'and we can get Diana Baker to play piano.' Diana's dad played clarinet in my dad's band.

'What about me?' I demanded.

'Susie, you will play the bass.'

I had no choice. From that day on we were a band.

I went back into the TV room and enquired, 'Hey, Dad, do you have a bass guitar?'

'Sure,' he said.

Destiny knocks yet again. While all the other girls made do with cheap instruments, my dad gave me (pay attention, guitar anoraks) the Rolls-Royce of bass guitars – a 1957 original Fender Precision, gold scratch plate, with a stripe up the back of the neck and a beige Fender bassman amp too! (*Well, you sure fucked up that bass case, didn't you, Susie? You did go through a 'jerky' stage – tell 'em what you did.*) Okay – but I call it my 'hippy' phase. I was looking for the meaning of life when I splodged brown paint all over that wonderful original Fender case. The spots of eternity are square, so maybe 'jerky' is the right adjective. This was the time when I lived in the basement of our house in Grosse Pointe, burning incense and devouring every sacred phrase that Bob Dylan uttered. But to this day I've kept that bass guitar, which now hangs on the wall in my front lounge. John Entwistle of the Who, an avid collector of basses, once offered me a thousand dollars for it. Well, John, that's one you didn't get!

The Fender Precision has the widest neck of all basses and is the most difficult one to master, but back in 1964 I didn't know this. I practised, using only my thumb on my right hand, until it was blistered and bleeding. Then a guy in one of the local teenage bands, showed me how to use my index and middle finger to pluck the sound out – any 'real' bass player knows that this is the only way to play. James Jamerson (my hero, and Motown's studio bass player, founder member of the Funk Brothers) played all those wonderful bass lines with just one finger. Picks – aka plectrums – were not an option. Imagine how wonderful it was when I changed to a slightly slimmer-necked guitar – I was like greased lightning. Always tackle the steepest mountain first!

The local dance hall, the Hideout, was just off the expressway in Harper Woods (my Devil Gate Drive). It was just a plain, one-roomed building, but at night it burst into life with teenagers doing the pony and the jerk on the beer-stained, cigarette stub-filled dance floor. This is where I met my very first boyfriend, Chris (until the day she died my mother kept asking why I didn't marry him), and after sharing a slide around the floor he asked me to go steady. But the truth is that I was never good enough for his parents.

Chris grew up in a richer family than mine. They lived in a very big house with a manicured lawn and were definitely upper-class – hell, they even had Napoleon's silverware on the dining room table. Chris was quite square in a way, and very sweet. Every year he gave me another charm for my silver bracelet, and we smooched until our lips gave out. Yes, he was my first love and yes, he was my first lover – and that's something you never forget. I was so lucky, because he wasn't the 'wham bam and thank you ma'am' type. He was tender, he was gentle and he was attentive. In truth he spoiled me, and throughout my life I have accepted nothing less.

Chris's parents never really regarded me as his girlfriend. One particular Thanksgiving however, I was actually invited into the inner sanctum of his home to dine with the family. This was a big deal – it meant that after two years they might be starting to accept me. I wore a conservative blue dress, not too short, fixed my hair nice and was on my absolute best behaviour. I made small talk with his mom till dinner was served. I did everything right, put the napkin on my lap, sipped daintily from my wine glass, picked up the correct knife and fork – and then proceeded to send my turkey leg sliding right across the table, knocking over his dad's water glass. I will never forget the look that passed between his parents.

One night Chris and I went to see James Brown live at Cobo Hall. We were both huge fans, and he didn't disappoint. Seeing his cape routine for the first time was unforgettable, and his dancing – right across the stage in one movement – was amazing. But the best part came at the end of the show when he said, 'Okay. Turn on the lights. James Brown wants ta see da people.' Chris and I looked around at the packed stadium: 'Oh, honey, guess what – we're the only white people here.' And then James began to sing, 'Say it loud, I'm black and I'm proud.' He called on all the audience to get up and sing it with him.

'Shit! What do we do now?' I said in alarm.

Chris replied, 'Stand up and sing!'

It was with Chris that I had my first motorcycle ride. Against his dad's wishes, he had purchased a 50cc Honda with his own money. Remember, these were the days when helmets were optional. It had been raining and we decided to go across a golf course – really stupid, since the grass was still wet. All of a sudden the bike started to slide. Chris lost control and we went right into a tree. I was flung into the air and remember thinking how nice it felt to be floating – then *bang*, I landed on my ass. But I wasn't hurt. Chris *was* hurt – big time. The bike had fallen across his leg and the gas tank had gashed it open deeply. We stood the bike up, climbed on and sped to the nearest hospital, blood spraying the road all the way there.

When his dad was informed he came to the hospital and drove me home. Fortunately my mom and dad never found out, or they would have killed me.

Chris and I were a couple from 1964 until 1967, and he kept in contact with Mom and Dad for many years. We met up again a few years ago and reminded ourselves how good that relationship had been. And of course he will always be linked in my mind with the Hideout, where I did my first gig.

We girls had been a band for about a month when we went to the Hideout for our usual Friday night frolics. There were different bands every weekend, mostly local, and while watching the Underdogs, a very popular group, Patti turned to the club owner, Dave Leone, and said, 'You know what, Dave? That band is crap. We can do better than that.' And so that very night we secured our first booking. We had two weeks to get serious.

First, a name. Many were bandied about before someone got hold of a dictionary, and as we thumbed through we came across the word 'hedonist'. When Nan got to the bit in the definition about 'seeking pleasure' Patti said, 'That's it – the Pleasure Seekers! Now let's get down to the basement and start rehearsing.'

We learned three three-chord songs – not very ambitious, but safe: 'Latin Lupe Lu', 'Twist and Shout' and 'Louie Louie'. My dad had loaned us an old radio-style microphone, and since we had no mic stand it was propped up between two guitar cases. God, we were awful – Arlene has since confessed to standing at the top of the stairs, crying with laughter. Anyway, we learned our songs, I sang lead on all of them 'cos they were 'ballsy', and, before you knew it there we were, on stage at the Hideout about to do our first gig in front of a live audience. We were dressed in English-style clothes: Beatle boots, skin-tight corduroy pants, white shirts, waistcoats and ties. Chris was standing right at the front, glaring up at me and not very happy about it – he always thought it was a 'hobby'. But as 'Oh Little Latin Lupe Lu' ended to huge applause I was high as a kite.

At this point in the story I must give a prayer and a thought for our drummer, Nan Ball. Every town has its local beauty, and she was ours: five foot one, long blonde hair, small slanting blue eyes, full lips, breasts to die for. Nan was a top student too – but her passion was rock and roll. I'm sure there are still guys out there who remember Nan's rendition of the Troggs' 'Wild Thing', on which she sang lead vocals. There was never anything more sexy as she beat her drums, swaying back and forth, whispering the words like pillow talk, and all this without a bra! Yep, she was a hard act to follow. But as much as Nan lived and breathed playing drums in the Pleasure Seekers, her parents were dead against it. After all, their daughter was very bright and they wanted her to have a college education. So, a few years down the line, Nan was forced to leave the band, and I feel she never truly recovered. She eventually got a degree in child psychology and set up a practice in Grosse Pointe. But she avidly followed my career, making a guest appearance in 1999 on my *This Is Your Life*, and we remained good friends until her tragic death in 2004, when she was crushed between two cars on the expressway while coming home from work. I always felt her end reflected her life – trapped between two conflicting vehicles. Bless you, Nan – I hope they have a drum kit up in heaven! The beat goes on.

Way back then, the Pleasure Seekers got their first recording deal with Hideout Records. We recorded two sides, both originals written by Hideout owner Dave Leone: 'Never Thought You'd Leave Me', which Nan sang, and 'What a Way to Die', a song all about drinking beer, which I screamed my way through. When I listen to it now I think it's not bad for a first try, not bad at all.

We did our first TV on the local station, a show called *Swing Time!* They announced us, the cameras pointed at me, but instead of playing the opening bass riff I froze. Patti nudged me in the side and hissed, 'Play, you idiot. And smile.' I finally managed a little movement in my index finger but then my lip started to twitch uncontrollably – another Elvis link! When we watched the show back at home with my parents Dad said nothing, which really said it all. I never suffered stage fright again.

Our first single bit the dust – as did Hideout Records and Dave Leone. Enter local Detroit label Golden World with another offer. Boy, two labels in a year and I was still only fifteen years old! We recorded 'He's a Rebel', which Marylou sang, and 'Long White Line', an original tune all about riding that long white line down the highway on the back of a motorbike, which of course I sang. (*Seems to me like you had no choice but to evolve into me with all those songs about beer drinkin' and motorbike ridin'. You know, those Golden World records are the only things missing from the Ego Room – that's a damn shame.*) Attention eBay users. I would reward anyone who can find these tapes.

Around this time I became a go-go dancer on television. The show was called Club 1270 and went out live every Saturday afternoon, hosted by Dave Prince, a popular local DJ. Since this was Detroit the show featured all the Motown acts, and we had top chart hit artists too. It was a real learning curve. Every week I was within touching distance of my heroes – the Temptations, the Supremes, Martha Reeves and the Vandellas, Little Stevie Wonder, the Four Tops – and I was able to learn the dance steps first hand – or should I say first foot! Even today, put on a Temps' record and I'm up and dancing, just can't help myself. I also saw the Shangri-Las, whose lead singer, Mary Weiss, left a lasting impression – sexy as hell, and wearing leather. Then there were the Ronettes (another sexy-as-hell lady), the Cookies and from England acts like Paul and Barry Ryan, the Walker Brothers and Long John Baldry. The show's producer liked me a lot and so I was placed at the front of the 'regular' dancers, jerking, jiving, swimming, ponying my ass off. Every time a DVD comes out from this period, I search for my face in the crowd. So far, no luck.

Soon we were booked into dance halls all over the area, doing gigs with other up-and-coming bands from Detroit and the surrounding suburbs including MC 5, Ted Nugent and the Amboy Dukes, the Knack, the Rationals, SRC, an early version of Iggy Pop and the Stooges (Iggy was still on drums), Alice Cooper, Bob Segar pre-Bullet Band (Bob was always good, with original material, but 'older' than the rest of us), Mitch Ryder and the Detroit Wheels, and Catfish and Dallas Hodge. We were all friends at that time, jamming and hanging out together. We even rehearsed in the big farmhouse that Alice Cooper and his band rented on the outskirts of the city. In this line-up we played just about everything from Motown and Beach Boys to early Beatles and Stones. In fact Nan was such an English Invasion freak that we ended up with a very British set of songs.

Those early gigs are some of my fondest memories.

Marylou (who played cello in the school orchestra while I played percussion) sang some of the leads in her very soulful, Motown-sounding voice. Lou's one big complaint was having to do the Rolling Stones' 'Off the Hook', on which she played tambourine and sang backing vocals – non-stop 'It's off the hook . . . smack jingle . . . it's off the hook . . . smack jingle' which she said made it the most boring song in the world. Patti sang a few Motown numbers, like 'Dancing in the Street' and 'Baby Love'. But I always got the male songs – anything hard, heavy and growly was my domain.

I remember doing a gig in the early days at a school dance. There was no stage, so we set up on the floor. Things were going well, but the audience was starting to get annoyed that they couldn't see the lead singer. 'Put her up on the table!' they shouted. So up I went – a defining moment in my development as a performer. We started 'Do You Love Me' by the Contours, then right in the middle of it, feeling the audience surging up towards me, I let out this beast-like, unearthly scream: '*Wahhhhhhhhhhhhhh.*' It was pure instinct, and I just let rip. The crowd went wild and I thought the effect was so good, that I'd keep it in my repertoire.

As in many industrial cities there was a burgeoning music scene in Detroit born out of desperation: a 'gotta get outta this place' feeling – but until we do let's escape into the music. My hometown had the best pedigree of all – those exciting, energy-laden white rock bands and Motown. I'm a self-confessed Motown junkie. My natural style is somewhere between the two genres – a kind of black/white boogie/rock and roll. And at the tender of of fourteen, as a bona fide Pleasure Seeker, I was about to extend my experiences to the smoke-fuelled world of marijuana.

There was a coffee house-cum-music venue called the Chessmate on the east side of town. It was funky, dirty and totally atmospheric, filled with teenagers bent on rebelling, and it featured some fantastic out-of-town bands like the Blues Magoos, who hailed from New York City. Chris, my boyfriend, would not be seen dead here. Armed with my fake ID so that I could pass for sixteen, the rest of the band and I took my dad's Cadillac and drove to the club. It was packed to the gills, but we were able to get seats right in the front of the stage. I had never experienced psychedelia before. The band came on looking stoned and cool as hell, with long hair, scruffy clothes, strobe lights, echoplexes and loud amps. They went into an extended version of the Nashville Teens' 'Tobacco Road', jamming away for at least ten minutes. The sound was like an earthquake and made my body tremble with desire, though not in a sexual sense – I simply wanted to be part of that 'power'. The Magoos were incredible – riff after riff, lights flashing, hair flying, pumping away, the bass sound hitting me in the solar plexus or even a little lower. I was in love with Ronnie 'Magoo'. He didn't play that low-slung bass so much as ride it, rocking back and forth on a natural (or unnatural) high. I adopted this stance soon after, and it became one of my trademarks. Every time the boys appeared in town, we were there in the front row. My parents had no idea I was a regular customer. 'Too, too young,' my mother would have said. Too, too right, Mom.

One night after the show everyone paired off, leaving me with my hero, Ronnie. We began to talk and he invited me up to his hotel room, presumably to see his 'strings'. Once there he produced a joint of marijuana, the popular poison of the sixties.

'Have you ever smoked one of these?' purred Ronnie.

'Yeah, sure!'

So he lit up and off we went. I had the first one, then the second, taking big puffs, holding it down and letting it out slow as instructed. 'Big deal! What's this supposed to do? I don't feel anything.' Then I had the third one.

Ronnie put the latest Bob Dylan album, *Blonde on Blonde*, on his portable record player. 'Oh mama, can this really be the end?' sang Dylan, drawing me in. I got high on the music, and then high on the weed. It hit me *pow* – my brain exploded on to the ceiling and I was flying around the room.

'Oh, my God, Ronnie, I think somebody's coming up the stairs! It must be my mum. Better take your shoes off – let's hide. This is strange . . . why is the room spinning? Oh, my God, do you hear sirens? Is that the police?' And then he kissed me – as his face swam in and out of my vision. I liked the kiss, but not the fact that I couldn't focus on anything.

Thankfully, Ronnie was a perfect gentleman. He backed off, laid me down on his single bed and went to sleep. I spent the entire night trying to come down – I was really, really scared. The next morning, after a sleepless night, I mumbled into the phone asking Leo (Arlene's husband number one) to come and get me. When I came out of the house I looked like I had just attended the wildest orgy ever, and he slapped me across the face: 'Don't ever do anything like that again, Susie!' And I didn't – well, I never got *that* stoned again, anyway. When I returned to normality, I wrote a poem. Catholics major in guilt, you see.

A Good Catholic Girl

A good Catholic girl, in a whirlpool of desire
Trapped.
A mass of contradictions
When she's good, she's good
When she's bad, she's great

Her own sense of time, her own right and wrong
Her own rhythm, a system that's allowed
What's not allowed, she pursues,
Despite consequences

Then in a darkened cubicle, all is revealed
And all is forgiven.

The rhythm of lust beats slow and steady
And touches a good Catholic girl

(Susie Quatro, 1965)

I'm no angel, and I tried other drugs like every teenager of the time did – but I don't like the feeling of being out of control. I did smoke a little again, from time to time, but it always spelled disaster. Once, after we had moved house to Grosse Point Farms, Arlene and I smoked a little weed behind the garage. (Much later we actually tried smoking banana skins, a 'Mellow Yellow' suggestion which we took seriously – much to Donovan's amusement when I shared this story with him in the 1990s. And no, it didn't work!) My big sister and I were mid-marijuana-induced giggle when the back door flew open and our mom said, 'Come in to dinner, girls.' I stared down at my steaming plate of spaghetti, a little confused about the next step, and just couldn't get the fork to my mouth. Arlene was stifling her laughter, trying to look normal. Somehow we managed to get through the meal.

Dexedrine (speed), another poison of the day, masqueraded as a diet pill and was supposed to suppress your appetite. A friend of mine had access to them in her part-time job after school at the local drugstore (aptly named). So I popped a couple of pills in the hope of losing some weight. That day in physics class I surprised myself, raising my hand to answer a question on relativity. I didn't know the answer, of course, but just continued to wave my hand around every time a question was asked. I was loud, confident and wrong. The warning on the label should have read: 'Drugs and Susie – a bad mix!'

Back to the music. Diana Baker was first to leave the band, at the 'request' of her boyfriend Ron. She is still married to him today and we remain friends – indeed, she was another guest on my *This Is Your Life*. To take her place we recruited Priscilla, a big-busted, big girl with long blonde hair who didn't last long. Marylou was next to go and we replaced her on rhythm guitar with Eileen Biddlingmeyer. (God, what a name!), who stayed for several years. When Priscilla left, my dad suggested we looked within the family. So Arlene came in to play piano, and hubby Leo quit his job and became manager. Nan's parents had been dead against the band from the start, but agreed she could play until she went to college, when the drums would have to be sold. What they didn't know was that Nan had saved up enough money to buy herself a secret kit, and the band continued right under their noses. While Nan was at the University of Michigan at Ann Arbor she was able to keep us busy with a series of college weekend dances called TGIFs, (Thank God It's Friday).

It was at these gigs that I began to learn how to handle hecklers – every performer needs a few tricks up their sleeve to shut these idiots up. It was Friday night and the college kids were letting their hair down big time. Beer, vodka, gin, anything drinkable was consumed in vast quantities. Halfway through our second set some drunken asshole started to dance wildly right in front of me. That wasn't the problem – him sliding and wiggling his tongue in and out in an unmistakeably suggestive manner *was* a problem. So I lifted my bass – what a useful instrument to have at hand – and smacked him over the head with it. 'Oh, sorry. Didn't see you there.' Problem solved.

(*Susie, can I just make a comment at this point? It seems to me that you might have a problem with men. You know – touching, getting too close, not being respectful . . . Am I right?*) Yes, you're right. But I have my reasons. Let's go back a year or two . . . .

I was twelve years old, and starting to expand in all the right places. We had just returned from church when Mom decided to stop at a department store that, unusually, was open on Sunday. As she and her sister, Aunt Izzy, disappeared down the clothes section, Nancy and I went off in search of the toys. From out of nowhere a foul-smelling old man appeared, stubble on his face, yellowing teeth, and wearing a creased jacket over stained trousers (I am very observant). He followed us up and down the aisle staring, leering, edging closer and closer, until finally he leaned over and whispered in my ear, 'Hello, honey. Would you like me to buy you a dolly?' '*Wow* yes please!' Nancy, although younger, sensed the danger and ran away. I stayed, wanting my free toy. At this point he grabbed my hand and pushed it into his pocket, where I felt something round and thick. I reckoned it was a wad of money, and that must be good. We stood there for about a minute, his sweaty hand clutching mine, making small circular movements, when it suddenly dawned on me that something wasn't quite right. I pulled my hand away and ran off, suddenly desperate to find my mother. I was crying hard as I blurted out the whole story to the store security man. We searched every single aisle but the man had gone. Back home, mother tried to make light of the incident, which hurt me deeply. But in retrospect I can see she wanted to lessen the impact of what had happened. Unfortunately, this was not an isolated case.

Fast forward to the Roostertail, the happening place in Grosse Pointe Shores situated on 'Millionaires' Row' (Lakeshore Drive) and owned by car industry magnates the Sheoneth Brothers. It was 1965 and Leo had achieved a real coup and got a booking there for the Pleasure Seekers, now his sole source of income. You had to be eighteen, so I'd borrowed an older friend's driver's licence. The evening came, we'd played our second set to a packed house and I was happy and working hard, dressed in my black top hat and silver micro-skirt. It was time for a break, so we told everyone we'd be back in fifteen and I jumped off the stage in desperate need of a toilet. On the way there, some drunk approached me, stuck his hand under my skirt and grabbed me – and I mean *grabbed me*. Shocked, I stepped back and slapped him across the face as Mom had taught me to do. Guess what? He slapped me back. Leo was just behind me, saw what happened and tried to goad the guy into exchanging blows, but the man was just too drunk. Well, Suzi Quatro, are you beginning to understand. No? Well, read on.

Fast forward again to 1974, touring Australia. The boys in the band and the road crew were all big, mean-looking, moody guys, not to be messed with and very protective of me. After our concert in Perth we were invited to a private club, although I never liked going to these places because we invariably ended up fielding autograph-seekers and gawkers and basically we had to keep performing. We were sitting in the roped-off VIP section, drinking and unwinding – which takes at least an hour after the show. It's nice to come down slowly instead of crashing back to reality.

Laughing and joking, I got up and excused myself to go to the toilet – maybe in the future I should try and 'hold on'. Having edged my way past the band and crew, I had to go under the rope and squeeze past a few 'regular' customers who were a little the worse for wear. One of them quite deliberately lifted his leg, pushing his knee between my legs.

'Did you see that?' I shouted to my party, and immediately I saw seven faces full of fury, especially Len's. Up he jumped, grabbed the guy by the shirt and lifted him off the ground.

'Why did you do that, you bastard?'

'It's the truth – I didn't do anything at all, honest,' spluttered the Aussie.

'*Why* did you do that? Tell me. *Why, why, why*?'

Until Mr Jerk finally said, 'Sorry.'

'You *did* do it, you idiot!' *Smack*. Len punched him straight on the chin. He went down. We all left. Not a pleasant evening after all.

Hey, Suzi Quatro! Let me ask *you* something for a change. Why does this always happen to me?

3

CH-CH-CH-CHANGES

....

Donald and Helen Ball made a decision. 'Let's drive up to Ann Arbor and surprise Nan this weekend.' Good idea for them, bad idea for the Pleasure Seekers. Her parents arrived late Saturday afternoon, and as they were walking up the stairs to her dormitory there was Nan coming down, lugging her drum kit to the van for that evening's gig. The shit really hit the fan. Nan was ordered to leave the band, and the drum kit was taken back to Grosse Pointe that very day and sold. As for Nan herself, she was beyond upset – her whole world disappeared.

The rest of the band too was devastated, for Nan was the heart and soul of the group and would be very difficult to replace. And what a contrast between the way her parents thought about our all-girl rock and roll band and the way ours did. Ours had allowed us to pursue our 'dream'. Dad got us equipment and a van and Mom put up with us rehearsing day and night in the garage, providing food, drink and sometimes an extra bed when needed. We were lucky to have such support from our parents when so many budding musicians don't.

Time to find another drummer. Not just a drummer, but a good one and a girl too, which made the task very difficult. But we did, and not far away either. She lived on the slightly less exclusive side of town in St Clair Shores. Her grand-mother (a beauty queen) came from England and lived with the family. She's important, because it was Grandma who hand-made all the Pleasure Seekers' costumes – leopardskin mini-dresses made out of plastic, black one-piece jumpsuits under a one-piece bathing suit-type top with holes for the 'bits' (all quite decent) and shiny silver mini-dresses (sexy but cute). Enter (*drum roll*) Darlene Arnone. I was a little jealous of her, for she was truly talented: strongly built, dynamite on the drums and blessed with a wonderful voice.

It's 1967 and this is the line-up: Patti (lead guitar), Eileen (rhythm guitar), Darlene (drums), Arlene (piano) and me (bass). Leo was now starting to look outside of the Detroit area for gigs. He flew to New York City and was able to get us a two-week booking at Trude Heller's in Greenwich Village for $1000 a week – when she only ever paid $800! School was out, and I was beside myself with excitement. Leaving Arlene and Leo's kids with my parents, we loaded up our equipment, jumped into the station wagon and began the long drive to the Big Apple. Chris was off to college, but *I* was off to New York! We arrived to the buzz of taxicabs honking non-stop and eagerly took in the crowds jostling for space on the sidewalks, the hotdog vendors and the skyscrapers nestled between brownstones. Wow, this was heaven! As soon as our suitcases were deposited in the hotel, Darlene and I went off to explore Broadway. The first visual to hit our eyes was a hooker dressed in a skin-tight red leather dress, with matching knee-high boots – she was there every day, and we called her

Red Boots. A couple of blocks down was a strange man standing in the middle of the sidewalk, next to his lunch bag and cup of coffee, and shouting, 'Change your underwear!' over and over again. Apparently this was his regular gig, and years later he made an appearance on the *Johnny Carson Show*. What a bunch of weirdos! This city has had a lifelong fascination for me. It's the only place in the world where you can be surrounded by people but completely alone – and always be entertained.

Both Trude Heller's, the venue, and Trude Heller, the owner, taught me a lot. The deal was five sets a night, forty-five minutes on and fifteen off, which we were obliged to play whether or not there was anyone there. The crowd didn't usually appear until the second set – the first set was used as a warm-up in which we did instrumentals and 'easy' songs that didn't tax the voice. There was a little ledge against the wall where regulars Carl and Carolou performed the latest dance steps worked into their own unique puppet-like style (Carl became my boyfriend for the duration of the gig – boy, did he have some moves!), also a small bar, several circular tables, a dance floor and a stage. A tiny greasy smelly kitchen was our 'dressing room'.

Trude watched us the first night, anxious to see if Leo's selling job had been accurate. It was, and we stormed the place. My big numbers at the time were 'Gimme Gimme Some Love', 'Do You Love Me', and 'Try a Little Tenderness'. But first nights never go without a hitch. 'Excuse us, please,' I said to the audience. 'We're having some microphone problems. Please be patient.' Well handled, I thought. Wrong. Trude marched over, shouting in my ear, 'Don't *ever* apologise – puts you on the defensive.' Her nickname for me was 'Little

Toughie'. Trude batted for the other side and had more than a little crush on me, which has been an ongoing thing in my career. If I was that way inclined, I could have had a smorgasbord! That first gig over, after having a pre-ordered prime rib with baked potato at the Stage Deli on Broadway we finally got to sleep around 6 a.m. I was in heaven – exhausted, yes, but so happy. I slept like a baby, and when I woke I ordered coffee and a Danish at midday. Boy, this is living!

Two weeks passed in a blur: gig, meal, bed; gig, meal, bed; no speaking in the daytime; losing my voice every night; spraying green liquid down my throat to numb the pain before every show. In fact it got so bad that Leo insisted I give some of my songs away to lessen the load. I was heartbroken but could see his point. I lost 10 lbs without even trying. Finally it was over and we were due to go home – me back to school to get my high school diploma. Both our parents were delighted that their kids were returning to the fold, but Mom especially wanted me back. She was always frightened about the 'temptations' of show business and didn't like me being on the road so young.

I remember sitting on my tiny single bed in the New York hotel room thinking I just couldn't go back. I picked up the phone and called home. It was Dad who answered. 'I don't want to go back to school,' I blusted out. 'There's nothing for me in Grosse Pointe, and . . . well, Dad, the truth is. I've found what I want to do for the rest of my life.'

Silence. Then, speaking in a voice that was just too soft. 'Okay, Susie. Is there anything I can say to change your mind?'

'Nope.' *Bang*. The phone went dead.

Very clever, Dad, cutting my lifeline. Is this what I really want. Am I sure? Am I really sure?

Now it was serious. Leo got us an agent, Joe Glaser from ABC bookings, who had handled many big stars including my heroine, Billie Holiday. Proper press photos were taken, with our stage names underneath. Susie Quatro became Suzi Soul (*spelling change noted, Susie Q*). With 'old school' Joe as our agent the gigs started to roll in, but he seemed to be content to book us into supper club after supper club – Boring! First set playing to the waiters, second set to the diners, third set to the drunken dancers, and always being told to turn down the volume. We thought we were a rock and roll band but Joe thought we were a cabaret outfit, which would prove a problem in the future. But in the big scheme of things it was all good training, and for now we all settled into our working life, 'work' being the operative word.

We had planned to take a couple of weeks off at home and then drive to Buffalo in New York State to appear at the Glen Park Casino, supporting Chuck Berry. This was the summer of the race riots, and all that first week the TV coverage was saturated. 'Newflash! There's been burning, looting and riots in downtown Detroit' – these were very, very scary times. Grosse Pointe seemed like another country, and even had its own police force. There were no African–Americans where we lived, but one morning we awoke to the shocking sight of soldiers with machine guns on top of the shops across the street, and took the sensible decision to leave early, in fact Mom, Dad and Nancy came too.

So here we were on opening night in Buffalo, supporting Chuck Berry. I was beyond thrilled to be on the same bill as him. So Chuck does his thing in his usual manner, making up the timing as he goes along, expecting his 'pick-up' band to follow. Duck walking, riffing, rockin' and rolling – he was *magic*. Now it's got to be said that Dad is prejudiced, although he strenuously denies it. He doesn't like the races mixing whatsoever, and firmly believes that we should stick with our own kind. 'Susie, if you ever bring a black man home I will disown you.' Anyway Chuck came off, we girls were hanging around the dressing room, and then it happened. Chuck took one look at Eileen (long blonde hair, big boobs) and grabbed her, lightly pushing her back on to the couch. He was only fooling around, but unfortunately my dad walked in at that very moment. He grabbed Chuck by the shirt, hauled him up to his feet and *bam*. God, Dad, you just hit Chuck Berry, and he wasn't even playing with his ding-a-ling. Years later I saw Chuck again in Bremen in Germany. I asked him, 'Hey, do you remember the Pleasure Seekers? We were an all-girl band and we supported you in Buffalo in 1967?' Looking at his face, it was obvious he remembered.

It was here in Buffalo at the start of our gigs all around the country, that I started my collection of hotel room keys (each key holds a memory) and I continued this hobby until the Pleasure Seekers disbanded in 1969, finally dumping all three hundred of them in the mail box. A funny thing happened when we were on the road in South Carolina. As usual we were staying at a cut-price motel: Leo and Arlene had one room, and we girls shared a couple of rooms quite a way apart from them. We returned late at night after the last show, said our goodnights and went to our room. Patti put the key in the door and pushed it open (see what I mean about keys and memories). She switched on the light and we all walked in, locking the door behind us. Then we heard one of the bedroom doors slam shut.

Christ almighty, were we scared! Patti screamed, 'Hurry

up, everyone. Get in the bathroom and lock the door.' There was a tiny window at the top of the bathroom door, so we climbed up on a stool and peered out. All we could see was a pair of shoes. We waited. We listened. There wasn't even a phone in the room. Five minutes passed, then we agreed to make a break for it and not stop running till we got to Leo's room. So suddenly there were four screaming girls all trying to get out the door at the same time, madly running for the other side of the courtyard where, we hoped, salvation was waiting. Afterwards we called the police, who searched the room and discovered our bras and panties strewn all over the place. Leo stayed with us that night, and in the morning they arrested the hotel owner. 'Change your underwear' – same theme, different guy.

Next stop Newark, New Jersey. Not a supper club this time but worse, much worse. This was a bar called Chez Charles, frequented by Mafia hoodlums and hitmen. Of course we weren't aware of this, and for the record I don't think Joe Glaser, our agent, was either. Then again, he had a reputation for being involved with the mob. . . .

The stage was behind the bar. Mirrors covered every surface. Young silk-suited guys started to trickle in and the place was soon crowded with heavy drinkers, shouting and joking with each other, completely oblivious to the 'entertainment' on hand. We continued to do our set, and then the strangest thing happened. The entire mood started to change – you couldn't put your finger on it, it was just something in the air.

It started with one of the guys in the audience swinging Darlene's boom microphone back and forth, smacking her in the face, to the wild amusement of his tough-looking friends.

Darlene finally decided she'd had enough and threw her drumstick at him, spilling his tumbler of whisky all over his shiny suit. Leo, noticing a bulge in the guy's waistline, started to look nervous. 'Something' was going on. I noticed several guys pointing at us, then having some sort of discussion, then pointing again. It made me feel nervous too.

We finished our first set and Leo ushered us into the 'dressing room' (we had graduated from the kitchen to the owner's office – yippee, it's the big time!). 'Okay, girls, we're in big trouble. These guys are hoods and they're packing guns. They've picked out which one of you they expect to sleep with tonight when the show's over. Now the main thing is to get out of here in one piece. Susie, it's down to you to lead the way. Here's how you play it. Look sick – really sick – and explain that you have to go home but you'll be back tomorrow. You gotta make it work, Susie – this is the only way we're gonna get outta here. And once you girls are outside don't look back. Here are the car keys. Just get in, quickly and calmly as you can, put your foot on the gas and step on it. Got it? Don't worry about me – I'll be okay.'

Well, I always knew I could act. I was brilliant. 'Hi, guys. Sorry 'bout this but I'm ill – got a fever. But I'll be back tomorrow, and then we can party – especially you, cutey.' (stroking his cheek, eyelashes fluttering). We made it to the car and back to the hotel. Leo arrived a lot later with the news that the club had been completely trashed, but due to the intervention of a hitman called Charlie our stage equipment was intact, standing on a postage stamp-sized oasis in the middle of the club. They put the owner in hospital. Leo was on the line to Joe Glaser in a flash, furious at what had happened and that Joe had put us in harm's way. Later that day Joe called back. His words chill me to this day: 'Those punks will never bother anyone again.'

And a little thank you to you, Charlie. All these years later and I still remember you. Yep, you were a nice guy – guess it was a good thing you had a crush on me. Charlie, bless his soul, said, 'Hey, wreck da place. Fine. I don't give a fuck. But what da hell did dees girls do to ya? Leave der stuff alone or ya gotta deal wit me. Know whadd I mean?'

Back in New York a few months later, once again at Trude Heller's, Charlie showed up to see the show. Halfway through the evening I got terribly sick (for real), with a temperature hitting 103. I fell off the stage and Leo and Charlie carried me out to a taxi which took me straight to hospital. No more gigs for me – a quick shot of penicillin in the bum and three days in the Gorham Hotel, fading in and out with damp cloths on my forehead. I have a hazy recollection of Charlie coming to visit with a bouquet of red roses. We did keep in contact for a couple of years – in my address book he was listed under M for Mafia – and I even went to visit him in his suburban home where he lived with his mother. How strange – hitman Charlie, killing people for money yet bringing me flowers and living with Mommy. You work it out!

Along with my growing collection of hotel keys I kept a list of the states we visited during that first couple of years of serious gigging. Reading it now, one phrase comes to mind: I did my homework.

Buffalo, New York (Glen Park Casino) appearing with Chuck Berry

New York City (Trude Heller's)

South Carolina (Caravan Club)

New Jersey (Chez Charles)

Toledo, Ohio (Peppermint Club)

York, Pennsylvania (Trail Lounge)

Athens, Ohio (Club 33)

New York City (Trude Heller's) appearing with Tiny Tim

New York City (8th Wonder) appearing with Patti Labelle and
  Gladys Knight and the Pips

Elgin, Illinois (Frankie Laine's)

Jacksonville, Illinois (Blackhawk)

Alpana, Michigan (Green's Pavilion)

London, Ontario (Brass Rail)

Toronto, Ontario (Friars)

Ottawa, Ontario (Carlton University)

Buffalo, New York (Glen Park Casino)

Lansing, Michigan (Grandmother's) appearing with Bob Segar.

Richmond, Virginia (3200 Club)

Miami, Florida (Jilly's)

New York (Anthium)

Detroit, Michigan (Roostertail)

London, Ontario (Cambell's)

York, Pennsylvania (Trail Lounge)

Dallas, Texas (Onyx Club)

Seattle, Washington (Teen Fair) appearing with the Boxtops,
  Canned Heat, Tommy Boyce and Bobby Hart, the Grassroots,
  Eric Burdon and Bryan Hyland

Los Angeles (air force base)

Denver, Colorado (LAPJ's)

London, Ontario (Brass Rail)

Detroit, Michigan (Arthur's) jamming live onstage with Ted
  Nugent and David Ruffian

Seattle, Washington (return engagement, playing everywhere!)
Kalamazoo (University of Detroit)
Home for Christmas – phew!

So I'm working in my band, travelling all over the country. Chris is away at college, but we're still a couple. I'm happy in my career and happy in love – or so I thought. Okay, here's that story, Suzi. But it ain't gonna be easy digging up that emotion all over again.

DC and I met at Trude Heller's. He was the A&R man sent down by Mercury Records to see the band with a view to signing us up. Nine years older than me, married with a kid, six foot four inches tall and gorgeous with his long black hair and long, long legs, dressed in the latest style with black T-shirt, black suit and black boots . . . oh, yes, the man in black, so cool. We did our set and he was impressed, mainly with me as he told me over and over again: 'You're the star of the show, Suzi, and some day you're going to have to say goodbye to the rest of your sisters.' How perceptive of him. I was smitten immediately – you can't stop chemistry, and the two of us had it for each other in spades.

About a week later the Pleasure Seekers were at Mercury Records' head office, having a picture taken for *Record World* as we signed our first major record label contract. Once the business was over we discussed the way forward. Plans were made to record two tracks, 'Good Kind of Hurt' (Darlene's song) and 'Locked in Your Love' (mine). The studio was booked and I was given a demo to learn my tune. There I was in the little single bedroom, part of the apartment we shared at the Gorham Hotel. It was the only 'private' bed and I claimed it for my own. I had a portable record player and was going over and over the song when the phone rang. It was him! Now DC was an alcoholic, big time. So, in this loosened state of mind, he began the flirtation.

'What are you doing, Suzi?'

'Trying to learn the song.'

'What are you wearing, Suzi?'

'My sleepsuit.'

'Describe it for me.'

'Well, you know the kind that little kids wear? One-piece with feet and a trap door in the rear.'

'Yeeeees, I get the picture.' (I have always been a pyjama girl, which can be quite sexy in a little-girl way – especially for dirty old men!)

We talked and talked for hours as DC got braver and braver, finally saying, 'I'm going to come up there, Suzi. And do you know what I'm going to do to you?'

Whoops! Time to hang up. I was only seventeen and out of my depth. This was grown-up. Was I ready for this?

In the meantime we returned for another two-week run at Trude Heller's with one new member in tow, Pam Bedford, as Eileen Biddlingmeyer had left (again at the request of a boyfriend). Pam was probably the best girl guitarist I ever heard – and I really hate to say 'girl', but it's true. She was a big Jimi Hendrix fan and did a perfect imitation of 'Purple Haze' on her blonde Byrdland guitar, which had cost her an absolute fortune. She was anal-retentive about this guitar – carried it to the stage, opened it, strapped it on, played the set, put it back in the case and carried it home, placing it next to her bed while she slept.

Even though the Pleasure Seekers had been working hard non-stop since 1964, I couldn't help but feel lucky that we had landed ourselves a major record label deal this early on. And finally the big day arrived. At the studio an orchestra was in place, with DC behind the console, and we five girls waited eagerly but nervously to begin. It's the only recording on which we didn't actually play our own instruments – it just didn't happen back then. Darlene went first, doing a great job. She had a grown-up voice reminiscent of Lulu, with great vibrato. Then it was my turn: uh-oh, shit, wrong key. DC was angry that I hadn't pointed this out, but hell, I was so green it should have been his job to tell me. 'Locked in Your Love' should have been the A-side, but due to it being too low Darlene's track became the single and I was relegated to the B-side. And before you say anything, Suzi Quatro, this was not perception but a fact. I had been pushed aside, and I was heartbroken.

DC and I continued our nightly phone calls down in Miami, where the band were booked into Jilly's Club, owned by Frank Sinatra's pal. DC decided we needed to redo the vocal on my track, so he flew down from New York. We were staying on the beach at the Blue Horizon and I was having a lot of trouble sleeping, even after five sets a night. My heart and mind were in turmoil – what exactly was happening between DC and me? I knew this was wrong (Mom didn't raise me this way), even though we hadn't actually done anything yet.

After the show we returned to the hotel around 3 a.m. and DC announced he felt like going for a walk on the beach: 'Anyone want to join me?' Hoping no one else wanted to go, I said, 'I do', and off we went. For the first time, he held my hand. We walked barefoot in the sand until the sun started to appear over the water. Funny how I wasn't the slightest bit sleepy. Finally we sat down, DC put his head in my lap, gazed up into my adoring eyes and said, 'You know, Suzi, I'm in love with you.' I was flying, and then it happened – he kissed me!

I wanted him so badly, but DC refused to consummate our relationship until I was legal at the age of eighteen, which was several months away. So as the sun rose in the sky we walked slowly back to the hotel.

'You'd better get some sleep, Suzi,' DC said.

'No! Don't leave me yet,' I cried.

So we went into the bar, which was being cleaned, and persuaded the bartender to give us some drinks. I was trying to hold on to the moment and the feeling for as long as I could. Tony Bruno singing 'Yesterday' in the background set the mood.

'Please, please make love to me,' flew out of my mouth. I don't possess an edit machine.

'No way, Suzi. Not until you're eighteen.'

'I can't wait that long. Please, *now*!'

'No! Now listen, here's my room key. Go and get some sleep – you have another show tonight. But I must warn you, don't be there when I return or I won't be able to help myself.'

Frustrated, I went to his room like a good little girl and lay down. But sleep did not come. I lay there with my daydreams hoping for his return, even arranging myself in what I thought was a sexy position on his bed. He didn't come back, so eventually I went to my own room to get ready for the evening's performance.

The next morning I got a big surprise. I was sitting on a chair in front of the hotel, just daydreaming, when whom did I see driving up the road but Chris, my 'official' boyfriend and the last person I expected or wanted to see given the current state of my heart. He had driven all the way from Detroit and bounded up the stairs with love in his eyes. But I stepped back and said, 'I'm sorry, Chris, but it's all over between us. I've fallen in love with someone else – and it's serious. So, you'd better go back home.' He just turned away, got back in his car and drove away, broken-hearted. I felt terrible sending him away like that, but being honest was the only way to do it. I can't help but feel that Chris knew something was wrong anyway, otherwise he wouldn't have driven all that way without even letting me know he was coming. And I'm pretty sure he had his share of girlfriends at college. Ours was a schooldays love affair which had run its course.

3 June 1968, Dallas, Texas. It was my eighteenth birthday and I was legal – horray! I was actually standing on the driveway of the hotel waiting for DC to arrive, sanity far away, consumed by a sexual desire I had never felt before and have never known since. In the distance I saw a green Mustang slowly coming up the road. I waved frantically as he pulled in. We didn't touch, didn't speak. Once inside the room, DC silently drew the curtains. We undressed, fell on to the bed and made love. It was like floating in a sea of pleasure. I wasn't a virgin any more, having done the deed with Chris – but I might as well have been, for nothing was ever like this. Nothing mattered but being together. He touched my mind, he held my heart, he possessed my soul . . . and I never gave myself so completely to anyone ever again.

Dallas is, of course, the place where John F. Kennedy was assassinated; and strangely enough, while we were lying in bed after the gig, watching the evening news, Robert Kennedy was shot on TV, right in front of our eyes. I spent the week-long engagement sleeping with DC – another first for me as I'd never spent the night with anyone before. I loved curling up against his back, feeling so loved, so protected. The insomniac Susie was non-existent and I wanted it never to end.

For the next couple of years we met wherever and whenever we could. Canada, Florida, New York, even Detroit, where he booked in at a hotel five miles away from my house. We talked constantly on the phone, never running out of conversation, and really were soul-mates. Arlene, at this time, had become my best friend and confidante. She was very unhappy in her marriage and had begun to 'fool around'. More than once we snuck off to New York together, me to see DC and her to see Alan, a guy she'd met at Trude Heller's. 'I just need a little space, honey' was Arlene's excuse to Len. I always felt bad about that – cheating and me just don't mix. (*Well, that's just a bit hypocritical, Susie, if you don't mind me saying so.*) Hey, what did I know – I was so young!

Mom, do you remember 'that' day? You must. I was planning to fly to New York for a rendezvous, and of course you knew – your instincts were infallible.

'Where are you going, Susan Kay Quatro? Off to see that married man? Shame on you – shame on him!'

'Yes, dammit, I am, and you can't do anything about it. I'm eighteen, so there!'

Slap right across the face. It left a big red imprint and I stormed out of the door.

Two days later, while lying in a hotel room with DC, I called home to let them know I was okay. Dad answered. 'Where the hell are you, Susie? What do you think you're doing? Do you know how upset your mother is?' Then Mom got on the line. She didn't speak to me. Oh, no – it was far worse as she began, 'Our Father who art in heaven, hallowed be thy name . . .' She was so worried for me. I held the phone out so DC could hear what was going on.

Hey, Mom, you were right and I was wrong. I deserved that slap, and more. And I'm so sorry to have put you through all that pain and worry. When they say 'parents know best' it's true. This affair ended in a pregnancy, a termination (Arlene by my side the entire time, as she always was), and finally so much heartache. I thought I would die. When I get to those golden gates (hopefully) this is the sin I will pay for. Not a day goes by that I don't think about who that baby would be now. Children are a gift. 'I'm sorry, Father, for I have sinned . . . please forgive me, Lord.' (*You shouldn't be so hard on yourself, Susie. This is not an unusual tale – it's happened to lots of young girls. You know what I think? You should put another poem in here – you know, the one you wrote about your children.*) Okay – but Suzi, I gotta tell you. It still makes me feel so sad.

It's a Small Wonder (for Laura and Richard)

It's a small wonder
Unlike any other
Special gift of God
A loving bundle
Father and mother
Made by each other
Love creates another
Small wonder

(Suzi Quatro, 1985 . . . lesson learned!)

I completely lost touch with DC in 1971 after moving to England. Everytime I went to the States I called various likely numbers in New York, looked in phone books, asked around. Finally an old songwriter friend of his told me he had gone to Miami and was remarried (it could have been me)! Via the Internet I was finally able to track him down some time in 1999. Should I call or should I not? I did, and got the answering machine. I left a message: 'Hi, this is an old friend of DC's. Can you get him to phone me back on this number?' Then, not happy with the message, I called again: 'Hi, this is Suzi Quatro—'

'*Suzi*!' DC blurted out, breathlessly. 'I was sitting out by the pool and heard your message. I knew it was you immediately. I've just knocked over a table getting to the phone. Oh, my God, how are you?'

And so, our reconnection began. As it turns out, he was the one that never got over it. Always thought it was the other way around. Today he's a reformed alcoholic and drug user. One day during a psychotherapy session he blurted out my name. The doctor said, 'Who's Suzi?' and the process of exorcising his demons began. DC and I had so much catching up to do. Finding him enabled me to have closure. And thank you to my husband Rainer, who is sure enough of himself to have allowed me the freedom to meet up with DC while we were in Miami, and have a drink (well, I had a drink, he had a Coke – the soda pop version!). These are the words my heart had to write all these years later. And, stranger still, after sending this to DC he sent me in return a nearly identical piece that he'd written back in the seventies as part of his therapy!

Miami Sunrise

That still Miami sunrise casting shadows in the sand.
You gazed into my soul, I smiled and held your hand.
So terrified, so mystified, it was all so new to me
As the tide washed over us, we pledged eternity.

I remember how we kissed as we melted into one
Music in the waves, two children in the sun
A whirlwind of emotions, caught in time, evermore
Soon to be forgotten, two strangers on the shore.

That still Miami sunrise, a moment we shared
It seems so long ago, we touched, we cared
Now so far apart, I send you love from this distant heart
That still Miami sunrise, one moment, we dared.

We found an empty bar-room, in a hotel by the sea
I sat so close there was no space between you and me
I begged you to release me, electricity . . . so strong.
Your wedding ring burned my hand . . . oh yes, this was wrong.

I stumbled to your bed, bathed in twilight's finest hour
Waiting for your light, like a rare and precious flower
We could not know our fate, no guessing destiny
Waves rolled in and washed away what was not meant to be

(Suzi Quatro, 1999)

Alongside this huge personal life-changing event, falling in
love with a married man and everything that came with it,
there was another huge professional one – Elvis's comeback
concert in 1968. I was glued to the set, having loved him since
the year dot. I always knew I would be like him one day – hell,

I'd been doing Elvis hits in my set since the very beginning. What I didn't know was that his 'outfit' would also become mine, and it was directly after this show that I got my very first bona fide black leather jacket.

'Hey, girls,' said Patti, 'guess what? We're going to Vietnam to entertain the troops!' First stop the passport office. Let's see: name, place and date of birth, address, occupation. Now what do I put here? Oh, yes, of course: entertainer. The other girls put 'musician'. I was excited about my first trip overseas, of course. But Vietnam . . . hmmmm. I was only eighteen, and the idea of war was alien to me, even though lots of boys my age were dying there. This would be a trip to remember, for sure.

First we flew to Hawaii, staying a couple of nights crammed into one bedroom, sharing two double beds. I always hated having to share – had my fill of this as a kid – so I slept on the beach instead. We did one gig in a club, then got ready for our first journey overseas. I didn't sleep because I don't like flying much. I was amazed at the long expanse of never-ending water, hour after hour with no land in sight, until finally we made landfall on the Pacific island of Guam. Upon arrival we were greeted with the news that our officers' club engagement had been cancelled due to the club itself being bombed. So what now, Patti? Do we just turn around and go back home? Nope. What happened was that the booker asked us if we would mind, since we were there anyway, grabbing our guitars and walking through the hospital just to cheer the boys up. No problem. Let's go, girls.

I led the way into the first ward where – shock horror – a young man lay in bed completed covered in bandages and with blood still visible. His entire right side seemed to be missing. God, he couldn't have been more than eighteen years old. Biting back tears, I said, 'Hi.' (How pathetic!) 'How are you doing? We're here to sing for you.'

This guy was flying high on painkillers. 'I'm doin' okay. Wounded a little. But I can't wait to get back there and kill some more of those little slit-eyed Viet Cong bastards. Just get me back out on the field. I'll show 'em we fucking mean business. Get me back there! Get me back out there now!' I left him to his ranting and raving and moved on down the row of beds. We walked, talked, sang a few songs. In bed after bed it was so sad to see legs missing, scarred faces, arms in slings. And so much blood. We found out later they'd all just been lifted off the helicopter and not properly cleaned up yet. Finally, nearing the end of this 'walk of death', which is what it felt like, I came upon a black man lying quietly, very quietly. I paused, and was able to 'stare' closely at him – he couldn't see me because he had bandages covering both eyes. He'd been blinded in battle.

'Hey there, soldier. I'm Suzi, and I would love to sing a song just for you. Is there anything particular you'd like to hear?'

'Cool, man. Do you know "Try a Little Tenderness".'

We were finished, mission accomplished. We walked out the front door and I fainted.

On the flight home I made friends with Tim, who was on a two-week leave from his duties in 'Nam. With him was an ex-Viet Cong called Tong, who had switched sides and now worked for us Americans. 'He's never been out of his village before,' Tim explained. 'I'm taking him back as a reward. He saved my life! We were on duty together, walking through the jungle, trying to find any booby traps. Tong was walking ahead of me, as this was his job. All of a sudden he seemed to disappear, falling halfway into a pit lined with pointed spears. Luckily he caught himself on the edge before going all the way, or he wouldn't be here now. Lift up your shirt, Tong – show Suzi the scars.' Tim and Tong later spent a few days at the Quatro house, where I delighted in seeing Tong's reaction to just about everything. Hot and cold running water, television and *food*! One morning he took himself across the street to Blazo's café and actually managed to order breakfast. Both of them came to a Pleasure Seekers' gig. Riding back in the van late at night, Tong proved himself to be yet another who reinforced my 'don't touch me' attitude. (I hope you're making a list, Suzi Quatro.) He grabbed my breast, so I gently brushed his hand away. He grabbed again. I brushed him away again. Finally he gave up and went to sleep with his head on my shoulder. Tim and Tong were due to fly out the next day to Cleveland, Ohio, where Tim's family lived.

'What happens to Tong after this?' I asked Tim.

'Well, Suzi, I'll probably never see him alive again.'

'Why, for God's sake?'

'Because he's bad propaganda. He's seen too much. They'll get rid of him for sure.'

I heard from Tim, but as predicted Tim never heard again from Tong.

While the Pleasure Seekers were busy entertaining the troops in Vietnam, the anti-war peace and love movement was alive and well. I watched as hippies wore flowers in their hair and took LSD, dropping out of everything their parents stood for. Somehow I never felt a part of it. I guess being in the band isolated me in a way. My world was 'on the road'.

Jimi Hendrix was a good example of everything the Swinging Sixties stood for. I remember when my brother

Mickey put on a concert with him and my dad's prejudice reared its ugly head again. My brother had a limo booked to pick up this legendary guitarist from Detroit's Metropolitan airport, but it broke down. Panic! Mickey quickly phoned dad and asked if he could do the honours in his Cadillac, and I went along for the ride. Jimi arrived – electric hair, colourful hippie clothes, a groupie hanging off his arm. We escorted him to the car, he fell into the back seat and we began the drive to the Ponchartrain, Detroit's premier hotel on the river. I was sitting in the front with Dad while Jimi was smoking marijuana in the back. All the way there Dad was muttering under his breath, 'Goddammit . . . I should be heading to the zoo . . . goddam monkey!' Whether Jimi heard or not I shall never know, but due to the fumes we all arrived a little higher than when we left.

Some time in 1969 our drummer Darlene Arnone left the group – she never forgave Arlene for divorcing Leo. The truth is she was a little in love with him herself. Enter Rogers, who hailed from Kalamazoo – an excellent drummer, properly schooled. Timpani, kettle drums, guitar, even trumpet – yes, she knew her stuff. Our first engagement with this line-up was in Miami, which is where Arlene met hubby number two. She left the band a couple of months later to get married again (get ready to change that photograph, Dad).

I was angry with Arlene for leaving – after all, she was my buddy and I would miss her. Since the day she joined the band we had been soulmates, sharing our deepest fears and wildest dreams. We discussed every details of the various loves in our lives, giving each other advice. I felt then, and feel today, that Arlene is the only one who truly understood/understands my 'destiny' as I did/do, and harboured not one ounce of jealousy. She knows me better than I know myself sometimes, and doesn't let me get away with a thing!

Minus a keyboard player, we needed a serious rethink of the band. It was decided that we needed new blood – someone younger, with their finger on the pulse of today. And so the final Quatro joined. Nancy Jean was about to become a Pleasure Seeker, and would in fact become the main singer in the band. Okay! That's okay! That's fine. (*Hey, come on, Susie. You can't just sweep over that one without explaining. You must have been upset to be relegated to the back line again. So let's have it – time to share the pain!*) Boy, oh boy, you don't let me get away with a thing, do you? So this is what happened.

Festivals were the new big thing. After Woodstock, every promoter in the land tried to cash in on these new 'love-in' musical extravaganzas. Among them was my brother Mickey, who had become one of the most successful promoters in the Mid-West. Since Leo was no more, Dad had talked my brother into helping out by kind of managing us. Mickey had a big show coming up – Arthur Brown, Dr Tim Leary, the Frost, Alvin Lee, Ted Nugent and the Amboy Dukes, the MC 5, Alice Cooper, the Stooges, Pink Floyd, Savage Grace, Teegarden and VanWinkle, SCR, Fruit of the Loom, Bob Segar, Bonzo Dog Band, Coven and, right at the bottom of the poster, the Pleasure Seekers. We rehearsed with Nancy like crazy. I still sang a few of my biggies like 'Try a Little Tenderness', 'I've Been Lovin' You too Long' and 'Jailhouse Rock', but Nancy sang the rest. Basically we did the supper club act we'd been doing for the last few years, albeit as a four-piece, and guess what happened? We bombed, we absolutely bombed. It seems the whole scene had moved into this new cool, hip phase, with hippies, beads, sandals, patched blue jeans and tie-dyed T-shirts. There just happened to be another all-girl band on the bill, called Bitch. They weren't even on the poster, but were added at the last minute just because they were friends with the Frost (Dick Wagner's band). Dressed in blue jeans, T-shirts and barefoot, they took the stage. There was no 'show' to speak of, just four girls 'jamming'. And I tell you, they could play – they were ballsy and then some. I'd have thought it was a boy band up there if I hadn't seen them with my own eyes. What a wake-up call for us. We went home very downhearted and asked ourselves: where do the Pleasure Seekers go from here? Answer: nowhere.

Patti didn't pull her punches. 'Suzi, I think your time is over. You're old-fashioned. Nobody wants soul music any more. They want heavy, they want riffs, they want jammin'. God – Hendrix, Cream, Vanilla Fudge! We are so outta touch. I think the best decision is to let Nancy completely take over the singing. You can still do a couple of numbers – you know, "All Shook Up" and "Jailhouse Rock" – and you can play bass.'

All right, Suzi Quatro, before you put your two cents in let me say this was the best thing that ever happened to me. We changed our name to Cradle, started to write our own songs and proceeded to tour Kansas non-stop. For some reason they loved us there – a more boring place doesn't exist, but it had its uses. We jammed – boy, oh boy, did we jam! Taking a page out of Cream's book, 'Spoonful' became our showcase number. We all took long solos, sometimes lasting five minutes each. The couple of years of Cradle's existence enabled Suzi

Soul the 'entertainer' to merge with Suzi Quatro the musician. I got good on my bass. I mean seriously good. But Cradle was a non-starter. To save money we fitted out the van with mattresses and lived in it. We wrote lots of songs, but no one could agree on the direction. And personality-wise it just didn't work. No one was happy in this band: there was no spark, and I knew *this* all-girl band had to end. For all the reasons the Pleasure Seekers deserved to make it; this band did not.

We toured for about eighteen months, while I gigged, watched, learned and waited. Here I must give credit to a couple of girl musicians, Brodie and Carol. We were in Washington and heard of this group playing in town that was a real knock-out. We went to see them, and they gave me a totally different take on what I was trying to do. It was during Brodie's rendition of Janis Joplin's 'Piece of My Heart' that I overheard one of the customers saying, 'Jesus Christ! That girl has *balls*.' Indeed she did – great voice, and a good bass player too. As all artists do, I gathered this up to be used at a later date. Thank you Brodie (*Hey, don't forget the other 'gift' she gave you*).

Oh, yes . . . Brodie had a flower tattooed on her wrist. I thought that was so cool, so in South Carolina I visited the tattooist and had a tulip put on my shoulder and a star on my wrist. (*Simply 'not done' for a girl in those times. You were in the downstairs bathroom washing your face, wearing a strappy top, when Dad came in, noticed your shoulder and said, 'Get that silly decal off, Susie.' He tried to wipe it away while you continued to scrub your face, and finally the penny dropped. 'Oh, my God, you idiot! You've gone and permanently disfigured yourself.'*) Leather jacket, tattoos, bass guitar and attitude – seems like I had the whole package and just needed somebody to discover me.

Do you believe in magic? I do. I have always felt 'entities' around me since I was a child, and have kept my mind totally open to this phenomenon even though it scares me. Okay we were at a club in Somewheresville, Kansas. Cradle was up on stage, and the dance floor was crowded with people groovin' and having a good time, when suddenly right in front of us appeared a very handsome blond young man. He had this unearthly, unnerving stare and remained stock still. Then, as the music swelled, all of a sudden the floor seemed to disappear, leaving a big black pit. The only visible person was 'blondie', and everything else was swimming in front of my eyes. Was I hallucinating?

Patti called a break, and as soon as we got into the dressing room she said, 'God, did you see that?'

I was so happy that someone else had seen it too. 'What was it? What's going on,' I demanded. 'I don't know,' Patti replied. 'Maybe someone spiked our drinks or something. Anyway, let's just forget it, get back out there and finish the set.' We filed back on stage, and found the man had gone.

During the next break I went over to the pinball machine and it was pinging away when I felt someone looking over my shoulder. Oh, my God, it's that guy again and he's standing right behind me. He really was a beautiful-looking boy – almost angelic.

'Do you want to have some fun with that pinball machine?'

'Sure,' I gulped. And I swear that ball began bouncing all over without me touching it. Up, down, in and out, *bing bing bing*. The score was getting higher and higher . . . and then it stopped. The man was gone. Weird? You bet it was. We finished the evening and went home to bed without further incident. Or so we thought!

Knock knock. 'God, who the hell is that? It's two o'clock in the morning. Susie, you get the door!' Why is it always me? Natural-born leader, huh? . . . It was him and, crazy as it seems, we let him in.

'Hello, girls. Sorry for dropping by so unexpectedly. And just in case you're wondering who I am, I'm a white angel and I'm here to protect you.'

From what? That would come later. We sat and talked about religion, good versus bad, for a couple of hours. I was fascinated. Funny how I didn't even question who he said he was – he just felt real to me. Finally we fell asleep, although I don't remember dropping off. When we woke the next morning, he was gone. He did leave a note, though. 'Nice to meet you, girls. My warning to you is always stick to the good side of things. Don't dabble. Don't play around with forces you don't understand. It's dangerous. Keep safe. Stay out of harm's way, be happy and God bless you.' It was signed 'The White Angel'. Next stop the city with a long history of witches, aptly named Wichita.

We were bored – that's all it was. 'Hey, why don't we have a seance? You know, see if we can call up a spirit from the past. That would be fun, wouldn't it?' So we lit some candles and sat on the floor in a big circle. I began, 'Calling all spirits out there. We would like to communicate with someone. How about Janis Joplin? Janis, are you there? Come in, Janis. Come in.'

We sat in silence for a few moments, waiting for something to happen – and it did. The air in the room changed and it got freezing cold. You could feel the presence of 'something' . . . and it didn't feel very friendly. I was petrified. Suddenly Patti leapt out of the circle, stood up, swaying back and forth, and said in a voice that was nothing like her normal one, 'Why did you call me here? What do you want?' Then sister Nancy's friend CeeCee jumped up, screaming, 'I'm blind. I'm blind. Help me!' as she crashed into the lamp, knocking it to the floor. That was it. I found the light switch. Patti didn't seem to remember anything, saying, 'Okay, girls, let's stop playing and get some sleep. I'm going to bed in the other room.' But of course we didn't go to sleep. 'I don't like this,' I worried. 'I think we've called something unholy into our midst. Let's get the Bible and try to get rid of it.' I was adamant. We sat down, lit the candles again and Nancy took the Gideon Bible in her hands. 'Whoever you are, we want you gone. Leave us. God is protecting us now. Go away. We don't want you here.' As the dark, cloudy atmosphere started to swirl around us yet again, getting closer and closer, the hairs on the back of my neck rose in warning. Nobody dared breathe. . . . The phone broke into the tension and we all screamed. Then someone found the light switch again.

It was Patti, the Leader Who Must Be Obeyed. 'I don't know what you guys are doing there, but stop it right now and get over here – all of you. I just heard a crowd of voices going by the window, and I don't feel safe.' We just sat there, dazed and frightened, and noticed that the Bible had been flung aside but with one page ripped out and still in Nancy's hand. 'Though shalt not dabble in the unknown' was written across the top. We just ran to Patti's room, too scared to sleep alone. Squeezed up together on top of the bed, we told her breathlessly what had happened. Then the strangest thing started to happen. As we were yapping away, one by one everyone fell into a deep, almost coma-like sleep. Except me: little Susie was left all alone.

Evil seemed to permeate the atmosphere, and I clasped my hands together in terror as I gabbled the Lord's Prayer. This went on all night as 'forces' pressed in on me from every direction. I felt heavy, as if I was sinking down into the bed, and reckoned my faith was being tested. Only when the sun finally started to peek through the curtains did the mood lift and I felt safe again. I had won the battle, whatever it was.

One by one the girls awoke, and again nobody remembered much. Nancy and I decided to go for a walk in the nearby woods – after all, it was daytime now and the night's dangers were fading away. But deep among the trees we came upon a very strange dwelling, with the remains of a fire and red paint splashed on the trees depicting upside-down crucifixes. That was enough to convince me never to walk that road again. . . . Okay, so I lied. I *did* walk that road again, many times. My abilities to channel are very acute, and when the mood hits I can't resist. But since this nightmare experience in Kansas I have been a lot more careful about how far I venture into the unknown.

As 1970 rolled on Cradle were gigging, travelling and even spending some time in Grosse Pointe. We started to get some good gigs in the Detroit area. We'd supported Mountain a few times, and became friends. Patti actually has a very valuable gold Les Paul given her by Leslie West, a lovely mountain of a man. We once invited the band over for dinner before the show. When Mom saw Leslie walk in she burst out, 'Oh, my God! I hope I made enough spaghetti.' On another occasion we were supporting Jefferson Airplane, and this time we invited the boys to come to the house and jam. It was 2 a.m. by the time we plugged in and turned on. Since my dad had turned over to us the garage at the far end of the house we didn't think we would be disturbing anyone. Wrong! Out comes Art Quatro in string vest and boxer shorts. 'What's going on out here? What's all that goddam racket?' I was mortified – street cred out the window. Then Dad plonked himself on the Hammond organ, saying, 'Hey, guys, do you know the B flat blues?' And off he went. Surprisingly, everyone joined in and had a great time.

One day between gigs I was bored to tears and decided to drive to Eastland, the local mall (I am a mallaholic). It was at the make-up counter than I started to talk to 'Linda'. We somehow connected and decided to meet up the next day for lunch. Over our Big Boys (the best hamburgers in Detroit) Linda told me about this lady she knew called Mrs Beasley, who was a spirtualist and could tell you your future. You didn't have to pay her anything, but just donate whatever you felt was right to her spiritualist foundation. Who could resist that? (*You know, all your life you have followed you instinct. And hasn't it led you to some interesting places!*)

The house was small, just two bedrooms, but situated in a nice suburb in Royal Oak, Michigan. The lady herself looked like an absolutely normal grandma. We sat down together at the breakfast table, and Mrs Beasley 'listened' and wrote, 'listened' and wrote. I watched, sipping a cup of coffee. Afterwards, she read the contents of the notepad to me. It was up to me to interpret it – she was just the messenger.

First, she explained, I would go to England (right – like that's gonna happen.) Mom must put her feet up (I found out when I got home that Mom had just been diagnosed with serious arthritis in her feet). Someone called Mary was looking down and guiding me (grandmother Sanisley). She went on to name several people whom I was not familiar with, but again, when I returned home Mom confirmed they were all relatives.

Mrs Beasley continued. 'You are guided by a violin player named Ezra. Your first car will be a blue sports car.' It was – a blue Mercedes 280SL purchased in 1974 from Mike Chapman. And the last thing, in fact the only thing that to my knowledge hasn't happened, was that she saw big success with the number five, and pink roses all around. I thanked her and put in a small donation. She was such a warm, lovely woman, and so sincere, that you couldn't not believe her gift was genuine. Mom was so impressed with my 'notepad' of information that she and Dad made several visits themselves, although, they never shared the information they gleaned with me. Mrs Beasley, I'm sure you are now on the other side. Thank you. You got most of it spot on. But maybe you can explain number five and pink roses – just send me an email.

I think the best thing Cradle ever did as a group was to write a mini-opera. Pretentious? Moi? We were so intent on being 'serious' musicians. But in reality by 1971 we were nearing our end as a band. We went into the studio to put down several original songs and sent the tapes out to record companies. There were a few bites, including one from Elektra Records. Its president, Jack Holtsman, came to see a gig and came away liking only me. That same week (enter my old friend Destiny) my brother Mickey found out that legendary producer Mickie Most was due in Detroit to record Jeff Beck at Motown Studios. Somehow he persuaded him to come and see us play at the Grandee Ballroom, *the* gig to play at that time.

Now I was a huge Donovan fan, especially of the production. But I'd always wondered about the ego of a producer who printed on the back of his albums 'produced by Mickie Most . . . a Mickie Most production'. Did he have to say it twice? Mickie was actually the most successful independent producer of the sixties with acts like the Animals, Herman's Hermits, the Nashville Teens and Lulu to his credit. Anyway, the evening came and Cradle took the stage. Nancy was lead singer, but in due course my turn came dressed in T-shirt, cut-off Levis and barefoot, I strode to centre stage and said, 'Okay, here's something I wrote,' and went into 'Brain Confusion'. Then I screamed into the mic, 'Goin' to a party in the county jail', did the song, stepped back without another word and we finished the set.

As we came offstage Mickie crooked his finger at me: 'Come here. I want to talk to you.' I followed him and a hotel bellhop to the back of the venue, where, before sitting on a couple of old cinema seats, the hotel employee placed a pillow under Mickie's royal arse (my mother's expression) and poured him a glass of champagne. I learned in that moment about Mickie's strange sense of humour.

'How would you like to make an album in England, Suzi?'

I honestly thought he meant the whole group. 'Yeah. That sounds good. Who are you?' Instinct told me to play it cool.

'I'm a producer.'

'Oh, yeah? Who have you done?' I knew every single act he had produced, of course.

He listed his credits, then invited me to join him at the studio alone.

'Okay. Just let me tell the girls.'

Off we drove in a huge black limo to that most sacred place in Detroit's history, Motown Studios. I didn't know quite what was happening, but didn't question it; I was going along for the ride, wherever it took me. Jeff Beck, Cozy Powell and I ambled into the pit and began to jam on 'Cissy Strut' – I was flying. We all went into the control room as the engineer set things up for their session, but then I started to feel a little uncomfortable at being the only female there.

'Can I call my sisters, Mickie? They have to come and get me.'

'Sure, no problem.'

Patti and Nancy picked me up, and all the way home we giggled wildly about what was going to happen to Cradle.

Mickie went back to England, but not before having a meeting in New York with my brother to discuss his offer. He wanted to make a record, oh yes, but only with me. And he added that he was reluctant to break up a family band. My brother promised to relate the entire thing to all concerned – as indeed he did to everyone in the family but *me*.

For the next few months I bombarded Mickie with tapes, pictures and phone calls – 'He likes you, Suzi. Keep calling.' (It must be said that we all have a different version of these events. I'm fifty-seven years old and we're *still* talking about it.) Anyway, no contract was forthcoming, of course, and as time went on we all started to get very downhearted. And them the inevitable happened – the band broke up. I rode my bicycle over to Arlene's house (still with husband number two). Ever since the Pleasure Seeker days my biggest sister had always seemed to give me the right advice.

'God, what do I do now? Music is my life. The band is my life.'

Arlene replied, 'Why don't you give Mickie Most a call? You know, he wanted to sign you as a solo act!'

'What the hell are you talking about? I don't know anything about this!' A wave of excitement hit me in the gut – but with another wave of guilt just behind. I phoned immediately, and told him the band was breaking up – which is exactly what he was waiting to hear.

'So are you ready to come and record for me?'

And again those waves – the first of anger, the second of regret. How could they nearly deny me the chance of something I had been waiting for my entire life? How unfair! How selfish! If the band hadn't broken up the entire thing would have passed me by . . . Yet what a shame we didn't all get the offer. I wasn't the only girl in the band with a dream – Patti especially would be gutted.

Now that Cradle had disbanded, two solo offers appeared on the table. Jack Holstrum wanted to take me to New York City, form a male band around me and, in his words, 'make you into the new Janis Joplin'. Mickie wanted to take me to England, form a male band around me and 'make me into the first Suzi Quatro'. It was a no-brainer really.

4

DESTINATION LONDON

....

It's the summer of 1971, I'm now twenty-one years old, every decision is my own and I take total responsibility for my own life, good and bad. ('*Excuse me, Susie, but methinks you're gathering quite a lot of emotional baggage.*) Oh, yes, I was aware of the hole I was digging emotional baggage-wise, but the over-riding need to succeed took precedence. This is my destiny, this is my destiny, this is my destiny . . . Maybe if I said it enough times it would stop the guilt bubbling under the surface of my excitement – guilt that in some ways is still with me today.

Mom, Dad and I are sitting in their bedroom, Mom in her rocking chair, Dad in the 'power' seat and me – well, I was standing (ready to run if I had to).

Dad: 'So, Susie, what are you going to do? You have two offers on the table. I would prefer you to stay in New York.'

Mom: 'Yes, Susan. You don't want to move to England. You'll be all alone, no family, nothing. I don't recommend it.'

Me: 'Okay, Mom, Dad. I've thought a lot about this – and I *am* going to England. I'm twenty-one years old, and legally you can't stop me.'

Oh no! Mom burst into tears. 'I knew it. I knew you'd leave. Oh, my God – you'll be on the other side of the world!'

She was clearly very upset, but this is the part I remember most. Dad said quietly, 'You do realize your sisters will not make it without you.' Pretty heavy statement to lay at my feet.

Nobody spoke for a few minutes. The only sounds were my mother's tears, the creaking of the chair and the ticking of the clock. Finally, I broke the silence.

'Dad . . . I'm going!'

The proposed contract arrived, along with two round-trip tickets to England (Arlene would go with me for a few days as my 'manager', i.e. best friend). She didn't seem to have any problems about me leaving the band – remember, she too had quit a couple of years earlier. And for my part, I was keenly aware that leaving behind everything that was familiar would be difficult enough, so I wanted somebody with me for as long as possible. With the contract came an advance of two thousand dollars: 'Wake me up, I must be dreaming!'

We were due to leave in a couple of months, so I began serious preparation. Up at five every morning, then cycle five miles to Farms Pier to lie in the sun for a few hours. Diet diet diet. Even permed my long brown hair into ringlets. And wrote songs constantly, completing thirty to take to Mickie.

I was so wound up in my own little world that it nearly slipped past me that I had to leave a thousand dollars of my advance with the family. Cradle 'debts'? Excuse *me*! We worked all hours, we lived in the van, we existed on one hamburger a day. *What* debts? But in the end I thought it was a small price to pay. In a way, it lessened the deep guilt I felt about leaving everybody.

I packed carefully: two pairs of blue jeans, four T-shirts,

my yellow hot pants, mustn't forget my leather jacket, teddy
bear pyjamas, one sweater, two pairs of boots, the guitar
alarm clock from Mom, a few personal photographs, my
Billie Holiday and Motown Hits album, and my extremely
heavy Les Paul recording professional bass guitar. Mum
nicknamed me Suitcase Lizzie, which I turned into a song.

Suitcase Lizzie

Looking for something incredibly new,
Had no particular mould
Met a magical man with a perfumed hand
Wavin' away the road
Pinched her arm, maybe she was dreaming
Woke up with a stranger, and he was singing

There she was, fresh outta school
Lonely hearts answer to super-cool
She's Suitcase Lizzie from Detroit City
Out to try her wings
She's Suitcase Lizzie from Detroit City
And she can do 'anything'

Floating way up in the sky on his magic carpet
Clouds so white, rushing by
Lay back girl and enjoy it
You'll never get another ride like this
Smiling sweet he made her sleep with a kiss

Hands encased in silver gloves
Barely touching her fingers
Electrical waves all through her veins
Imagine what he might bring her!

They walked together just above the ground
Tried to speak, but there was no sound.

There she was, fresh outta school
Lonely hearts answer to super-cool
She's Suitcase Lizzie from Detroit City
Out to try her wings
She's Suitcase Lizzie from Detroit City
And she can do 'anything'

(Suzi Quatro, Sept. 1971)

I was ready to go, but the mood in the house was sombre and it felt like someone had died. It was the end of Patti's hopes and dreams as she saw her future going out the door. The Pleasure Seekers was her baby – she wanted success every bit as bad as me, maybe even more. But this is not the way the story was written, and we must all accept our fate. Patti, Nancy, Arlene and I jumped into Dad's car for the journey to Detroit Metropolitan Airport. First stop for Arlene and me New York City where we would stay for one night, see a lawyer, sign the contract, then hop on a BOAC flight for our journey overseas. I sat in the back with a silent Nancy while Patti shot me murderous looks in the rear-view mirror. The goodbyes were painful, but nothing could curb my excitement. Nerves, happiness, anxiety – I felt so many conflicting emotions that I couldn't possibly name them all. (*Hey, you do realize that I'm about to take over the story – because you are about to become me!*) Not quite – let's not forget how difficult it was for the first eighteen months. I didn't really become you until just before the first hit.

We boarded the plane for Europe at 6.30 p.m. on 30

October 1971. As we went up the gangway I realized it was a jumbo jet. I'd never seen one before, let alone been on one – and I just hate flying. We strapped ourselves in and I sent up a silent prayer, promising God I'd be good (*you lied!*). Arlene slept all the way there, but I sat up the entire night with the stewardess holding my hand. As we neared England, our destination, the pilot announced, 'Well, everybody, I hope you were able to get a little sleep. It's a beautiful day. Look down and you will see a wonderful view of the City of London. The time is 7:15 a.m., Greenwich Mean Time. You may want to adjust your watches.' Adjust my watch? I was about to adjust my entire life!

We disembarked, went through passport control ('Visitor?' 'Yes,' I replied, as instructed by Mickie Most), got our bags and wheeled our way through customs. I looked eagerly around, expecting to see photographers and journalists waiting for me. Imagine how I felt when I spotted one little man with a sign which read 'Quantrell'. No limo – just a small Ford of some description. As we drove through London I took in the sights. 'Where are all the bowler hats? The umbrellas? The rain? Look how tiny everything is – isn't it quaint? Wow, look, there's Big Ben! . . . Excuse me driver, is this the river Thames?' I pronounced it not 'Tems', but to rhyme with 'games'. We pulled up eventually in front of a building called Aston House Villas in the Earl's Court district – a tiny little house pretending to be a hotel. Hardly the welcome I expected, but at least I was here at last. I had five hundred dollars in my pocket, and I had my dreams in my heart. Arlene and I checked in, went to our tiny room and feel into a blissful jet-lagged sleep.

In the morning we were woken by a call from the front desk: Mr Most was here to pick us up. Wanting to look my absolute best, I quickly applied a little mascara and some rouge and put on my yellow hot pants – well, they were in fashion then. I grabbed my bass guitar and my cassette of songs, and down we went. Mickie was dressed impeccably in pressed blue jeans, blue leather shoes and a powder blue V-neck sweater over a sparkling white T-shirt. Longish blond hair and beautiful blue eyes completed the look. As he stood there, leaning against his gold Rolls-Royce, I thought, '*This* is the welcome I expected.'

Mickie's face was a picture as he took in *my* outfit: 'Get in, *quick*.' Having been brought up in the land of Cadillacs, I slammed the door and was promptly admonished. 'This is a Rolls-Royce, Suzi. You don't need to do that.' Good beginning, eh?

We drove to Oxford Street where Rak Records was located. Mickie shared one large office on the third floor with Led Zeppelin's manager, Peter Grant, Dave Most (his brother) and an accountant. We all sat down and he began to outline his plans for me.

'This is how I see it. We'll go into the studio as soon as we've settled on the right songs. I'll get the top musicians, we'll record the album and then Suzi can go back home.'

What? Go back home? You must be joking! I was screaming to myself. I had no intention of doing that. Mickie didn't know it, but I was here to stay.

'Now,' he continued, 'you're probably a little the worse for wear today. So why don't you go back to the hotel, get some rest, and in the morning we'll have a listen to what you've written.'

'Oh, Mickie, I've been thinking – what's going to be my stage name? I have some ideas.'

'What are you talking about, Suzi? You have a great name – Suzi Quatro. I don't want to change anything about you.' In that moment I knew I had made the right decision.

The next morning arrived, and since Arlene was leaving that day I had to move to a single room with no bathroom. I would now be sharing one some distance away with the rest of the floor – yuck! As we said our goodbyes we were both in tears. So before I continue the story I must address my best friend in the whole world and partner in crime, sister Arlene. Over the years we had shared everything – how would I survive without her by my side?

As the eldest child, Arlene was witness to the rockiest part of Mom and Dad's marriage. Dad was not keeping it zipped up, and our mother suffered constantly. Mom kept Arlene in the house, making her do hundreds of household chores – no wonder she wanted to get married so damn young. Arlene knew, as she was walking down the aisle on Dad's arm, that she'd made a big mistake. She loved Leo like a brother, not as a lover. It took seven years and three children before she broke out.

And somehow, even though I was only a teenager, I became the expert on sex. Did I enjoy it? What did I do? How did it work? I remember one time at the Gorham Hotel in 1967. I was sitting in her bedroom while she was putting on make-up for the evening show at Trude's and we got gossiping about some of the cute guys at the club. There was one in particular who had caught her eye. 'Mmmm – I would *love* to sleep with *him*!' *Bang* – the door to the bedroom flew open. It was Leo with a face like thunder. He'd been listening at the door and looked ready to kill. Brusquely, he ordered me out. I heard shouting, arguing, crying. Next morning she told me, 'I said it was just silly girl talk and I didn't mean a word of it.'

In the middle of my affair with DC and Arlene's with 'that' dancer from the club, we decided to take one of our trips. She told Leo, 'I need to go away for a couple of days – just to get some space, honey.' He seemed to accept we were going to one of her friends' houses but something must have made him suspicious. We packed two small overnight cases, opened the bedroom window at the Quatro house and put them on top of the air conditioning unit before making our way out of the garage door to the car. Leo was standing there, both cases in his hands. 'Where is it your're going, girls?' I don't know how, but we did manage to get away that night, drove to Chicago, left the car at the airport and grabbed a plane to New York City. The next day, while walking down Broadway with DC, I was amazed to see a stubble-faced, shattered-looking Leo glancing wildly from side to side and obviously looking for his missing wife – the writing was on the wall. I had always loved Leo, had had a crush on him since I was a child, and I did feel bad. But, it has to be said, not bad enough to stop – after all, I was only seventeen and we were having a great time!

Finally the day came that she decided she could take no more and told Leo she wanted a divorce. We were playing the Richard Harris album with all those Jimmy Webb songs: 'This time we almost made the pieces fit, didn't we, girl? This time we almost made some sense of it, didn't we, girl?' At that moment, Leo appeared at the door. I shall never forget the look on his face; and when I faced my own divorce, all those years later, I saw that look again. It's heartbreaking – it takes a lot of courage to walk away.

This time, it was Arlene walking away from me. She was

gone, and my first day alone in London was about to begin. While I was getting ready, I turned on the tiny radio over my bed. I was shocked by what I heard. Where was the rock and roll? Where was the fun? Why are these DJs talking and talking and talking and hardly playing any music? And when they did play music – my God, this is radio in Britain! I felt my first wave of homesickness for all things American.

I walked to Earl's Court Tube station, bought a ticket to Oxford Circus and then walked the couple of blocks to Mickie's office. After lugging the heavy bass up the stairs, I breathlessly sat down with him once again. Wisely, this time I had my blue jeans and leather jacket on.

'So, let's hear what you've got.'

I took out my little cassette, he put it on his player and the first song started. Five seconds in, stop, fast forward, next song began, six seconds in, stop, fast forward. Shit! Doesn't he like anything? This went on and on until we were nearly at the end of the tape, when a little six-bar ditty made an appearance. Boogie woogie piano: 'I'm getting bogged down, and tired of ya, pretty boy . . . keepin' your body fed is gettin' me mighty annoyed.' End. Mickie stopped the tape machine.

'That's the one, Suzi. Work on that. Don't like anything else. Who do you think you are? Carole bleedin' King?'

So, armed with these wonderful words of encouragement, I said goodbye for the day and returned to the hotel. Then it hit me. I was alone for the first time in my entire life. I went up to the roof and gazed at the sky. Gee, I wonder if they're seeing the same moon in Detroit. I felt a million miles away from everything and everybody I ever knew. This was not going to be easy. I went back to my room, got undressed, brushed my teeth, put on my pyjamas and for the first time cried myself to sleep. It wouldn't be the last.

Eighteen long months were to pass, and somehow I learnt to survive. Mickie rented me a rehearsal room in Finchley, equipped with a piano and a small amp for my bass. Every day from 10a.m. till 5p.m. I sat and wrote. The first song I completed was 'Ain't Ya Something, Honey' from my ill-fated 'showreel'. Coffee and cigarettes (well, I puffed anyway) were my sole companions. Mickie clearly knew what I wasn't, but it was also clear he didn't know what I was. The only obvious thing was that I didn't fit into any of the accepted female modes. Shit, I'd known this from the very beginning. I was desperate to deliver what Mickie was asking for: 'We need that one magical song. Once we have it, everything else falls into place. When I can visualize you on *Top of the Pops*, then we've got it. And don't forget – it's gotta grab you in the first thirty seconds. Right, now get busy!'

Olympic Studios were booked with big Jim Sullivan (guitar), Alan White (yes, drummer), Rabbit on piano and me on bass. I was playing with some of the best. And the songs: 'Brain Confusion' (an early composition from my Cradle days), 'Ain't Ya Something, Honey' (out-and-out boogie-woogie), 'The Wick That Was', 'Curly Hair for Sale' and 'Sugar Flash Rapper'. These tracks were obviously well played by musos of this calibre, but the direction was unclear. Something wasn't gelling, and both Mickie and I were losing our way. The harder we tried, the harder we fell – and for me that fall was into a deep depression.

I had no money and no friends. I existed in my little bathroomless room (now on Cromwell Road in the Atlantic

Hotel), in the rehearsal room or in the studio. There was no other reality. Too proud to ask for help (*Well, Susie, to be fair, he had given you two thousand dollars to tide you over. Why didn't you tell him the truth?*) I was embarrassed – there were enough problems trying to get me into gear without giving him my tales of woe. It wasn't his problem to solve; it was mine. The food part wasn't too difficult – I would 'borrow' it from local pubs. My altar training as a child would come in handy after all (remember those candles?). In pubs I would go to the toilet, which usually meant passing the kitchen, and just grab whatever I could and shove it in my pockets. As for smokes, luckily I had made friends with Victor who worked on reception and he let me wander around behind the desk. I searched a little and located the hotel's supply of cigs – another problem solved. But the no-friend situation was a little more difficult. So I drew pictures of children whom I called Tommy, Sarah and Vanessa, and hung them on the cracked mirror over the stained basin. For some reason I felt safe to share my secrets, my tears and fears with these drawings. Although I wasn't a child myself any longer, emotionally I still felt like one. It was a long wait for fame.

England was a foreign country to me in every way. It would be quite a while before I got to grips with the sense of humour, the various accents, the legendary reserve, the tiny streets/food portions/milk bottles/cars, the lack of television stations and the radio. Oh, my God the radio! It came crackling out of the tiny speaker above my bed and I couldn't find a decent station. But by twirling the knob back and forth, I managed to hear various hit artists of the day. Marc Bolan's T Rex was huge at the time, and Rod

Stewart and Slade were just beginning to take over the British charts with hit after hit. I was overjoyed when I heard my old friend Alice Cooper blast out of the airwaves with 'School's Out'. But most of the time it was middle-of-the-road crap. I used to go downstairs to the hotel lounge and see *Top of the Pops* with people like Chicory Tip doing 'Son of My Father' and Benny Hill singing 'The Fastest Milkcart in the West', and wonder what kind of 'pop' music this was supposed to be. Everything about my new enviroment was different from what I had grown up with – countless TV shows featuring all the hits artists of the day, and so many radio choices it made you dizzy! I had never realized how spoiled we Americans were.

Although I was lonely and broke, my life wasn't entirely without light relief. I quickly found myself a boyfriend who was a disc jockey on BBC Radio 1. He squired me around to a few parties, including a get-together given by Paul McCartney and his wife Linda. It felt pretty amazing to meet a Beatle at long last. My boyfriend shared a flat with another DJ, Ed Stewart, who was dating Eve Graham from the New Seekers at the time, and we became friends. She took me along to one of their concerts in Hemel Hempstead. I also attended a concert by Don McLean (American Pie), and one by David Bowie just before he broke big. I watched the show wide-eyed as this gender-bender wowed the audience, then I went backstage to David's dressing room where his bisexual wife Angie tried to pull me. I made my excuses and left. Aside from a few months of companionship and dates (this particular romance hit the dust when the said DJ tried to take over my management and Mickie showed him the door) I was still waiting for my dreams to come true.

Sometimes Mom and Dad would phone me and ask how I was doing.

'Great. Everything's wonderful. Success is just around the corner!'

'Do you need some money, Susan?'

'No. Mickie is taking care of everything.'

Lies, lies and more lies. I didn't want anyone to stop believing in me, especially myself. But sometimes, it was hard to keep believing. Most nights I pounded the floor in tears, asking God to help me be strong. It's hard to explain how lonely I was. Remember, I came from a big, noisy family. There was a car, food, heat, hot water, bathrooms, a telephone and people – everything that was missing from my everyday life. I was in emotional limbo. Here are some lyrics I wrote while in this state of mind.

Mind

I do believe, I can clean out my head, if I can dream
There comes a time I may melt, a time I may bend, love my friend
. . . love my friend.
Lately my hands get lost . . . running cross my face.
I tried to cry last night . . . for the human race.
Racing like the wind, just to beat him to the end.
Oh what a way to kill a day.

Mind mind mind don't let me down
In this crazy cold world we live in
You're all I got, all that I need
After everybody's gone away
I can't make it. Don't let me down.

Circus ride, mama's child did I go wrong . . . it's been a long
   lonely time
Long time to wait before, someone unlocks the door, my friend
   . . . I need a friend
Can't understand, it's like living in a cage
Permissive society, what a messed up age.
Ageless my desire, smouldered in the fire.
Now I got nothing left to say.

(*Hey. While you're wallowing in self-pity don't forget the tape.
Remember Thanksgiving 1971? As if you weren't having a hard
enough time surviving! Tell 'em about it, Susie.*) Okay – though
I'd rather forget. Thanksgiving is always the fourth Thursday in
November, and it's a big celebration in America. It's a national
holiday celebrating when the settlers made peace with the
Indians. Families get together for a huge turkey dinner, and
there's a big televised parade at Macy's where Santa makes his
first appearance. And 1971 was the first holiday ever that I
wasn't at home. Mom, for some reason, stuck a small picture of
me on the candles at either end of the dining table. Strange – like
I was dead or something. Dad decided to tape the festivities with
the idea of sending it over to me in England. (*Nice of him – or
was it? Why didn't he tell everyone he was taping?*) In the
background were the normal noises: Mom turning on the water,
shutting the oven door, yelling at someone, kids arguing, doors
opening and closing. I could pick out various voices. Patti was
there, my brother, and my one true ally, Arlene, always sticking
up for me. Then Dad started to conduct the orchestra. The
following is the conversation on that tape.

   'So how about that Mickie Most signing little Susie up, eh?
What do you think of that!'

Mickey: 'Yeah . . . goddammit, who'd have thought it? I flew to New York to try and get the girls a deal, but he didn't want 'em – just Susie.'

Dad: 'The thing is all you kids are talented. *Why* he picked Susie I just don't know. Hell, I don't think she's even that good a bass player.'

Patti: 'Oh, my God, Dad, Suzi is sloppy, very sloppy – she would tell you that herself!'

Arlene: 'Well, Mickie Most thought she was talented.'

On and on it went. Imagine how I felt, sitting alone in my room, excitedly playing the tape, anxious to feel my family around me once again. It really hurt, and I struggled for many years to find a reason for this conversation even taking place.

Looking back on it now, Dad always wanted a big career in showbiz. But destiny dictated that he would have five kids and so he needed a day job. But this didn't stop him from dreaming about what could have been, and I guess I was living the dream for everyone. Once, in an unguarded moment, Dad said to me, 'Susie, you did what I never had the guts to do.' I think that said it all.

It was now December, and I had absolutely nothing to show for it but a growing debt to Rak Records. It all added up – the flights, the advance, the hotel, the studio, the rehearsal room – and some day Mickie (rightly so) expected it to be paid back. Christmas was coming and it would be my first Christmas away from home – it wasn't a nice feeling. Dad suggested I should just jump on a plane and fly home and he'd pay for the ticket. How sweet of him. And what did I say? 'No thanks.' (*I think you were afraid that if you went back you'd never get away again. Isn't that the truth?*) Got it in one.

When Chrismas came I was so very alone that I couldn't

95

stand it, so I went for a walk down to Earl's Court. What's that I hear? Singing? I followed the sound. There, inside the tube station, was a choir of children singing Christmas carols for charity. I couldn't resist sneaking unnoticed into the back row and joining in. Big tears rolled down my face as I sang my mother's favourite, 'Silent night, holy night, all is calm, all is bright . . .' This was my all-time low, and years later for the album *Rock Hard* I would remember this time and write the song 'Lonely is the Hardest' – and it was. Mom always said that this was the period in which I got tough – that I had to get tough to survive. And she was right, as usual.

In the New Year it was time for a 'strategy meeting' with the boss.

Mickie: 'Suzi, we don't seem to be getting anywhere, do we? Maybe you should go back to Detroit.'

For the first time I felt fear. 'Listen, Mickie, this is an unnatural situation for me. I've always been in bands, I miss the gigs. I work so much better in that environment.'

Mickie studied me for a few moments trying to make up his mind – and, I guess, trying to decide whether he had wasted his money. (*May I say that was strictly your perception. He was merely testing you – scaring you a bit, intimidating you, frightening you. Get the picture? I know for a fact he never considered sending you back – he believed in you right to the end.*) Mickie said slowly, 'Riiiiiight. A band, eh? Okay, let me think about that one. Maybe we can do something about it. I think we need to start the publicity machine rolling, get some kind of buzz going. I know just the man – used to work with the Beatles up in Liverpool. His name is Bill Harry.'

And so my fifteen-year association with Bill began. At our first meeting we talked for hours while he took down all my details. After that I often went to his West London flat and babysat his son Sean, while he and Virginia went out for the evening. Soon I began to get headlines in loads of publications: 'Mickie's Latest Discovery' and 'The New Female Marc Bolan'. Before every interview Bill would brief me about the kind of publication it was and what kind of angle he had sold them. I was marketed as tough little streetwise Suzi from Detroit.

So, aware of this agenda, I began one encounter with a journo like this. 'It wasn't long after the race riots. Downtown Detroit was still considered a very unsafe place to go. One evening, around midnight, we sisters decided we all wanted some Top Hat hamburgers (cheap, disgusting and delicious). So I got the keys to Dad's Cadillac and volunteered to go – by myself! Stupid, yes? I got to the hamburger stand, got out of the car and walked inside. "Hi, can I have twelve hamburgers to go?" The grease sizzled as he flipped the meat and fried the onions . . . mmmm, smelled good. Actually I don't know what he was flipping – the ingredients were always a bit dubious.

'As I stood there waiting for him to load my burgers into a large paper sack (which would come in useful as a sick bag later on) I noticed another car pulling into the otherwise deserted car park. Six very large, mean-looking black guys got out. They noticed me. I noticed them. It was one of those moments when time stands still. "Oh, holy shit. What do I do?" The weedy-looking cook was going to be no help whatsoever. So I said to myself, "Susie, you can do one of two things. You can scream your ass off and hope help comes. Or you can get your burgers and very slowly walk to the car." Decision made. I paid the guy, gathered up my acting skills and attitude, and walked out slowly but purposefully. "I have a right to be here" was silently flashing in my eyes, and, "Don't fuck with me, boys."

'The group of men parted without a word as I neared my car. I carefully put the key in the lock and opened the door, laid the burgers on the passenger seat, did up my seat belt, put the key in the ignition, turned on the engine and put my foot flat on the floor, burning rubber on all four wheels as I hauled my sweet little white ass outta there.'

The journalist loved my story and requested a suitable picture to go along with it. Next month, I noticed his magazine on a newsstand. 'Suzi the Knife' was the headline, and in the picture of me looking mean and dangerous my hand was stretched out holding . . . a butter knife.

Bit by bit, we were building the image that would become Suzi Quatro. Bill often told me, 'Suzi, you are *so* quotable and *so* interesting and *so* different – you make my job easy for me.' Oh, yes, I was definitely different – trying to carve out a path for female rockers at a time when girl singers were sweet/ pretty/cute/feminine as per Dana, Lynsey De Paul, Mary Hopkin and Olivia Newton John. I, on the other hands, wore blue jeans, T-shirts and a black leather jacket, played bass guitar and belted out rock and roll with the best of 'em (and I mean boys!).

We did many different stories: me hanging out at a pool hall (I am an excellent player, as Alex 'Hurricane' Higgins will tell you); standing in Carnaby Street, leaning on a lamp-post cigarette in hand, pretending to smoke (thought it made me look cool, you see); and various 'rock chick' orientated stuff. Little bits of press coverage appeared everywhere and this pleased Mickie, giving him a new boost of energy. I was generating quite a lot of interest, and things were looking up.

It was March 1972, and I'd been away from home since the previous October. Mom and Dad were coming to visit me in London. I was so looking forward to it, but was actually worried that I might not recognize them – my 'other' life seemed to have been a million years ago. But when the day came I just fell into their arms, hugging and kissing and crying, quite overwhelmed with emotion. They were on a special tour with everything provided, so we got on the bus and headed down to their hotel in Bayswater Road. Both were surprised at how tiny the room was, but by now I had become sufficiently anglicized not to notice. We had breakfast and then made our way to Rak Records, which by this time had relocated to an office just off Berkeley Square. I hoped the nightingales would be singing that day – guess I was more than a little nervous because you never know how parents will react in any given situation. (*I'll say! Won't it be just dandy if Dad starts on about how wonderfully talented all his kids are, and how Mickie should have signed the whole band, and how Dad doesn't really understand why he chose just you . . . and oh, yes, your brother's God-given talent on piano going to waste. Such a shame, such a damn shame. Well, good luck, little Susie from Detroit!*)

We arrived right on time and Judy, Mickie's secretary, led us up to the third floor. Dad was charm personified, Mom shy as always. They all shook hands, and tea was ordered. We sat down on his brown leather couch (many a photo of me was taken lounging on this couch, dressed in my leathers). Mickie's office was tastefully decorated, but what impressed most was the walls – lined with silver, gold and platinum discs. I noticed my father taking it all in. Mom was quietly studying Mickie.

Niceties were exchanged first ('How was the flight over? How long are you staying? What sights are you planning to see?') Then the real conversation began. Straight in at the deep end Dad said, 'Mr Most, when do you think Susie will be able to come back home?'

Without missing a beat (although *my* heart was pounding), Mickie replied, 'Well, Mr and Mrs Quatro, let me tell you what my plans are. I know it's been several months now, but things don't always go without a hitch. We haven't found the right song yet. It's all a matter of putting the right picture in the right frame, and we're still searching. Have a look at these press cuttings – you can see that we're starting to develop an interest in Suzi here. For the first time I think we can see the light at the end of the tunnel. She's a star, and I'm the one who's going to make her dreams come true. Isn't that right, Suzi?' (Yes, Master.) It was suggested that I take some time off from my song-writing duties and go off and enjoy a visit with my family. Grateful for the invitation to 'get out of there', we left.

The three of us did all the normal touristy things that day – Big Ben, Madame Tussaud's, a trip down the Thames, even taking in a movie in Leicester Square – until finally it was bedtime. I just could not bring myself to go back to my room in Cromwell Road, so I asked Mom and Dad if I could sleep on the floor in their room. Without asking any questions they agreed, and for the next week this is where I spent my nights. I was so desperate to feel close to someone again.

The next day Mom and Dad wanted to see where I was living. I was dreading it. So we took a cab ride (well, he could afford it) to my hotel, where I threw open the door for them. The three of us just stood there for a moment – actually, it was so small that no one could move. Then, *pow!*, my dad slammed his fist into the wall.

'Goddammit, Suzi. I never thought you'd be living like this. You have a beautiful home in Grosse Pointe. You call this a bed? And where's the bathroom, for Christ's sake? How can my daughter be living under these conditions?' Then he started to cry. Mom just stood there saying nothing, pain etched into her face. (*This was the moment, wasn't it, Susie? This was the 'test'. The only time you ever considered giving up. It broke your heart to see your parents so disappointed.*)

'Okay, Dad, tell me what you want me to do. If you really insist I'll pack my things now and come back home. Is this what you want?'

Miraculously, the sobbing stopped. 'No, Susie. Mickie Most has made an investment and he believes in you. You stay put and finish what you started.'

The rest of the visit was uneventful. After they returned home I went back to my single room.

The tracks we had originally recorded were sitting in the vaults at Rak gathering dust as the search for the ideal song continued. One day, Mickie called me to his office. 'Sit down, Suzi, and listen to this. I think I have a song for you.' It was a tune written by Phil Denny, called 'Rolling Stone'. Catchy little pop tune, I thought – terrible lyrics, though. 'Now I don't like the lyrics,' Mickie said, reading my thoughts, 'so what I thought we'd do is this. You get yourself over to Erroll Brown's house tomorrow, and together you can rewrite it. You know – make it your own.'

So, excited by this new assignment – anything to get me out

of the non-productive cycle – I got myself over to Hampstead Heath. I was already acquainted with Erroll, who was a very nice, talented man. We sat at his piano and began.

'Okay, Suzi. This is about "you". Let me see. How about something like "Age of sixteen, was on the road . . ."'

"Doing things you've never seen," I added. And we were off.

'You've got great eyes and a great smile – let's try and get that in."

"I've got my sunshine's eyes and I've got my sunshine smile."

A few hours later we were done. Happy with the day's work, I prepared to leave.

'Erroll, can I ask you a favour? I'm broke. Can you lend me some money to tide me over? Just enough to get home on the Tube and maybe get a snack or something?' This was the first and last time I ever borrowed a red cent from anyone.

'Sure. Take this five pounds with my blessing. And Suzi – I don't ever want it back.'

Thank you, Erroll, thank you very much. God bless!

Another session was booked, this time at Morgan Studios. The musician line-up was a little different: Peter Frampton on guitar (Peter Frampton's Herd), Mick Waller on drums (Rod Stewart's band, the Faces), me on bass and lead vocals, with Erroll joining me on backing vocals (you can hear him clearly, wailing away, 'Rolling stone . . . rolling stone'. I was pleased to be working with some of the artists I had grown up listening to. After all, I was a teenager in the sixties when the British Invasion took America by storm. The session went great: it was a good track and I sang with conviction. The wheels were set in motion for my first single release. *At last*! I thought. Fame, here we come.

I used to go quite often to a local swimming pool, and it was here, a few weeks later that I overheard a transistor radio playing my record. 'Hey, that's me!' I shouted to no one in particular, beside myself with excitement. It was what you call a 'turntable' hit, which meant it got played but didn't sell. It did reach number 1 in Portugal, but it bombed everywhere else. The thing that really bothered me, though, was that my name wasn't on the writing credits. Phil Denny had written the original song, and then Erroll was brought in and we worked together on it, of course; but Mickie told me it would have to be credited just to Brown and Denny so as not to upset Phil by splitting the credits three ways. That was shitty – but really it was the least of my worries. What would Mickie do now? Would he want to give up again and threaten to send me back to Detroit? My hopes had been raised, and then dashed to the ground. Welcome to the wonderful world of showbusiness.

It was now mid-1972 and I was desperate to start a band, so Mickie and I placed an ad in *Melody Maker* and booked a rehearsal room in King's Cross. With a list of four drummers, and three guitarists, auditions were held. I chose Keith, one of the best drummers in the country at the time (ex-Deke Leonard band with that Bill Haley feel, sitting way back on his stool and hitting that shuffle rhythm exactly right) and on guitar Jeffrey, a flash American who was full of himself but really, really good. I had my trio and I was happy.

Now we began to rehearse in earnest, working up a set of my originals – and before we knew it Mickie got us a booking as first act at the Rainbow in Finsbury Park, arguably one of the most important gigs at that time. We would be supporting the Kinks, who'd had a string of hits in the sixties including 'You Really Got Me', 'All Day and All of the Night', 'Tired of

Waiting' and 'Dedicated Follower of Fashion', more recently 'Lola' in 1970, and were now in the charts with 'Supersonic Rocketship'. Also on the bill were an all-girl American band, Birtha (their blurb proclaimed: 'Birtha has balls'). This was a very important moment for me, an opportunity to prove what I could do. Dave Most, Mickie's brother and record plugger extraordinaire, attended with instructions to report back to him as soon as the show was over.

As soon as we started the first number *bang* – my amp blew up! Oh, for fuck's sake . . . I had no roadie, so I slipped off my bass and went to see if I could repair it myself. Jeffrey took advantage of this unexpected halt in the proceedings to begin his own set, launching into one of his original songs, 'My Whiskey'. Amongst the confusion I eventually plugged into his guitar amp and we limped to a finish. It had been a disaster, and we came offstage to a splattering of sympathetic applause.

Not a word was said, though I was furious with Jeffrey for taking over my set. I just walked to the dressing room, put my bass away and crossed the street to catch the Tube home. As I was heading down the stairs who should I see but Bill Harry, my publicist, rushing up. 'Suzi – sorry I'm late. Have you been on yet?'

'Yep, we have,' I told him, swallowing my tears . . . 'Goodnight, Bill.'

I rode home deep in thought. One step forward, two steps back. (*You know what, Susie, The way I see it is this. If you can't stand rejection get outta the business – know what I mean?*) I grabbed a box of cookies (comfort eating big time). went up to my room, undressed and put on a cassette of Neil Young's 'After the Goldrush'. I lay down on the bed as the lyrics began: 'My life is changing in so many ways . . . I don't know who to trust any more.' I kept going over the evening in my mind – my first English gig – fighting back the tears until finally they burst out in one great sea of emotion. And then the phone rang. It was Mickie.

'I've just heard from Dave. He said you were useless. What the hell happened? You begged me to let you form a band – and now this. How embarrassing for me! I tell you what, Suzi Quatro, from now on you're going to follow my direction to the letter. What I say goes! Do you understand? . . . *Do you understand?*'

Sniff. 'Yes.'

'Now go to sleep and be at the office first thing in the morning. We have things to discuss.'

One step forward, two steps back. Would I ever reach my destination? (*Funny, the way I remember it is that this was a character-building experience. You found your balls.*) Yeah, I guess I did – it was a turning point for me. I made another deal with myself. No more being down. No more allowing myself to be shouted at. No more bullshit. I came here to do something – and I was going to do it.

Next morning I turned up at Rak Records, as commanded, for the showdown with Mickie. My eyes were swollen and red from all the crying, but I was armed with a brand-new attitude: I was well and truly ready to fight my corner. After all, nothing that had happened was *my* fault – I mean, why hadn't he hired us a roadie or something? Then I wouldn't have had to stop in the middle of the show to repair my own amplifier. I was a little scared as I climbed the stairs, wondering if I would soon be finding myself back in Detroit. But, more than that, I was angry.

Luckily, the entire situation was defused because Jeffrey had left a message that he was leaving the band, and this new turn of events took precedence. To make matters worse, he was refusing to give back the stage outfit Mickie had bought – thought he deserved it in compensation. Mickie being Mickie (love this about him) took a cab over to his flat, grabbed the clothes and returned. Exit Jeffrey. The Rainbow disaster was forgotten for the time being, but in later years whenever Mickie and I discussed it he always referred to it as 'character-building'. Okay, Mickie!

It fell to Keith and me to sort out the situation. It was around midnight, and we were playing Scrabble on the floor of his flat in Acton.

'Suzi, you know I have a friend called Len Tuckey who's an excellent guitar player? He's with the Nashville Teens at the moment. He's really, really good – and a nice guy too. Why don't I get on the phone and ask him to come over so you can hear him play?'

'Not interested, Keith. I'll put another ad in. Don't worry, we'll find someone. Don't want any friends of friends – don't trust that way of doing things.'

But Keith was relentless, and about thirty minutes later he made the call that would change my life yet again. For some reason (probably instinct) Len got out of bed, grabbed his guitar and hauled himself over to Acton. I was still on the floor playing Scrabble and pretty much ignored Keith's attempts at introductions. Then my eyes slowly slid from the visitor's green platform boots to the patched blue jeans and up his never-ending legs: Levi shirt, long black beard, long hair. So far, I liked what I was seeing. Finally I arrived at a pair of kind blue eyes. He was a giant of a man and could easily have looked menacing, but as soon as he smiled the sun came out.

We talked for a little while, then jumped into Keith's car and headed for King's Cross (luckily we had an open-ended booking and I had made friends with the owner – hell, he never slept anyway.) So, arriving at three in the morning, we plugged in and started to jam.

'Okay, Len, why don't we do a Chuck Berry number? Do you know "Johnny B. Goode?"'

This is my 'tester' song – you can play all the right notes and still get it wrong, because 'feeling' is something that cannot be taught. Yep, it was perfect. He was good without being flash. I had found my guitar player – and he was cute too!

The next day I was at Rak bright and early, ready to report this latest development to Mickie. 'I've got my band now. Found the right guitar player. You gotta come down and hear us at the end of the week – we'll have a set worked up by then.' Mickie had never heard me so 'positive', and caught the mood.

'Okay, Suzi, go get rehearsing. Next week I'll send down Dick Katz – he's a big agent. If he likes what he hears he'll get you some gigs pronto. Then maybe you can start earning your keep around here.'

We practised for hours on end, doing mainly original stuff but with a couple of Chuck Berrys and Elvises thrown in for luck. Then someone had the brilliant idea of getting a second guitarist, so we put the word out and scheduled auditions for one week's time. After we'd seen a couple of hopefuls in walked this guy with a Wurlitzer piano under his arm. Didn't say a word, just plugged in and started to play. Bemused, we all joined in. At the end of the jam Lennie said, 'Excuse me, but who are you?'

'Well, I heard you were looking for a keyboard player, so here I am.'

'We weren't – but we are now.' We looked at each other, beaming. 'You're in.'

Enter Alistair. My line-up was complete, or so I thought. (*Hey, Susie, you know we always said, you and me, that we could write a complete book about Alistair? Sex, drugs, and rock and roll – you know, the stories everyone 'expects' to read. They were all about him – well, mainly all about him, though we had our moments of devilry too!*) Yeah, you're right. Don't worry. I'm going to devote an entire section to him – he deserves it.

The following week Dick Katz appeared, listened, nodded and left. Next thing you know, I've got me an agent. I was on the Mad About Music roster – wow! We started doing lots of university gigs, mainly booked by John Giddings – founder of Solo, now a huge agency. I stayed with MAM well into the eighties, even after Dick died. We quickly got the band together as a working unit, going up and down the M1 in a van and gigging, gigging, gigging. It felt like old times back in the States.

In November that year some more good news came our way. Mickie was good friends with Chas Chandler (bass player of the Animals), who was now managing Slade. They were a brand-new force in British rock and roll who would dominate the UK charts for many years – a real kick-ass group of musicians who wrote their own songs, fronted by the unique vocal talents of Noddy Holder. This was the true beginning of what the world remembers as glam rock. Slade were about to do their first big nationwide tour, and Chas agreed to let my band be the opening act. We would get fifteen minutes to strut our stuff, followed by Thin Lizzy and then Slade.

We rehearsed non-stop: 'Free Electric Band?', 'Ain't Ya Somethin' Honey', 'Brain Confusion', 'Curly Hair for Sale Ain't Got a Home', 'Monkey Mama' and 'Sweet Little Rock and Roller', which has remained in my set to this day. But before we began, Mickie called a band meeting.

'Okay, kids, here's the story. You'll be paid forty pounds a night, out of which you'll have to pay for petrol and hotels – nothing fancy, just bed and breakfast. We'll supply the van. I'm going to advance you the cash for some good equipment. Suzi, since you're the star we'll get you some acoustic gear.' This was the loudest and best bass amp at the time – reflex cabs, great for throwing the sound out. 'Chas will supply the PA system. Now, clotheswise. Boys, you'll dress in black. Suzi, my wife will go shopping with you today. You need something really special, and Chris will make sure you stand out. (*I'm certain anyone who was at any of those gigs will remember the little pink-haired girl with the purple and gold-striped bomber jacket and white flares pumping away on the bass guitar. Kinda hard to forget!*)

And so the tour began. The tour dates are framed and are still hanging on the walls of both my house and Len's. It was the beginning of 'us'.

Opening night in Newcastle was sold out. The place was filled with screaming fans dressed in glittery clothes with top hats and platform boots. Streamers and hand-made ribbons stretched across the balcony declaring, 'We love Slade!' And again, so different from the music scene in Detroit, where most bands wore T-shirts and blue jeans, and played high-energy rock and roll peppered with political slogans. We weren't even on the bill but I didn't give a shit – we were *there*. Noddy Holder watched me from the side of the stage that first night. He had heard about this little bass player from Detroit and was curious. Years later he told me, 'Slade fans were notorious for not liking our support acts. They would heckle and even used to throw stuff. But you won them over – I was impressed.' As I was with you, Noddy – you were special, and so were Slade. I was delighted to be asked to write the foreword for their book, published in 2006. It was the least I could do – after all, they'd taken a chance on an unknown and let me share the stage on their hit tour around the UK.

I always say the seventies were the last great era for 'real' musicians. We did the gigs whether the audience wanted to see us or not, drove the miles, ate the crappy food, got no sleep and very little money – in fact we just did it 'cos we loved it. We drove miles every day, from Cardiff to Brighton to Edinburgh, staying in one shit-hole after another.

Lennie and I had hit it off immediately. I was single at the time – hadn't really made any friends in England, and aside from a couple of short-lived romances I was still very much 'alone'. I knew I was vulnerable for friendship, and indeed love, so I was cautious – didn't want any unnecessary problems to occur. But I really, really, really liked him a *lot*! On the road we two always seemed to wake up at the same time, and ended up walking and talking – we had so much in common that we never ran out of conversation. He was living at that time with a Finnish girl whom he was about to finish with. He told me later, 'You know, Suze, I had a huge fight with my girlfriend. She said she didn't know what I was looking for or how to make me happy, to which I replied, "I want someone like Suzi." ' He added that this admission surprised both her and himself.

During the course of the tour all the musicians hung out together. Phil Lynott of Thin Lizzy, whose eventually fatal addiction problems were obvious throughout – he was either drunk, high on marijuana, or both – kindly invited us all to stay at his mother's guest house when we played in Sheffield gotta say though, Mrs Lynott, it was *fffffrrrreeeeezzzzzing*. But thanks anyway – you didn't charge us a penny! On 8 November we were in Liverpool. Dave Hill fell off his platform boots, broke his ankle and had to finish the tour sitting on a golden throne. It was also the gig where something else happened and— (*Excuse me for interrupting, but can I say, Susie, it was bound to happen, wasn't it? Inevitable, really. You guys were like . . . seriously attracted*). Shush, now – let me tell it my way.

So, lots of gigs, lots of parties, lots of groupies, lots of fun – but Len was always lurking behind me to make sure no one hit on me. Every time we meet Noddy always reminds me, 'I watched you guys fall in love, Suze.' Our feelings were growing stronger and stronger. One night, while I was bent over the snooker table in my green moleskin trousers, making a shot, Len came out with, 'You've got a great ass, Quatro.' Somehow it wasn't offensive, which was unusual considering my problem with men misbehaving. Anyway, back to *that* night. The show was over, and we all retired to our separate rooms. Problem was my bed was broken, and so was the electric heater. So I phoned Len. 'Hey, Lennie, do you mind if I sleep in your bed tonight?' Easy as that. It felt like coming home, and for the remainder of the tour and indeed for the next twenty years we were together.

When we hit Wales, Keith talked us all into staying at his parents' house in Llanelli. *Mistake*! As soon as he walked into the place he went into 'Pamper me – I'm not feeling well' mode. Halfway through the night, Len snuck into my bed to try and keep warm. Next morning we happened to see into Keith's bedroom, where he was surrounded by no fewer than five electric fan heaters.

After Bristol on 5 December it was all over and we began the drive back to London. Len, lying with his head in my lap (memories of Miami), looked up at me and said, 'I love you, Suze.' I was so surprised to hear him blurt it out like that, and my initial response was: 'You do?' Then, 'You know you're coming home with me tonight!' That was it. Done deal. We were officially a couple. Lying in bed as the sun came up next morning, I said to Len, 'Wouldn't it be funny if we actually got married?' I guess it's fair to say I proposed to him, and the very next day we pooled our money and purchased two gold wedding rings at the cost of £8 each. I knew we would be married, and I knew he would be the father of my children. But first we had to tell Mickie about our plans.

I don't know why, but I told Lennie to stay across the street in a café while I saw Mickie alone. It proved to be a good move, because Mickie just exploded.

'Who is this guy? You don't know anything about him. You're lonely, that's all, and you've grabbed on to the first guy that came along. I didn't bring you all the way over from Detroit to have you run off and get married. It would be bad for the image we're trying to create. Do this, Miss Suzi Quatro, and you and I are finished!' Then he calmed down and continued in a more normal voice. 'Here's what you do, Suzi. Live together for a while, see how it goes, and if he really is the one *then* you can get married.'

(*You do know, Susie, that Mickie was acting as a 'father'? He always took this role seriously – you were his responsibility. Try and see it from that angle.*) Yeah, whatever. All I know is that I walked across the street with a heavy heart, and relayed the entire conversation to Len. We were both in tears, but agreed to play it Mickie's way. We were in love, but we weren't idiots.

The two of us were invited to spend Christmas 1972 at Len's parents' house in Romford, Essex. This little girl from Detroit was about to meet the folks. During the course of the Slade tour I had had a chance to hear lots of phrases that were peculiar to my ears – words like 'bollocking', 'wanker' and 'poxy' – and eventually I asked Len to explain their meanings.

'Bollocking means to yell at someone, poxy means not very good, and a wanker is an idiot.'

Okay – got it!

So there we were sitting in Len's parents' front room having a very civilized cup of tea when Mr Tuckey asked, 'So, Suzi, how was the last gig?' to which I replied, 'Oh, it was poxy. The roadie was a real wanker and I had to give him a bollocking.' That evening, Len sat me down and told what I had actually said. What an impression they must have had of me!

But, oh boy, what a difference from the last Christmas – I had presents and a turkey dinner, and I was surrounded by the warmth of a family once again. Even though Len and I were living together, I insisted that we sleep in separate rooms for the holiday period. Well, that's how my mom raised me

(*Ahhhh! Remember Christmas Eve? Len's parents had gone to bed, and the two of you put on the radio, wrapped in each other's arms, and so very much in love. On came Gladys Knight's 'Help Me Make It Through the Night' and you danced and danced and danced. Sounds like a story for Suzi's romantic rendezvous, a regular part of 'Rockin' with Suzi Q', on rockin' Radio 2. . . . Commercial over, back to the regular programme.*)

5

'CAN THE CAN'

....

Soon it was 1973, the year everything finally came together. The Slade tour had really whipped us into shape and we were now a nice, tight, boogieing rock and roll band, ready and raring to go. Mickie took us into the studio where we cut two tracks, Albert Hammond's 'Free Electric Band' and Clarence Frogman Henry's 'Ain't Gotta Home'. No good – Mickie had no idea how to record the band. (*Hey, Destiny, are you ready? It's your turn to knock at the door again. Everyone's waiting for the next move.*)

So Mike Chapman (one half of Chinn/Chapman, hitwriters for a decade of music) is sitting in Mickie's office at Rak Records. 'Who's that girl I keep seeing in reception? She looks "interesting".'

'Aha – that's my secret weapon. That's Suzi Quatro, and she's going to be a big big star,' said Mickie as he put 'Rolling Stone' on the turntable.

'Oh, that's a surprise! That's not what I thought she'd sound like. I thought she'd have some balls.'

This must have been the pivotal moment for Mickie, and before you could say, 'Number one' a band meeting was called.

115

'Okay, guys, here's what I would like to happen. Now you've got a good set of original material worked up – some nice stuff in there, and you've developed your own sound – I'd like these two new songwriters I've just signed to see if they can come up with that "elusive" single that's needed to launch you. What do you think, Suzi? Is that okay with you?'

I didn't have a problem with that – anything to get us off the ground. So next day the band set up in the tiny basement at Rak and went through our entire set while Mike took it all in. Then he went back to Nicky Chinn's flat and they began to write. The very next day Chinn and Chapman came in and played a rough demo of 'Can the Can'. Then Mickie surprised us all by asking Mike to take over production. (*It must have been very hard for him to just turn over the reins like that – but smart at the same time. He knew deep down that he couldn't do what was needed.*)

To answer a frequently asked question (what does it mean?) 'can the can' is an American expression; 'can it' means keep it safe, put it away where no one can find it (put your man in the can, honey – get him while you can). As for '48 Crash' – well, that was all about the male menopause. So now you know.

Bandwise, all was not well. Keith was jealous of Len's and my growing romance and was causing all kinds of trouble. 'I want extra money. I'm doing all the driving and it's not fair.' This may have been true, but it was Len and I who were always on time and had to load up the van all by ourselves. No one was really owed anything – we were all working together. Len got really angry and raised his fist as Keith hid behind one of the amps. Just then Mickie walked in, saw what was happening and called another band meeting at which he admonished us: 'Stick together, be a band, don't argue. Oh, yes, for the future there will be no band name as such. And gigwise I think it's fair that Suzi gets fifty per cent and the rest of you share the other fifty.'

Once again we set up down in the basement at Rak, this time to routine the single. Mike played the demo, with multi-tracked screeching voices over multi-tracked screeching guitars – very rough but very exciting. Keith came up with that wonderful drum intro. Len played along creating that nice middle bit. I added 'Ooo can the can, ahhh can the can' over it, accompanied by a tasty little bass riff. Alistair, tinkling away on the piano, created that great 'answer' riff on his Wurlitzer – never met anyone who could make a Wurlitzer sound like he could. As far as I was concerned, Alistair was the 'muso' of the group and the rest of us were simply 'rockers'. We had something. We definitely had something. I always say you know when you've got a hit record, because the hairs on the back of your neck stand up, and that's how it felt when we laid it down in the studio the next day.

Chapman was sitting behind the console, a little bemused as he began his first solo production. Oh, yes, he was being tested by Mickie, who'd had more hits than I've had hot dinners. We were being tested too, and the band rose to the occasion. It was raw, it was edgy – it was 'different' and exciting. Track down, it was my turn. Mike had put me at the very top of my chest voice range, something he would continue to do for the rest of our association (which is still ongoing today). It wasn't easy – maybe I should have used a ladder. Anyway, it had the desired effect – electric! Vocals done, Mike fast forwarded it to the middle section.

'Now, Suzi, I need something really special here. You know, to lift it into the stratosphere.'

'Right, Mike. Start the tape. . . . *Whaaaaaaaaaaaaaaa*.' That put the seal on it. Now for the most important job of all: mixing!

Mickie was due to fly off to the States soon, but before he went we had one last important meeting, alone. (*I'm waiting, Susie. It's nearly my turn to take over now*).

'Okay, Suzi. I think we'll have a big hit with this song. It's time to discuss "image". How do you see yourself?'

'I want to wear leather,' I stated.

'No . . . no leather. It's been done many times and it's old-fashioned.'

'Yes!' I insisted. 'It's what I want. And it hasn't been done by a girl before.'

Back and forth we went until eventually I won. Then Mickie suggested, 'What about a jumpsuit?'

'Great, Mick. Perfect. I won't have to worry about tucking anything in. No ironing. Just great!'

The 'image' was born. A designer was found, I was measured up and the outfit was created: skin-tight black leather jumpsuit, cut off at the knees, long silver zipper down the front, snakeskin knee-high boots, and to top it off Mickie loaned me his collection of silver-chained tiger's claws.

Next step was picture time. Well-known and respected photographer Gered Mankowitz was called in. We sat down and discussed ideas while Mickie played him a rough mix of 'Can the Can'.

'How do you see her, Mickie,' asked Gered. 'What are you looking for exactly? What are you trying to represent with these photos?'

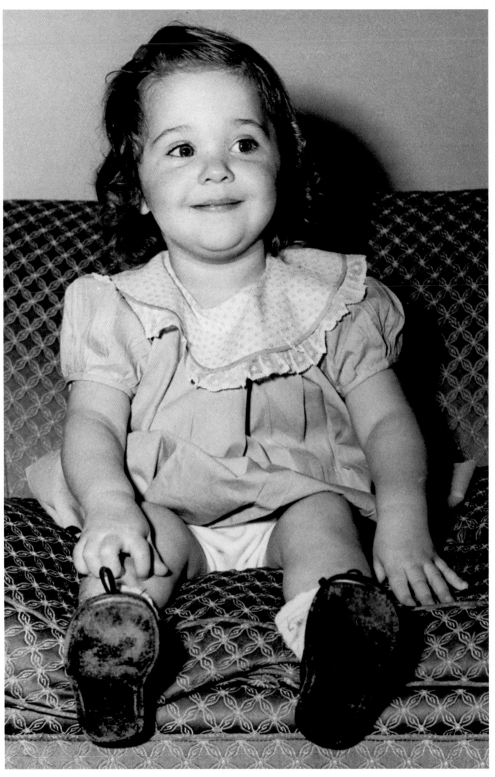

This is me aged two. It's all in the eyes . . .

My one and only formal dance. Check out the white gloves.

Low slung bass, top hat, pink and green micro mini: someone call the fashion police.

All our dresses were made by the drummer's grandmother. Fun clothes, fun days.

1972, waiting for success. Lonely is the hardest – I was trying so hard to look tough.

Showing off. I flew Mom and Dad over to London. I could afford it at last.

The constant protection of Mickie (on the right). I miss him.

Backstage at *Top of the Pops*, Christmas '73. I'd just said fuck in front of my dad . . . oh shit.

Me and Len, when we were happiest.

This was at a huge award ceremony in Germany. Mickie didn't smile like this very often. I was living the dream.

Me and my boys making a hit record.

At home in Detroit with Mom. I went home a star, thank god.

Lenny and me, having
a discussion.

Wedding number one, in London.
Bad hair days all round.

Wedding number two, in Japan.
Slightly different outfit!

A couple of friends dropped by my recording session. Debbie Harry on the left and Joan Jett on the right.

Me and Alice Cooper having a discussion on the neverending Welcome to my Nightmare tour.

A very normal picture. Me, Len and my parents at the house I still live in today.

'Suzi is one of the boys. In charge, ballsy but female. The photos must skirt both genders – it's all about "attitude".'

We set the session for two weeks' time.

Gered, I discovered, is a very organic photographer who gets right in there and creates his vision. Credit-wise he had already done everyone from the Rolling Stones to the current trends. Mickie often said, 'He's expensive and a little artsy-fartsy, but he's good.' This is another association that has lasted to this day – my current album, *Back to the Drive*, was photographed by Gered.

But while my 'image' in all senses was well in hand, all was not well within the band. Keith was increasingly unhappy and relationships were suffering. That night, as Len and I drank a bottle of Chianti together, we made the decision to fire him before any more problems arose. It was a hard decision to make, but neither of us felt we had any choice. The problems were poisoning the atmosphere big time, so we decided Keith had to go. Just then the phone went. It was Keith, and guess what? He was quitting the band. He went weeks before the single was due out, and must still be kicking himself. We gave Mickie the news as if it was no big deal, then frantically advertised for a replacement.

On audition day the first drummer to appear was Dave Neal, and after playing a little together we looked no further. He would stay with me well into the eighties. He wasn't a fancy drummer, more of a basher – but good-looking and very easy to get along with. Dave's memory of that day centres on me saying hello and then spitting my chewing gum right across the room into a bin. That used to be one of my party pieces – quite impressive!

Now that the band was truly complete, we were off to get

our pictures taken. The boys wore black string vests and leather trousers. I was in my black leather jumpsuit and snakeskin boots, with tons of Mickie's chains around my neck and the minimum of make-up (always had this thing about looking natural). Since I didn't have the Suzi haircut yet I had put carmen rollers in my hair to achieve a fuller look. Gered had set up a large table, placing the boys in various positions around me, one with his head lolling off the side of the table, one peeking through my hip held-arms, and Len looking the other way. We were ready to begin. Almost . . .

Enter Suzi Quatro. Thank you, Susie. I think it's important that I now take over. After all, this is when everything clicked (pun intended), when *you* became me. (*Okay, Miss Suzi Quatro, but I reserve the right to pop in and out when I feel the need. Just to keep a little perspective – okay?*)

So there we were, ready to be photographed.

'Suze,' insisted Len. 'Let's just pull this zipper down a little bit. Don't worry – nothing will show! But it'll look really sexy.'

I was dubious, but allowed him to unzip me right down to my navel.

'Wow,' Gered said. 'That's great,' and went behind his camera. 'Now, Suzi, what I want is attitude. This is *your* band. *You* are in control. Come on, give me that Suzi look!'

Instinct took over. I looked the part, I felt the part. I pushed my weight on to one leg with both hands on my hips, thrusting to one side, looked straight into the camera and gave Gered 'the Look'. I was well and truly Suzi Quatro at last. Everything made sense: the journey had been worth it. Gered delivered contact sheets the next day for Mickie to study. Several were picked and printed up, but not before adding a little tattoo on Len's arm which read: 'Can the Can'.

The photo session and its results dealt with, Mickie flew to the States, arranging with Mike to phone him with the mix once it was ready. Mike duly called, played the song, and Mickie told him, 'We have a number one, Mike – great job! But one thing . . . just to make it slightly more exciting, try speeding up the track half a semitone – nothing more – just to give it that "dangerous" sound.' This is the one and only time it was done on one of my records, but it worked. We had the single, we had the image, we had the photos, we had the radio play lined up . . . and we had the release date. Five four three two one *fire*!

I was more than ready – all those lonely days in London were about to pay off. I was also relieved that after all the waiting. Mickie's faith in me was about to be justified – and, indeed, my faith in myself. Looked like I wouldn't be on that return flight to Detroit after all.

As the publicity machine got into top gear Mickie decided I should play snooker with champion Alex 'Hurricane' Higgins at the Victoria Sporting Club in London, with a prize of £1000 for the winner. He chose Hurricane because of his bad boy reputation: the two of us, he reckoned, would make a formidable team press coverage-wise. Not only that, but no woman had ever before graced this establishment – another first for Suzi Quatro.

So how did Mickie get this idea? Well, in the Quatro house there was a full-sized pool table and all of us could play. I have a good eye and a nice touch, and can sink 'em with the best. In fact, sometimes I used to be a hustler in downtown Detroit, playing and pretending to be terrible, then playing again for money. Mickie had got to know of all this.

I practised every day for a month in preparation. I didn't

win, of course, but my score was respectable seeing that I was playing a world champion. And there was that one very nice bank shot, from the far end back to the corner, straight in the pocket without touching the sides, which scared the shit out of Alex. Now that's what I call a load of balls.

Len had now moved out of his flat and we were sharing my hovel – so small that when we turned over in bed we could only do so in unison. We asked to move to a slightly bigger room on the first floor. It was in this environment, fuelled with Chianti, that we began to write songs for the planned first album – planned as long as 'Can the Can' was a hit. Please please please let it be so! These days were the honeymoon period of our twenty-year-long relationship, from which I have so many wonderful memories. We had a tiny little portable record player, loaned to me by my old friend on the reception desk, Victor. Besides my Motown and Billy Holiday we only had Ricky Nelson's greatest hits, which we played over and over again, jiving around the room, laughing, talking and getting to know each other inside out. I told him my stories and he told me his as we pledged to be together 'for evermore'. One of Len's favourite things was to get me to dress up in my blue mini-dress, put on my silver knee-high boots and do all the Temptation routines for him. He used to sit there for hours as I entertained him.

Privately, I had a few doubts. Man is man and woman is woman. How is this going to work if I'm earning more than him? It's bound to cause problems. The male ego is such a fragile creature.

'Lennie, I want to talk to you. I've been doing a lot of thinking, and I want to get it straight now before anything happens. If we're going to be a couple we need to share – and I *mean* share – the workload, the good times, the bad times and the money. Whatever I earn, whatever you earn, it's *ours*.'

I think Lennie was a little surprised at this, but he agreed. And I felt better having said my piece.

With the release date looming we had the radio on non-stop so as not to miss one single airing of 'Can the Can'. Radio Luxembourg played it first, and as we sat glued to the radio it sounded fantastic. Next day Radio 1 took over. We got Record of the Week on David Hamilton's show and one by one every DJ started to spin the disc. Then finally The Day arrived, 27 April 1973. The record was released, and sales could begin. I called home that night with the news: 'Hey, dad, guess what? I just sold seven hundred and fifty records in one day! Can you believe it?' Little did I know that on its biggest day 'Can the Can' would sell over 125,000 across the UK.

Next stop was *Top of the Pops*, where we were 'this week's tip for the top'. We had made it into the charts. Dave Most accompanied us to the television studio, while Mickie called me from America.

'Okay, Suzi, this is it. This is your big chance. The song is right, the look is right. Now you gotta do the performance. I want to you to give it everything – energy, energy. Make the cameras burn. Smile – you have great teeth. Don't forget to wear the chains. And I think you should use my white Fender Precision – it's in the corner of my office. Now go get 'em, girl!'

We arrived, at last, at *the* most important TV show of the time. It was 9.30 a.m., time for camera rehearsal. Glam rock was now in full swing, and for the first time I saw acts like Wizzard, with lead singer Roy Wood and his multi-coloured long hair (whom we knocked off number 1), Sweet (looking like rock and roll drag queens), Gary Glitter, Alvin Stardust (dressed in leather like me), Roxy Music, the Rubettes and Mud, all of them wearing more make-up than me. And, oh boy, the outfits! There were huge platform boots, striped bell bottoms, wildly painted jackets and glitter everywhere – except on me. I was bare-faced and dressed in my plain black leather jumpsuit, although I did give way to the fashion of the day with my knee-high snakeskin platform boots.

I always did and still do give my all, even for run-throughs. The way I see it, you've got to show the cameras what you'll be doing on the night or they might miss something important. Dress rehearsal was at 3.30, after which all the acts hung around in the bar until showtime, which was 7.30 p.m. 'Now, with her first hit record, please welcome Suzi Quatro!' Three cameras pointed at me, the kids cheered and I was gone, truly gone. What a shot of adrenalin – the only drug I'm addicted to. I stared into the camera, swaying back and forth, stroking the microphone, riding my bass, screaming, with hair flying and three heavy-looking 'hooligans' backing me. I don't think anyone was ready for this. People still talk about that first TV appearance now. It was a shock – no one had ever seen a girl like this before. I embraced this role with relish because I knew exactly how to play it. Hell, I'd been practising for a long time – since 1964 in fact, taking in New York and Vietnam on the way. And after all that travelling, the real journey was only just beginning.

The record began to rise rapidly up the charts. Mickie, now back in command position, checked the sales figures every day. And it was Mickie who gave me that wake-up call. I'll never forget it. It was on a Wednesday morning, chart day.

'Suzi,' the landlady called up the stairs, 'phone call for you.'

God! It was 8.30 in the morning. Who the hell could that be?

'Good morning, Suzi. You have a gig tomorrow night, don't you?'

'Yes, in Sheffield, Mick. What's the problem?'

'Well, I think you may have to fly.' (*Hey, this could be difficult, really difficult. We, you, both of us absolutely hate to fly. Tell him, Suzi. Just tell him.*)

'Why can't we drive up there, Mickie? The van's all booked. What's the problem?'

'Well, Suzi, there's no choice. You have to fly because . . .' He drew this out till it was painful '. . . you . . . have . . . to . . . appear . . . on . . . *Top* . . . *of* . . . *the* . . . *Pops* . . . because . . . you are number one in the charts!'

I dropped the phone and screamed. Len came running down the stairs as the landlady and her family looked on, bemused. 'We're number one. We're number one!' We laughed, we danced around their front room – the landlady even made some popcorn to celebrate. Unbelievable, really – after all this time, all the hard work, the stops and starts, the loneliness, I was not only in love but number 1 in the charts. I was beyond delirious, and the only fly in the ointment was that I had to get on a plane tomorrow!

Thursday came, along with a case of champagne and a congratulatory telegram from Mickie and Chris, EMI records, also, surprisingly, a telegram from Phil Lynott and all of Thin Lizzy – how thoughtful. We arrived at the TV studio, this time not until five o'clock in the afternoon (a privilege reserved for artists who had reached the number 1 spot), did the show and zoomed across London to catch a private plane which would get us to Sheffield in time to do the show.

It was a one-engine propeller job and I really was petrified. I was swigging out of a whisky bottle just to pull together the courage to board. Finally, when we were airborne, I tapped the pilot on the shoulder and asked where the toilet was. I should have known better – there wasn't one. The flight took about an hour – an hour of clenching my teeth and crossing my legs. When the pilot told me he could see the runway at our destination, I made the mistake of relaxing and breathing out. *Whoooosh*. Wonderful, I thought: number 1 in the charts and I've pissed myself!

'Can the Can' went on to sell $2\frac{1}{2}$ million records around the world, and 315,000 in the UK alone. That's a record that would be hard to beat.

Station Road, Finchley, 3 June 1973. I am twenty-three years old, it's 7a.m. and I'm sitting at our breakfast table having a cup of coffee. Len is sitting opposite. And this is what is going through my mind. I've fucking done it. Yeah, I've fucking gone and done it. I have a number 1 record charting all over the world. Journalists are calling me for interviews wanting quotes and photos. People on the street are stopping me for autographs. So a big 'Fuck you' to everyone in Detroit who thought I was a no-hoper. Shit, I'm feeling good. And I sure am looking good. And yes, it's official, I am the queen of rock and roll. I'm famous. I'm a star. I'm wonderful! (*Ah yes, Suzi. It was reality check time. Remember, you got up, went to the bathroom, looked in the mirror and who did you see? Little ol' me, Susie from Detroit. Yep, the ego trip was over. God, Suzi, what would you do without me here to remind you of who you truly are?*) I went to the table, sat down and picked up my coffee. Len looked into my eyes and simply said, 'Welcome back, Suze.'

As soon as 'Can the Can' hit the charts, Mickie instructed Chinn and Chapman to come up with a follow-up in the same style. Don't change a winning formula. It was decided that we would record our first album and '48 Crash' at the same time, and Mike would produce. This would be Dave Neal's first recording with us. The studio, Audio International near Baker Street, was booked for two weeks We worked from 10a.m. till 10p.m., every single day, in one big room set up as a 'band'. I always sat on a stool, bass perched on my knee, with the lyrics on a music stand, singing into a 'scratch vocal' mic. Len was in one corner with his Marshall amp behind a screen, Alistair on the other side with no amp but just hearing himself through his headphones. Dave could see us, but was screened off so that the drums didn't leak all over the track. It was live, it was happening, and if we got it wrong we started all over again.

That first album is still one of my favourites. Songwise, it represented some of the best Quatro–Tuckey originals, things like 'Skin-tight Skin' (weird and wonderful), 'Rockin' Moonbeam', 'Shine my Machine' (all about Detroit), 'Get back Mama' ('Get back mama you been holdin' me down too long), 'Sticks and Stones' (a crazy chant which ended up as a cover on a CCS album, and 'Glycerine Queen'. I still do the last-named of these today, because it incorporates my bass solo. (*Don't forget that story about the guy who came into your dressing room. After all, he was the inspiration for that song.*)

We were at a gig in Manchester when there was a knock on the dressing room door and in walked this transvestite wanting an autograph. At that time the boys used to grease themselves up with glycerine, which made their bodies shine – a great effect. Len, being Len, said, 'Oi, mate, do you want a drink?' The transvestite said yes please, happy to have become part of the backstage scenario. Len proceeded to pour glycerine into a pint glass. 'Here you go.' And he drank it straight down without stopping. (*Hey, while you're telling stories don't forget the recording of 'Skin Tight Skin' and 'Rockin' Moonbeam'.*) Oh, yes, a moment for Alistair. As I said earlier, he was the real 'wild one' of the band. He was from Bangor in Northern Ireland and liked a drink or two or several – actually until he fell over, which is what happened in the studio. First Alistair was supposed to put a piano solo on 'Rockin' Moonbeam'. He was already well into his alcohol-fuelled day. Chapman thought it would be funny to speed up the track slightly while he played. It was funny all right because Alistair had no idea – just happily banged away on his Wurlitzer and afterwards said, 'How was that, Mike?'

'Skin Tight Skin' up next. We were all sitting on stools grouped around a microphone as we added the back-up vocals: 'People are talking don't you believe it don't you believe it don't you believe it ah.' Alistair, still drinking, started to sway – and not because he was getting carried away with the song. Finally, mid-note, he tipped over backwards and fell to the floor. Session over.

All the tracks on the first album were similar-sounding to 'Can the Can', and it's fair to say at this point that we were a boogie rock and roll band. Chinn/Chapman and Quatro/Tuckey, perfectly in sync – sometimes I would forget who wrote what. Lyricwise, they really understood me. We also did the first of several Elvis covers, 'All Shook Up'.

When you're in the studio and deep into it, mad things can happen. It was one of 'those' days when Len decided to cut out one of the *Sun*'s page three girls and paste her on to the studio glass partition. Mike thought that was funny and added a suitable caption, also cut from the *Sun*. Next, Alistair pasted a picture of a petrol hose pointing up her backside. And then all hell broke loose! We just filled that glass with ridiculous pictures, headlines and jokes, until just as we finished Mickie Most walked in. 'Just came down to see how it was all going,' he remarked noticing our 'creation' at the same time. He said nothing at all – which was worse in a way than if he had gone crazy. Mike played him some stuff, Mickie asked if we were on schedule, and then he left. We ripped down the pictures and got back to work.

'48 Crash' was the next song to be recorded. Again, it was at the very, very top of my vocal range – in fact the 'crash crash 48 crash' was impossible. I tried and tried but just couldn't reach the notes, so Mike and Len went out and did the honours with the result that Lennie lost his voice for the rest of the day. Thank God it was a 'gimmicky' record – we just got away with it. (*Don't you think it's strange that you had to use this high, high voice on all your early recordings, when in the early Pleasure Seekers' days it was the 'low' voice that everyone commented on?*) Yeah, probably. But it was successful, so I didn't, couldn't and wouldn't argue. I used my 'normal' voice later on, and had success with that too. And some day, little Susie, I promise you I will do a soul album and a Billie Holiday album and a jazz album and something Chapman has always wanted to do: a country album. But for now I was a leather-jumpsuited, bass-playing rock and roller.

As 'Can the Can' and '48 Crash' started to chart all over Europe and the first album was released, TV show offers rolled in. I, of course, sent the finished product straight to Detroit, followed up with a phone call a couple of weeks later.

'Hey, Dad, did you get it? Isn't it great? What do you think? Have you listened yet? . . . And I have something else to tell you. I'm in love with one of the guys in the band—'

Mom on the extension: 'Oh, no. I knew it. I knew you'd meet somebody. Now we'll never see you!'

Dad simply said, 'Susie, please tell me it's not the guy drinking the bottle of beer with his hand down his crotch.'

'Yep, that's the one! But hey, Dad, don't jump to any conclusions – that was simply the "mood" of the photo. You know – rock 'n' roll and all that. He's a very nice boy, comes from a nice family, normal as normal can be. And I'm not lonely any more – isn't that great? Wait till you meet him, Dad. You'll love him.'

During this period it seemed like we resided permanently at *Top of the Pops'* studio, appearing over and over again with all the chart acts of the seventies. Besides the glam rock stars there were also acts like Boney M (member Bobby Farell threatened to bite my ears off – God knows why), Robert Palmer (who got drunk and pinched my ass), the Bay City Rollers and Hot Chocolate (my stable mates) And in all that time I never fancied another man . . . except David Essex. I must confess I had a real thing for him when he sang, 'Hold me close don't let me go . . . oh no'. That's exactly what I wanted to do. He was just so damn cute. I never told him, even though we met many times. So now my secret is out!

So hits meant travelling, and travelling meant flying . . . and flying meant terror. I refused, and took boats and trains everywhere. I even travelled on the Trans-Siberian Express to get to Berlin. I just would not fly. Just after the Christmas break we had a booking on the popular German show *Disco* (their equivalent of *Top of the Pops*). Mickie had somehow talked me into flying to this one, but as soon as Sonya, his secretary, phoned us with the flight times I was in the toilet with a nerves attack. On the morning we were due to go I was a mess.

'I can't do it, Lennie. I have a bad feeling, really bad. I don't think we'll survive this flight. Call the office, tell them I've got gastritis. Tell them anything. *I am not going!*'

So the booking was cancelled. *Disco* even called and offered us the chance to come the following day when the show was actually being taped, and do without a rehearsal, but I still refused. Mickie called me into the office for a meeting and I knew I would be in the shit.

'Now, Suzi, we need to have a talk regarding this flying business. I *do* understand – I hate to fly myself. But your records are about to be released in America, and you won't be able to take a boat every time there's a gig or a TV show. It seems to me you have a choice – either you get on those planes starting now, or you accept that you will have a very small career.'

I started to fly.

We now started to expand into Europe doing television, which included a show in Belgium where we appeared along-side the newly formed Abba. Len is still very proud that Agneta flirted with him shamelessly the entire time – okay, so she's got a great ass, but then so do I. Then in September Mickie decided to book a tester gig at a small club in Cologne in Germany to see if we would pull. The band flew out the day before, whisky bottle in tow, and in the evening we went out to see an all-girl band that was appearing in a bar in the old town. Now whisky is an aggressive drink – anyone who drinks it will tell you that. Len (like me, not a big fan of flying) and I had consumed quite a bit that day, which we topped up at the club that night. The all-girl band took the stage, did a forgettable set and went back to their dressing room. Len had the idea of going back and saying hello to them, which we did. Problem was that they were undressed, flashing their bits to all and sundry. I really hated it – didn't want to be there, felt embarrassed, angry and a little drunk too.

'Dammit, Len, get me the fuck out of here. This isn't right – all of you guys standing here while they're undressed. Totally out of order. It just shows a lack of respect for them – for me too. *Getmeouttahere!*'

And so we left. (*To be fair, Suzi, both of us suffer from possessiveness and more than a little jealousy. 'Childish' is the word that comes to mind. Groupies, temptations, rock and roll men on the road – didn't trust any of them, and in an argument we don't back down. Doesn't matter whether the warning signs flash, we just keep going. Mix that with a drop of alcohol and what does it spell? Trouble.*) Walking back to our hotel, Len was furious with me for causing what he felt was an unnecessary commotion, I was stubbornly refusing to back down, and this whisky-fuelled argument kept going until suddenly I felt a smack on the side of my head and ended up lying on my back on the pavement, still holding on to Len's hand. I was stunned into silence and didn't know quite what to do. When we got back to the hotel Len went straight to sleep, and nothing was said the next day either. Mickie was due to fly in to see the show . . . *mmmm*, this could be tricky.

We did the show – which was sold out – still not speaking of the night before. I have photos of that day in which I look confused and Len looks sad and just a little scared. Mickie, though, was none the wiser. (*I wonder what he would have said had he known what happened!*) Len and I acted as if nothing odd had taken place all the way back to Heathrow, then drove to his parents' house where we were due for Sunday lunch. I was still completely silent, trying to work out why it had happened and what I would do about it. (*You know, Suzi, you've been the same all your life. When you scream and shout it's almost comical. When you're silent it's serious.*)

Then, just before we sat down to eat, Len grabbed me on the driveway.

'Please, Suze, don't mention anything about this to my mum!'

So we ate, and then drove back to our flat in London. I remember thinking to myself, 'Okay, Suzi, so you made a mistake. He's not the guy you thought he was. Not too late to get out – just put it down to experience.'

Then, as if reading my mind, Len broke. (*Good for him he did, or the marriage and children might never have happened.*) He finally apologised. 'I'm so so sorry, Suze. Don't know what came over me. It'll never ever happen again, I swear to you. Please forgive me. *I love you.*'

On the road, pressures and whisky were not a good mix. The pressures would remain, but the whisky was soon banned from our lives. Wisely so!

Having successfully pulled our first paying audience in Germany, Mickie decided to book us a small tour with Lippman and Rowe, the biggest agency at the time. He and his wife Chris would accompany us. Several halls were booked, and although they were all memorable since this was my first proper tour as hit recording artist Suzi Quatro, the first one was the best. It was sold out. There was an unusual layout, with the stage at the bottom of a long staircase from the back of the hall. Soundcheck went fine except for one thing: Mickie went out to the mixing desk convinced that he could do the job. (*I remember. It wasn't the studio and he was out of his depth.*) So after our front-of-house guy had let him play around for a little while we readjusted the knobs.

Come showtime, Dave Neal was the first to take the stage. He walked on alone, twirling his drumsticks, went to his kit and slowly began to *boom boom boom*, teasing the crowd. Then, separately, Len walked out followed by Alistair. Once in place the band went into Little Richard's 'The Girl Can't Help It', after which Dave went into the drum intro for 'Can the Can'. The place erupted and I took the stage. The audience cheered and screamed as we went through most of the first album, though not actually doing 'Can the Can'. At the end of the last song, 'All Shook Up', I left the stage.

The plan was this. I would run up the stairs to the dressing room and change from my black leather jumpsuit into my gold leather one for the encore. It would have to be a quick change, because Dave was going to keep on playing until I returned. Chris Most would help me. She was great and had got everything prepared. So zip down the boots, zip down the suit, peel it off, step into the legs of the gold suit, zip up the gold boots, then zip up the rest of the suit. Problem: It wouldn't go up. I lay on the floor and Chris got on top, pulling and pulling, but it wouldn't budge. All the time we could hear in the distance *boom ba boom ba boom*. Finally it rolled up, Chris pulled me to my feet and I ran all the way back to the stage.

Mickie was at the top. 'Christ – what took you so long?' He pulled the curtain back and said, 'Go!' This was the culmination of all my dreams come true. I stood at the top of the long staircase, the spotlight blinding my eyes for a moment. Then I saw them, all on their feet cheering and screaming for *me*. So did I rush down to the microphone? No, I did not. I did the royal wave, taking my time to step down each and every stair. The journey must have lasted a full five minutes. Behind me I could hear Mickie shouting, 'Go, Suzi! Get down there! Hurry up.' Nope. I was gonna milk this moment for all it was worth, and when I finally arrived centre stage (much to the relief of Dave, who was sweating his ass off) we did 'Can the Can' and stormed the place.

There was one gig at the Musikhalle in Hamburg which in hindsight was very interesting. A local promoter, Peter Koch, had bought the date from Lippman and Rowe. Peter was there with his wife Margarit. A man named Rainer Haas was there with his girlfriend Hieke. Margarit became Rainer's girlfriend, and eventually in 1993 the girl on stage became Rainer's wife. Quite a cosy little group of people, wouldn't you say?

Things were good that first year of success. 'Can the Can', '48 Crash', 'Daytona Demon' and 'Too Big' all made the top twenty with ease; and there were lots of TV shows, concerts, photo sessions and interviews. Since I was the first serious female rock musician to open the door (*Come on, Suzi, you didn't open the door – you kicked it down*) the press were interested in talking to me. I swore, I drank, I smoked (well, pretended to anyway), I played with the boys and beat them at their own game. But when you have this kind of image there are bound to be problems every now and again. One day I was reading an interview with Lynsey De Paul, a very pretty piano player/songwriter who enjoyed hits in the early seventies with 'Sugar Me', and the Ivor Novello award-winning hit 'Won't Somebody Dance with Me', in one of the weekly music newspapers. Since we were contemporaries, I was interested in what she had to say from her domain, the softer, feminine side of the tracks. Imagine how I felt when I read, 'I don't need to jump around with a bunch of sweaty, hairy, greasy-looking guys to be successful. Anyway, I think Suzi Quatro is a dyke.' That made me mad, and I asked Mickie if we could sue. He calmed me down as he always did. 'Don't worry, Suzi. Today's newspapers will be wrapping somebody's fish and chips tomorrow.' Inside, though, Mickie was every bit as angry as I was.

Lynsey was in the charts, I was in the charts, and we were both booked on *Top of the Pops*. Len, Arthur Sharpe (ex-Nashville Teen) and I were on our way to the canteen. As we passed through reception I noticed Lynsey standing by the glass doors and immediately headed her way. Len grabbed Sharpe, saying, 'Let's go for a beer, mate, shall we?' So up I marched to a nervous-looking De Paul, grabbed her by the neck and shoved her against the glass doors. Her feet were actually dangling off the floor.

'So, Miss De Paul. You owe me a fucking big apology. How dare you call me a dyke!'

'I didn't, Suzi. Honest to God I didn't. I never said that – but I'm sorry it appeared that way.'

I put her down and left the scene of the crime. Mickie saw her soon afterwards and laid into her without mercy, making her burst into tears on the set. Lynsey again insisted she had been misquoted. End of story – or so I thought.

Some time in the eighties I went on a TV show hosted by comedian extraordinaire, ex-Goon Michael Bentine. Now Michael was a well-documented 'spiritual' man. In his auto-biography he tells how his son appeared to him at the bottom of the garden before he received the news of his death. He also spent many years studying ley lines – invisible lines connecting points of religious significance in the landscape – in Peru. I found these stories riveting, and the man himself fascinating. We got talking about departed spirits, and when I told him my 'black magic' tale from Kansas he explained it to me in a way I could totally understand. There are many 'lost' souls floating around who can't find the light. They can be mischievous and sometimes dangerous, and yes, my friends and I had called them to us. Michael also confirmed my suspicions that I was a natural channel, something I had known since I was a young child. I told him that sometimes it felt like Grand Central Station up in my head. He also warned me, as the Bible does, not to dabble.

For some reason Lynsey's name came up. He started to tell me how close they were, what a lovely, clever girl she was and what a tough time she had had growing up. I, of course, was a little reluctant to join in because I still held a grudge. He suggested I gave her a call because he saw us as very similar and potentially good friends. I never thought of this con-versation again until 2002 when I found myself sitting at the same table as Lynsey while collecting an award. Something, or perhaps someone, made me jump over my shadow. We started to talk, and before you knew it we were sitting at Langan's having lunch just like old friends. We were indeed very similar, often completing each other's sentences. And of course that interview came up – which was good, because it was time to put in on the table, discuss it, and then bury it in the past where it belongs.

'Listen, Suzi,' Lynsey began. 'I'm very honest. We're both Geminis and we say exactly what we mean.' I could only nod my head in agreement – she was right on the money. 'So if I'd said that word I would tell you so here and now and stand by my words. But how could I possibly call you a dyke? I knew you and Lennie were a couple. I may have said something about your image being a little "butch", which it is. Now, Suzi, the question is: Do you believe me?'

Can I just say here and now, Lynsey, in black and white, in my unretractable autobiography, that I do believe you – and you can quote me on that. I am so happy we are now the good friends that Michael Bentine predicted we would be. (*Some stories do have a happy ending, don't they?*)

At Christmas 1973 Len and I decided to invite my parents over and share the cost, which by this time we could afford. We had had four hit singles, I had paid off the debt to Rak and we both had money in the bank. We would all stay at Len's parents' house. I was so excited as Mom and Dad's visit approached. We had even booked a limo and arranged for the press to cover their arrival. (*This does stink a little of showing off, if you don't mind me saying so!*) Anyway there we were at Heathrow, black limo outside, standing at customs with numerous photographers waiting for them to appear. We waited and waited and waited, until it was obvious they weren't coming. That night my dad phoned to explain.

'We had to fly to Toronto to catch the connecting flight, and would you believe it? There was a huge snowstorm and the flight was cancelled. We'll be there same time tomorrow.'

And they were, arriving with no fanfare whatsoever. Len's mum had to go to the airport in a taxi and meet them – we couldn't do it ourselves because the band was otherwise engaged. So much for my dreams of them arriving in a blaze of publicity and seeing how well their daughter was doing at last. Yeah, I know. I'd set myself up for a fall.

Christmas was really great, though. I got to know both my parents on an adult level, and even heard my dad's huge catalogue of dirty jokes for the first time. He had us all in stitches. They seemed to like Len, who was on his best behaviour – it was another of those rare occasions when he had a haircut, and I did ask him to try not to stick his hands down his pants, or mine, while they were visiting! They bonded well with his parents, too. And, for a special treat for myself and my mom and dad, they got to go along to the number 1 Christmas special on *Top of the Pops*, where we sang 'Can the Can'.

My dad was a rascal, but with us daughters no dirty words were allowed. So I begged the guys to be respectful and not to swear. We had done rehearsal and were in the dressing room waiting for the show to begin taping, and to pass the time we played some poker. I was holding a really good hand, quietly sucking everyone in, and the pot was growing nice and large. Then Alistair threw in his hand. 'What the fuck did you do that for?' I shouted. *Whooops*. Silence. No one moved. The words just kind of hung there in the atmosphere, and finally Dad said, 'Deal the cards.' Phew!

Mickie told Chinn and Chapman that we needed another number 1, and they were that good they went and did it. This was the first time the Suzi Quatro haircut made an appearance, and I believe it was also the first time an actual choreographed dance step was done on television with a rock and roll band. David Toguri, who had done *Hair*, was brought in to work out a dance routine for me and the band. I could dance but they could not. Result: *West Side Story* gone wrong.

It was a stroke of genius on the part of Mickie Most, who was on the set during rehearsals at *Top of the Pops*. Unfortunately, Sweet were on the adjacent stage waiting to do their thing and trying desperately not to laugh at the sight of the band and me doing our thing! It got so bad that Mickie went over to them, fist in the air, and said, 'If I hear one sound out of you guys you're finished!' This clip of 'Devil Gate Drive' is one of the most played – me dressed in ripped blue jeans, white T-shirt, white gymshoes and black leather jacket, the boys in blue jeans and different-coloured sweatshirts. A worse bunch of hooligans trying to dance with something resembling rhythm didn't exist – you could seem them counting and watching my feet the entire time. And in the middle section, where Dave gets off the kit to join us in the dance, he and Len very nearly bang into each other. But, it worked, and the week after this *Top of the Pops* appearance it went straight to the top.

Actually the recording of this song was hilarious. It represented serious partying, motorbike riding and rebelling. Every teenager has a 'Devil Gate Drive' that they're not supposed to go to (though of course we all went) and we wanted it to sound authentic, so we went into the alley outside the studio and set up some microphones. Luckily, one of the engineers had a motorbike. Mike rolled the tape as a speeding motorcycle and four screaming musicans ran down the road to the amazement of local residents, who wondered what the hell was going on!

I was in the music papers constantly: *Melody Maker*, *Disc*, *Sounds* and the *NME*, which is how I met Chrissie Hynde. A journalist on that paper, she was told to join us on the road and do a story. Once we got to the gig we found it was too noisy to talk in the hall due to sound check, so we sat on the floor of the ladies' toilet and talked there. After the interview Chrissie told me she was a singer and songwriter too, and wanted to do what I'd done. I didn't really take her seriously – how wrong can you be! Years later, when she was at the top of the charts with 'Brass in Pocket', I sent her this telegram: 'Dear Chrissie, I thought you were a dreamer, now you're a winner. Love Suzi.'

Besides my growing collection of silver, gold and platinum discs I was collecting awards here, there and everywhere. In Germany I won the magazine *Bravo*'s coveted Otto, in *Music Week* I was number one best-selling female of the year. We were in the glory years, the heyday of the first phase of my success, and it was fantastic. But of course balance is important, and you can't have all that good stuff without some bad. The Good News Agency had booked us to play a few gigs in Switzerland, which I hadn't visited before. But when we got there and saw the advertising posters I hit the roof. An artist had done a drawing of me from one of my publicity pictures, but had seen fit to add really huge boobs. No way was I going to be marketed as a sex symbol, so I threatened the promoter with pulling out of the gig – and I meant it. Of course, after numerous apologies I did appear – ever the professional. And I swear that when I walked on stage I heard the audience gasp in what I translated as disappointment with my chest size. In compensation I did extra ass-wiggling that night – an area that I've never had any problem with.

But now, with Europe up to speed on all the Quatro hits, it was time for 'late nights and early flights'. Touring the world was about to start, and it would go on and on and on.

6

ON THE ROAD

....

Around this time, in 1974, Arlene's first husband, Leo Fenn, reappeared. It seems he had an outdated contract stating that he could manage me if I returned to the States. Even though it wasn't valid any more, Mickie decided it could do no harm to let him book us some shows. The first album had been released and was getting lots of airplay and selling quite well, although I hadn't had a big hit single there yet. 'Can the Can' and 'All Shook Up' went into the lower ends of the charts. We rehearsed, we packed, and I armed myself with a bottle of Valium, the latest line in 'numb me please' drugs for nervous travellers. I had been away from America for some three years, and now it was first stop: New York City.

How strange if felt to be back after all this time. We first played Madison Square Gardens with Grand Funk Railroad; it was sold out. Mike Chapman was there, as were Mickie and Chris Most. I finished my last number and ran off to change into the gold jumpsuit, then went quickly back to the stage for the encore. But it was silent – no cheering crowds, nothing. I was devastated, convinced we'd bombed. Leo said nothing but just pulled back the curtain. To my amazement, lighted candles filled the stadium. It was my first candle encore. Backstage, Mike was in tears: 'I was so proud of you tonight, Suzi. Makes me feel like I had something to do with it.' An understatement if ever I heard one. And, in case I forget later: I love you, Mike. Next stop Detroit. Stay tuned as the shit hits the fan.

One part of me was really proud that I was returning as a hero, but another part was dreading the emotion of it all. Would there still be jealousies, anger and resentment? Would I immediately turn back into little Susie from Detroit, insecure, begging to be seen and heard? At New York's La-Guardia airport we boarded our flight. It took one a half hours – not that long, but I still managed to get several sheets in the wind on whisky. Everyone was there to meet us – Mom, Dad, Nancy, Patti and Arlene. After hugging Mom she gently pushed me away, saying, 'Phew, Susan – you've been drinking.' The band went off to a hotel, Len and I back to the Quatro house. Back to my memories, my demons. . . . You get the idea.

Walking in was very strange. It was my home, and yet it wasn't. I was looking at it with different eyes now. Arlene was between marriages yet again and so was staying with her three kids at the family house. Sherry, my niece, lost her bedroom for a few days – sorry, honey. After we'd put our suitcases down the very first thing I wanted to do was to show Len my old bedroom down in the basement. I ran down the stairs two at a time, Len lumbering behind me, but where was it all? I was looking at an empty clothes rail, an empty album rack and empty drawers. Everything had gone. I didn't understand, so I asked Mom.

'Oh, well, Patti has altered most of your clothes. And the

records – well, they've been shared out between everyone. Don't know about the drawers.'

This was said as fact – no apology. I felt they had written me out of their lives. But the biggest shock was yet to come.

Late at night, in the borrowed bedroom, I decided to look in the drawers. Maybe some of my stuff was there and I could reclaim it. I was right. I came across the sheet music for some of my really early compositions. But then I did a double-take. Every page I turned was the same: in the right-hand corner, where it read, 'music and lyrics by . . .', someone had removed my name completely! I guess I could have confronted everyone about my disappearing wardrobe and albums, and the missing credit on my songs – but I didn't. I felt then as I do now, that it seemed a small price to pay for all my success. There was probably a bit of guilt over leaving them all behind mixed in there too. So I held my tongue and put my heart on hold. Sooner or later, that hold was bound to burst apart. (*Hey, while you're tripping down Memory Lane here – 'tripping' being the operative word – don't forget about 'Each Day I Love You More' that you wrote with your brother, which somehow ended up belonging only to him. I seem to remember Dad talking you into donating any and all ensuing royalties directly to Mickey. Isn't it funny, Suzi? You used to feel like the horse nobody bet on. Now you felt like the horse everyone wanted to ride on.*)

My first homecoming gig was at the Eastown Ballroom and Kiss was my support act: huge boots, made-up faces and weird-shaped guitars. Strange – but a good rock and roll band (hey, Gene, my offer of giving you some bass lessons still stands). Loads of old friends and family were there, including Mom, Dad and sister Nancy who had front row balcony seats

(Dad didn't want to be too close to the PA system), and we all arrived in a big limo. Yes, tonight we were doing it in style. Wow, what a great feeling when I took the stage: local girl returns a victor. The crowd went wild and it was truly magical. I gave it that extra mile that night, although it was a little embarrassing when they started to throw joints on to the stage, especially with my parents there. I didn't know it, but there was a whole different scenario going on up in the balcony. Later that night Nancy told me the story.

'God, Suzi, I nearly died. First of all, those joints being thrown on stage. Dad said, "What are those?" I said, "Marboros." Then someone started to pass a joint down the row – everyone was hitting on it, and it finally got to Dad. I was cringing under the seat. But guess what he did? Cool as can be, he passed it on saying, "No thanks, man, I already had one."' We laughed over that one for many years.

After the show we all rode home together. I was exhausted but satisfied. Mom and Dad were riding in the front as I ventured the 64,000 dollar question. 'Hey, Mom, so how did you like the show?' Many interviewers have asked me over the years: 'How do your parents feel about what you do?' And here is the answer, direct from mom's lips. 'Well, Susan, it was very nice but do you have to stand with your legs so far apart?' (*Yes, I do, Mom. Sorry, but it's the only way it works.*)

After Detroit we began a three-week coast-to-coast tour, hitting the Mid-west, down to Florida, back up for a few in Canada, then down below the Mason-Dixon Line, up north, and eventually ending up in LA. We did some great gigs at big rock clubs, theatres and even stadiums, playing alongside ZZ Top (supporting act), Edgar and Johnny Winter (supporting act) and Rufus (supporting act). (*You know, those days are a little blurry in my mind. Late nights, early flights, hotel, soundcheck, gig, sleep, then all over again. But there were a few highlights along the way – tell 'em that lip-curling tale about Memphis, Tennessee.*)

We were playing at a Memphis club that night and had just returned to the hotel after soundcheck when the phone rang. I thought I was dreaming when I answered.

'Ah . . . hello Suzi . . . ahh ahh ah . . . this is Elvis . . . and ah . . . ah just want you ta know that ah really like your version of "All Shook Up". Best I heard since my own.'

All I could do was breathe.

He continued, 'Would y'all like to come up to Graceland for a visit?'

This invitation was based solely on his hearing of 'All Shook Up' on my first album. He had never seen me live or anything. And believe it or not *I turned him down*! I made some excuse about having no time in the schedule due to gigs, interviews and so on, and said goodbye. He must have been totally amazed at my reaction, and I still can't believe it happened. But the truth is I wasn't ready to meet my hero. I was only one year into my success and didn't feel worthy. What a first-class jerk to pass up a chance like that – it wouldn't come my way again. (*A little pause for destiny, Suzi . . . If you had met him I don't think you would have written that tribute song 'Singing with Angels'.*)

Well, you may be right. The thing is, many years later when I was writing this tune I felt like I was taking dictation. I decided to use the names of some of his records and turn it into a story. So I got his box set out and perused the list of tracks. All I was doing was looking for rhymes, but when I'd finished I realized it was in chronological order. I may be clever, but not that clever.

Singing with Angels

I heard your voice late last night
I heard you say, are you lonesome tonight
I saw you crying in the chapel light
Love me tender and treat me nice

Lonely boy got the G.I. blues
That's all right mama's watching over you
Wise men say if you don't be cruel
You'll get to heaven wearing blue suede shoes.

Singing with angels, safe in God's promised land
Singing with angels, walking hand in hand
Singing with angels, it's part of God's master plan
There's so many angels, walking hand in hand
What a beautiful band.

I got a woman, she's my happiness
Don't leave me now, in my loneliness
Heartbreak hotel, I was counting on you
Thought I had a lot of living to do.

The blue moon of Kentucky shines,
Burning love makes suspicious minds
Mystery train heading for the light
Graceland's star, burning bright

Singing with angels, safe in God's promised land
Singing with angels, walking hand in hand
Singing with angels, it's part of God's master plan

There's so many angels, walking hand in hand
What a beautiful band.
(Elvis has left the building) end.

(Suzi Quatro, 2004)

In 2005 I recorded this song in Nashville, alongside the Jordanaires and James Burton on guitar. It was produced by Andy Scott (lead guitarist in Sweet). I have footage of this special event in my life, and some day soon both the film and the song will be release, this I swear! Every time I do this live I feel Elvis looking down on me – and Elvis, can I just say that without you Suzi Quatro would not exist. I hope you now have the peace you spent your life looking for. You are the King and no one can ever fill your shoes. I love you. Give your mama a kiss for me, and while you're at it give my mama one too – she'd love that.

We finally rolled into Los Angeles. Since most of the record labels were now on the West Coast this would be an important gig. We were booked to play the Whiskey-a-Go-Go on Sunset Strip, which had been sold out for weeks. At the airport our welcoming committee consisted of Rodney Bingemheimer (Rodney's English Disco) and various groupies and fans, complete with flowers, Quatro T-shirts and placards saying, 'Welcome to Los Angeles Suzi Quatro . . . we love you'. We drove to 'the' rock and roll hotel at that time, the Continental Hyatt House (renamed Riot House for obvious reasons). That day, in the hotel lobby, was the first time I laid eyes on one of my biggest fans. Joan Jett looked so cute, sitting there with 'my' haircut, 'my' leather jacket and 'my' attitude. In fact, she was always in the lobby waiting for me whenever I played LA. And yes, it is a compliment when someone loves you that much. I was so pleased when a couple of years later Toby Mamis, my American publicist, phoned to tell me that Joan had started her own band called the Runaways. At last she had an outlet of her own.

After we had checked in I sat on the bed in my room and I started to feel not so good. In truth I had been travelling non-stop through different time zones and was totally exhausted. Emergency action time – call the hotel doctor.

'Right, Ms Quatro. You have a serious throat infection. You really should have a couple of days off.'

'Not possible, doc. Not possible.'

'Bend over. Let's get this penicillin in you. Open your mouth and I'll spray some stuff to help the cords relax. Now you have a fever, too, so get to bed. No talking, no whispering, nothing until show time. Don't worry – we'll get you on that stage. It may not be a pretty sound, but you'll get through it.'

When it was finally time to leave my bed I felt like shit with a capital S. Oh well, it wouldn't be the first time I'd had to croak my way through a show, and it certainly wouldn't be the last. We drove down the Strip to the Whiskey-a-Go-Go and there in lights it read, 'Suzi Quatro appearing live tonight. Sold out.' And I swear I never saw such queue – right the way around the club and down a couple of blocks. It warmed my heart. Once on stage, with adrenalin pumping through my veins, I managed to put on a show. The album had sold well, so everyone was singing along. My voice sounded like Clarence Frogman Henry imitating a frog, but the people didn't seem to care. They were there to enjoy me, and enjoy me they did. Halfway through our set some little guy ambled on to the stage – he looked kind of familiar. It was Iggy Pop – I'd known him since the early days in Detroit, when he was a drummer. He stumbled to the microphone, trying to join in. Problem was, he was wasted, so we had to have security 'escort' him off. Sorry, Iggy, no offence. But if you're gonna get on *my* stage you'd better be 'together' – know what I mean?

And so the first American tour with my English band came to an end – and what a great time we'd all had. I had so enjoyed showing Lennie my country, and all that came with it: the endless TV stations, the hamburger and hotdog stands, the malls, the guitar shops (even better, the pawn shops where he picked up loads of cheap guitars), the streets of Detroit, Sunset Strip, the huge expressways. It was all so different from England. Len summed it up pretty well: 'You know, Suze, I became a kid again on this tour. I got my original enthusiasm back on guitar. What great audiences – they really appreciate and understand what we're doing. I love it here!' Next stop, Australia.

Australia always was and still is my strongest territory, and the 2007 tour is my twenty-third there. But in 1974 it was my first time down under. However, my records had already sold more in Australia than the Beatles' (although I was eventually outsold by Abba). Mickie had instructed me, 'I don't care what you wear on the flight, but when you step off that plane you must be wearing your leathers and sunglasses. There's going to be massive publicity, and you have to look the part.' We arrived in Sydney jet-lagged, of course, but as promised it was the fans' image of Suzi Quatro that walked down the steps. It was amazing – there were crowds of people leaning over the edge of the observation tower, screaming and waving. And there must have been a hundred photographers going *flash flash flash* (thank God for those sunglasses). I had not had a reception like this anywhere before, and I was loving it. Quickly down to earth. In the baggage hall we waited, waited, waited . . . for luggage that never arrived. Someone had to go out and get basics like toothbrushes, toothpaste, shavers and so on. Thank God I had my leather trouser suit just in case my stage clothes didn't get there.

We did a press conference at the airport, and mid-question there was an ungodly roar out on the road. It was a bikies' escort (Aussie hell's angels) coming for me. Apparently this is quite a rare honour. Finally we got into the limo, with a news camera in the front seat, and drove to the hotel – motorcycles leading the way. The bikies were enjoying their moment in the sun, swaying and doing handstands along the street, when suddenly one of the girls riding pillion fell off and unfortunately she wasn't wearing a helmet. I screamed at the driver to stop and we took her into the car. She was really shaken up, so I offered her a swig of whisky to calm her down and a couple of free tickets to the show. She was happy about that, and it was all over the news that I had 'nursed' her all the way to the hospital.

Finally we got to the hotel and fell into bed for a few hours' sleep. When we awoke we heard that our luggage had now been found – thank God. We turned on the radio and the TV to discover that our arrival was receiving saturation coverage. It was almost too much, so we switched off and started to prepare for our first show.

Sydney was sold out – six shows over three nights – (the promoter, Kevin Ritchie, actually asked on the last day if we wanted to add one more show. I declined). Although I had done some big gigs in Europe and America, nothing had prepared me for that first show down under. As I walked on stage I had never heard such a deafening roar. The entire sold-out crowd was screaming my name – my name! Every track was greeted with applause – the album was number 1 out there and we had had five hit singles. The bikies were being used as security – someone had the wise idea that this might keep them in check. Perhaps. During our extended version of 'All Shook Up', one of the bikies made an unscheduled appearance. He simply strolled on to the stage, handed each of us a bottle of beer, then strolled back off to the cheers of the crowd. No one did a thing to stop him – well, you don't mess with those guys, do you?

Throughout my many years of performing I have amassed various tricks of the trade. No one can teach you these things – it's trial and error. Some things work, and some things don't. And if they work well, you keep them.

When Dave went into the high-hat roll which signals the beginning of 'Devil Gate Drive' (Australia's absolute favourite hit) I wanted to drag this moment out, so instead of starting the words I paused and said, 'It's so great to be here in . . . *Shit*. I went blank. High-hat rolling. Pregnant pause. I looked round at the boys, then in a panic screamed at Dave, 'Where are we?' He screamed back, 'Devil Gate Drive'! Hilarious – one of my favourite on-stage moments.

Needless to say, that's not the bit I kept in the show. Towards the end of the song there's a bit of dialogue where I say, 'Come on boys, let's do it one more time for Suzi.' That night instinct took over as I went into some impromptu audience participation: 'All right, everyone. I want your hands in the air. Right now!' I nearly stopped playing as every single pair of hands went up in unison as if on strings – the word that comes to mind is 'power'. I felt like super-woman.

It's this that I've kept in my show ever since. I'm a really 'audience' performer. If I'm gonna sweat, then you're gonna sweat. I don't know how to 'coast' a show – you get 300 per cent or you get nothing.

I came off high as a kite. Someone threw a towel around my neck and shoved me into the waiting limo so I could get back to the hotel to try and come down – sometimes it takes hours. About twenty minutes after the show you get a horrible feeling. The cheers are fading away in your ears, the sweat is starting to dry and you begin to breathe reality again. Then, like an elevator diving to the basement, you crash. I *never* drink anything before a show; afterwards, just a glass of wine to make the return journey, to the real world a little less traumatic.

During my nightly prayers I told God how grateful I was. 'If you want to take me to heaven now – well, I can die happy.' Which is kind of strange considering what was happening back in England. Mickie was at Rak when he received a telegram from our promoter. He opened it and began to read, 'Suzi killed—' and then collapsed into a chair, shaking and white as a ghost.

'What's the matter, Mick? asked his brother Dave in concern. He picked up the telegram from the floor, where it had dropped out of Mickie's nerveless grasp and read out these words: 'Suzi killed 'em in Sydney'!

We hit Melbourne, Adelaide, Perth and Brisbane, and for the first time I experienced not being able to walk the streets: there were screaming fans everywhere and it wasn't safe. This is the 'not so nice' part of fame, and something I never liked. (*Remember our agreement, Suzi? You and me made a pact that we would be 'famous' but 'normal'.*) But normal was yet to come: on this tour I was anything but.

Brisbane holds a special memory for me. We had done the show and were already in bed when someone knocked on the door.

'I'll get it, Suze,' said Len. He was there for several minutes, and when he finally shut the door said, 'You won't believe it. That was a couple of girl fans – obviously gay.'

'How do you know that, Lennie? Did you ask 'em?'

'Nope, didn't need to. One of them had her breast out. She said, "Hey, does Suzi want to party?"'

So *that's* what took you so long!

The last stop was Perth, where were to play an outdoor show. We got rained off on the first day, but played the next. The stage was set up in a big park, behind an Olympic-sized swimming pool which served as a barrier. The mixing desk was on the other side. Our front-of-house guy told us later, 'You know, when you guys went off stage one fan jumped into the pool. And I said to him, "They aren't finished yet – there's an encore to come." So he got back out, danced around to "Sweet Little Rock and Roller", and then, yep, jumped back in.'

Australian tour completed, it was back to London where Mickie was waiting to greet us as we came through customs. For the first time he hugged me, hard: guess that telegram stuck in his mind! It was good to be back.

How can I explain life on the road to the uninitiated? It's non-stop flying, jet-lag, hotel rooms, dressing rooms, interviews, photo sessions, TV shows, sound checks, gigs and hangovers, not necessarily in that order. Then the show itself, of course. And afterwards the wind-down in someone's room, and hopefully a few hours of sleep before the same procedure starts all over again. I used to check the progress of the deepening dark circles under my eyes every morning; even when I slept well, they were still there.

It's a crazy, cocooned existence. Nobody gets out, and nobody gets in. Temptations are everywhere – groupies, drugs, like one big candy shop of pleasure. Thank God I never felt the need to go down that route. Been there, done that, got the T-shirt, and decided very early on that it was not for me. Even though I trusted Len, I still kept an eagle eye out for any trouble on that front. He sometimes resented this and made comments like, 'God, Suze, I just need to have some fun like the other guys', which used to infuriate me. (*Hey, Suzi Quatro, before you go any further why don't you get all those 'rock and roll' stories out of the way?*)

Okay. After that preview in the studio with Alistair we began to see cracks in his psyche. There was the time in Germany in the early seventies, for instance, when we were out to dinner with all the biggies from EMI. A very nice restaurant had been booked, with top-class food, wine, the works. Alistair, true to form, began to get legless. Problem with him was that he always went beyond legless, which was truly scary. The first course was soup. Alistair put his fist into the bowl and started to lick it off. Seated next to us was a nice-looking couple having a romantic candle-lit dinner for two. So the next thing you knew was that Alistair was on his hands and knees crawling under their table. Up he popped, and blew out the candle. The things we do when we're drunk, eh!

Fast forward to one of the sixteen tours I did of Japan (we were huge there too, like Australia). There we were, at the crack of dawn, waiting to catch a flight to Kyoto. Alistair was still drunk from the night before. As we stood amongst all the businessmen, Mr Wurlitzer tried in vain to get some coins out of his pocket. Finally, in frustration, he threw them all on to the ground. You know how polite the Japanese are? They were immediately on all fours, collecting them up and sweetly handing them back. '*Oragato*,' he said graciously, then *splat*, back down on the floor they went. After the third time the game finished: even Japanese patience can be tried too far.

Then there was Alistair's last Aussie tour. The first night we were all in his room playing poker. He was really, really drunk and halfway through a hand, he leaned over and threw up the entire contents of his stomach on to the hotel room carpet. Not a good memory. It was becoming obvious that Alistair's days with my band were numbered.

The last straw came during our marathon tour in 1975 with my old friend Alice Cooper. We had twenty shows on our own, then joined his tour for a further seventy-five dates as special guest on 'Welcome to my Nightmare' – aptly named. We had a day off in Los Angeles and had decided to go to Disneyland with one of the roadies and my sister Patti, who lived there at the time. When we returned in the early evening we noticed fire engines and an ambulance parked in front of the 'Riot House'. 'Alistair,' Len and I said to each other.

Dave told us what happened. Having finally got up at around 3p.m., Alistair began his usual daily intake of booze. Then he must have decided he fancied a dip. So up he went, completely wasted, to the rooftop pool and jumped in. There was one man sitting there, quietly reading a newspaper, and a few minutes later he realized he hadn't heard anyone splash around or get back out. Rushing to the edge, he saw a body lying at the bottom of the pool. Fully clothed, the man jumped in and dragged him out, giving him the kiss of life. Alistair finally managed to choke out the excess water, thank god, and, to show how grateful he was, he punched the guy in the jaw. The police were called and Alistair was taken to hospital, returning the next day with two beautiful shiners.

When we returned in June from this marathon of gigs I had no choice but to let him go. He was a wonderful musician and a very nice, intelligent man, but his behaviour was causing too many problems. The road is hard enough! Mike Deacon (ex-Ox) then joined the band. (*Excuse me. Let's not rush through this part. You yourself were not angel. Come on, cough up a few of your 'moments'.*) All right, all right. Balance at all times!

It must have been around 1976, in the middle of another non-stop world tour. We were having an after-gig get-to-gether in someone's room (it was never mine – I needed my sleep to keep my voice in tip-top condition). The wine, the joints (not me, honest) and the food were flowing when one of the roadies appeared with a beautiful groupie in tow. She was perfect: sexy short skirt over never-ending legs, big boobs encased in a tight T-shirt, long blow-dried blonde hair, beautifully made-up with long false eyelashes. The thing that annoyed me was she didn't join in but just sat in the corner looking aloof, which has always been like a red rag to me. I hate pretension of any kind. (*Mum's favourite quote. 'She thinks her shit don't stink, but her farts give her away'.*) Yes, Susie, thank you for reminding me.

Earlier, we had ordered a big cake due to it being some-body's birthday. But this wasn't just a regular cake, oh no. The joke was that we had asked the chef to put every bit of junk, stale food or whatever he could find into it to make it really disgusting (the things that amuse when you're bored!). So, a little tipsy, I decided to go to bed, and for some unknown reason picked up the entire cake, walked to the door and tripped accidentally on purpose, dropping the entire thing on top of Ms Perfect's head. I guess I was hoping for some kind of reaction. There was nothing. She didn't move – just sat there with this beautiful smile on her face as the cake dripped off her eyelashes. Now that *was* impressive. What a star! (*You know, I don't think the roadie got laid that night, do you?*)

Story number two. I always remember this because it was 1977 and we had been on tour for eight months, hitting Scandinavia, mainland Europe, America, Japan and finally Melbourne, where we taped a live gig for television. We were beyond exhausted. But the TV show had gone brilliantly: there is no audience in the world that roars like Melbourne. We were due to return to England the next morning. But first there would be an end-of-tour party at which we would be entitled to let off some serious steam – we'd earned it.

I remember sitting around quietly, talking about religion and politics, sipping from my tumbler of whisky – quite civilized for a rock and roll party. Then something snapped. Dave got up from his chair and poured his beer over the TV set, which blew up. That was fun! And then it started. We all began pouring liquid over every electrical appliance we could find, including the light bulbs which made a great popping noise.

After that, someone decided Alistair needed a bath. We

ran the water and threw him in fully clothed. Boy, was he pissed off about his new watch! Various bits of food flew through the air. Dave screamed, 'Careful! I have on my new shirt.' *Whoops* – some things should definitely not be said to a partying rock band. Len grabbed his shirt tail, dragging him around the floor until only the sleeves were left. That was fun too! Pictures came off the wall and were smashed on to the floor, mattresses were rolled off the bed. And then I decided that we should cut open the feather pillows and distribute their contents to make it like a snowstorm. But the pillows were so tough to open that I had to fetch a knife – must have looked like a madwoman as I sliced them open and flung them into the air. Finally, energy depleted, we went to bed.

The room belonged to Len's brother Bill, our tour manager, and in the morning there came a timid knock. Bill rose from the floor, covered in booze and feathers, and answered the door. The manager took one look and said the damage would have to be paid for, which we did with pleasure. It was worth it for the entertainment. He also said, 'I know it wasn't Ms Quatro, though. She would *never* do anything like this. But the rest are animals.' (*Thank you for that. But just one more, please, before we leave these tales of debauchery. Lennie . . . Scandinavia . . . remember?*)

How could I forget? we had just finished a tour and were due to fly out to Holland very early in the morning to begin recording with Mike Chapman. There was a band on at the hotel, so we stayed up drinking and jamming. It didn't bode well when Len begged me to go up and sing with them, then pelted me with ice cubes from the dance floor. We had decided that, since we had to get up so early, there was no point in going to bed. Len proceeded to get absolutely loaded. I was sitting in one of the booths when I noticed him holding his hand to his mouth, looking around frantically. Oh God, he was going to throw up. I shouted at the waitress, 'Where's the toilet, please?' Too late. Len's artistic technicolour contribution to the evening was now in the fireplace – at which point we were unceremoniously kicked out of the club.

Dragging him upstairs, I tried to undress him. The mess was all over his Levi's shirt, and he couldn't change it because all the luggage had gone on ahead. Somehow I managed to strip him, fling him across the bed and stick his clothes over the bathroom towel rail to dry. One hour later, we got our wake-up call. I gently nudged the comatose figure lying beside me and said, 'It's time to get up, darling', to which he replied, 'Fuck off, Suze.'

'Right, Len. Listen to me. If you don't get your ass out of bed this minute I am going to scream, and everyone will wonder what the hell you've done to me.' He saw sense and got up, and off we went to the airport like a good little band, boarded the flight, which was mainly full of businessmen, took our seats and got ready for take-off. Once we were cruising, the murmur of quiet conversation began. You could hear the newpaper pages turning as the stewardesses began the service. It really was a nice, normal flight. And it was just too good to last.

Len, sitting a few rows behind me on the opposite side, called out, 'Oi, Suze! This guy sitting next to me doesn't half honk.'

I ignored him as best I could.

'Suze, honestly. He fucking stinks.'

I kept my back to him, hoping no one knew my name.

Finally, about five minutes later, Len shouted, 'Oi, Suze. Guess what? It's me!'

That poor man! . . . Now I'm not saying that these are the only stories, not by a long stretch, and I just may belch out a few more later on. But for now it's second album time.

7

QUATRO AND BEYOND

....

We had now toured the world and were a bona fide successful recording act, and that felt good. London felt good too: it was becoming my home. Len and I moved into a much nicer flat across the street from Dave Stewart and Annie Lennox (of the Eurythmics), and this is where we wrote most of the new album, Quatro. (*Before you talk about that, don't forget the ghosts. They make an appearance all the way through your life – only this time it was Len who saw them every night like clockwork. At three o'clock he would wake and see a little kid standing on the stairs at the bedroom door, wearing an old-fashioned cap and coat. He got so used to seeing this figure that he would just go back to sleep.*) Well, that's the spirit, eh, Susie? So, back to the new album.

Great picture on the front – a live shot, Precision in hand poking out the front, pouting mouth, with Len bringing up the rear – taken by nearly blind *Bravo* photographer Boobi. My deal with Rak was that I would provide 50 per cent of the songs, and much to our annoyance it didn't happen on this album. We had recorded what I consider to be one of the very best things we ever wrote. 'Angel Flight' was a seven-minute

163

epic depicting the changes of the season, completely orche-
strated, absolutely beautiful and truly before its time –
reminiscent of a Queen track. Chapman really got into the
production of this one as we all stretched our creative wings.
But this angel was not to take flight. People from EMI
Germany were in England for a preview of our next product,
and this track was played. It was not typical Quatro, of
course, and they were a little confused. Seeing their reaction,
Mickie took the decision not to include it on the album and to
rethink the tracks we had already recorded – guess he thought
it was too soon to change our style so drastically. To this day
Len and I think he made a big mistake, and that this track
would have stunned both listeners and critics and elevated us
to a new status. (You can actually hear it on the 2004-released
As and Bs and Rarities on EMI.)

The album also included a slow version of 'The Wild One'
because Mickie, with his fear of changing too quickly,
thought it needed a completely different treatment. Len
and I had to work hard to convince him to release the up-
tempo version – which became another hit. 'Devil Gate Drive'
and 'Too Big' represented our hits. Coverwise we did 'Keep a
Knockin' (Little Richard), a track I still do today, 'Move It'
(Cliff Richard), 'A Shot of Rhythm and Blues' (the Pirates)
and 'Trouble' (Elvis Presley). This last track was particularly
interesting, going into an impromptu jazz routine at the end.
Len and I ended up with only two originals, 'Cat Size' (a song
I wrote all about leaving Detroit, and one of the most popular
live songs for years) and 'Klondyke Kate'.

I wasn't happy with this selection but we swallowed it
down – no point rocking the boat just now when things were
successful. We vowed we would rectify the situation on the

next recording. It must be said, though, that we felt our creativity had been stifled. Nevertheless it was a good album and sold well around the world. So, with this second album out, we began another year of touring, taking in Australia again and America with Uriah Heep, interspersed with the UK, mainland Europe and Scandinavia. And this was also the year we did our first tour of Japan.

I couldn't tell my story without talking about Japan. It's by far the most interesting place I have ever visited, because it's like landing on the moon. Everything is so alien – the crowds of people like ants, rushing here, there and everywhere; the incredible sound of pachinko – once you hear it you never forget it; the karaoke bars filled with worse-for-wear Japanese businessmen, singing either 'Diana' or 'Dream Lover' (the Japanese cannot drink – they're missing an enzyme or something) and of course Kobe beef. This was in the seventies, when it was still one cow, one owner, massaged and fed on a crate of beer a day. You didn't need to chew – it literally melted in your mouth. (*Hey, don't forget the sake. Methinks there's one more debauchery story to tell here.*) How can I forget *anything* with you sitting on my shoulder, little Susie?

Okay, the sake story. I was so popular there that they named a sake after me: it's called Sake Rocks. But that stuff is dangerous. It's so smooth going down that you don't even feel like you're drinking. Then you step outside, get hit by a blast of oxygen smack in the head, and you're gone.

One particular evening we were having a Korean barbecue – very popular there – and the sake was flowing like water. We didn't have a show the next day, so we were really enjoying ourselves. I couldn't then (and can't now) handle much alcohol. Basically I'm a cheap date – under the table after two drinks. We were eating, drinking, laughing and having a great time when it hit me. The last thing I remember is saying to Len, 'Take me home, please.' The rest is a blank – but the roadies kindly filled me in on the details next morning. As we left the restaurant I collapsed in a heap, unable to walk, so the boys carried me home singing 'What shall we do with the drunker gaffer?' At the hotel they deposited me in the luggage cart and wheeled me up to my room. Unfortunately on that tour we were sponsored by a sake company, and bottles were delivered in great numbers to every dressing room. Can't touch the stuff today.

How strange that first show in Tokyo seemed. We were waiting to go on and the audience was completely silent, which to us was really odd. Dave went out . . *thump thump thump* (still silence). Then the boys, plugging in and getting ready (still silence). Then me. Eruption! They went absolutely berserk! It was like turning some kind of volume knob – very weird.

Cultural differences manifested themselves in other ways, too. One night we were having yet another EMI dinner, and Len had had a word in my ear about things I shouldn't discuss. 'Now, Suze, don't mention the war whatever you do.'

Well, one or two glasses of sake in and I began, to the older man sitting next to me, 'So . . . what did you do in the war?'

'Ahhhhsoooo . . . well . . . I was kamikaze pilot.'

Great! Who said you Japanese don't have a sense of humour? 'What did you do? Miss?'

He went on to tell his story . . . 'Ah no. I was trained for the mission, and the day I should fly Japan surrender.'

File this one under 'Whoops'.

On a more serious note, I'll never forget our first trip to

Hiroshima. Again, I was warned not to mention the atom bomb. This time I listened and said nothing at all. Imagine my surprise, as I travelled by cab back to the hotel, to see pockets on the back seat full of pamphlets urging 'Come see where the A-bomb fell'. It was a tourist sight. And we did actually go on to the bridge over the 'red' river, so named because of the amount of blood that had been spilled. I stood there on the bridge and felt the pain of all that wasted life deep in my soul.

A little word for Tats, who passed away in 1999. He was known as Mr Japan, and controlled the main publishing company in the country. Confession time: I had a huge crush on him. He was cute and intelligent, with a well-developed sense of humour. I am a one-man dog by nature, but I was sorely tempted with this guy. One night, sitting at his favourite little Kobe beef house, we began to flirt. It was innocent – and, after all, Lennie was sitting right next to me. I felt safe to play the game and flex my female allure. We traded stories of our lives. Boy, was he impressed that Joe Glaser who had been Billie Holiday's agent also used to be my agent. Tats for his part had me riveted with stories of his great friend Nat King Cole. When the evening came to an end we all piled into the waiting limo to return to the hotel. It was in the lobby that I got a little shock. Tats turned to me and quietly said, 'So, Suzi, let's go.' What had I done? He was expecting to go to bed with me! I went into my best cover-up – total innocence – and luckily it worked. Could have been most embarrassing otherwise.

Years later in 1992, after my divorce, we met up again. I had butterflies in my stomach – after all, I had nurtured this attraction in my mind over the years and had built it up out of all proportion. Sitting there having lunch I confessed to my feelings and he owned up to his, but too much time had passed and the moment was gone. Do I regret not having slept with him? Absolutely. Attraction is not a frequent visitor to my door. If you don't touch my brain you ain't touching anything else. A kiss for you, Tats. You were a cutey and will forever remain in my heart, filed under 'If only'. (*Ahhhhh, that's so sweet – ain't love grand! Hey, Suzi, tell 'em about that club, and that guy. You must remember!*) Who could forget it?

We were at Biblos, the 'in' place to be in Tokyo – me, my band and various EMI male representatives, having a grand time dancing the night away. Len doesn't dance, although on this night it would have been better if he had. One of the EMI reps just leaned over and whispered in his ear, 'I want to fluck you.' A panicked Len leapt out of his seat and started to run around the club – on to the dance floor, over the seats, scattering people and drinks everywhere – with the besotted Jap in tow, pinching his ass in the chase. Len, you should have just told him to 'fluck' off.

Although I was flying all the time now, I still hated it and on this tour insisted that wherever possible we take the bullet train. It was great travelling through the Japanese countryside this way. You miss so much when you fly – in this case miles and miles of paddy fields with Japanese rice pickers wearing those triangular straw hats, bent over their task. You could sleep, you could eat and you could relax. I loved it, except for one particular journey. There was a large group of sumo wrestlers with us up in first-class; in Japan they are revered as *very* special VIP's. In came this tiny little Japanese girl with the tea. She leaned over to pour and spilled a minuscule drop on one of the guys' shirts. Up he jumped, slapping her across the face. She bowed over and over again, tears falling from her eyes. He hit her several times, and with every slap she bowed lower. I could stand it no longer and jumped up in anger. Len pulled me back down immediately, pointing out that it was their culture and there was nothing I could do. How strange it was that the people of this country, where women were second-class citizens, had made me, who represented the complete opposite, their heroine.

I also ran into my old fan Joan Jett again, on tour with the Runaways. This is the tour that really cemented 'the act' for Joan. Every night she would do her gig with the band, then grab a cab over to my show and stand at the side of the stage taking in every detail of my performance. I pulled out every trick in the book to impress her. 'See how a pro does it,' I thought to myself – yes, my ego was flying high. Well, Joan, you learned your lesson well – perhaps too well. Years later, in 1982, as 'I Love Rock and Roll' hit the charts (great record, Joan) I had numerous calls after her appearance on *Top of the Pops* – 'God, Suzi – it's great to see you back in the charts!' Imitation may be the most sincere form of flattery, but sometimes it can be kind of spooky.

Just before we leave Japan, one word of warning: never play poker with them. It really is impossible to read their faces. I lost so much money on those tours that I began to deal instead. Sometimes I would wander around the room while someone else took over, and on these trips as a non-player I got the chance to peek at everyone's hand. I watched one night as Massa, our EMI representative, played a hand with four-aces without moving a muscle!

Remembering all these tours makes me wonder how I ever managed it all. I performed with throat infections, flu (throwing up in a bucket at the side of the stage) and a raging fever. The worst experience of all was on the way to New Zealand after a long Australian tour. I had had no sleep on the flight and on arrival went straight into a press conference, lifted up with a Buck's Fizz (a steward's advice). Then I began to feel really wobbly – and we had three sell-out shows starting that evening. As I lay down with a view to catching some much-needed sleep I noticed a bump on my leg. Was it a bite? I touched it, and screamed in pain. Len didn't like the look of it and called the hotel doctor. He said my leg was full of poison from my ankle to above my knee. The reason? I was simply run down. The doctor actually had to lance it (you wouldn't believe what came out – yuk!) and put a poultice on it, which Len had to change every few hours. That was how I performed that evening – out of my brain on pain pills, and full of penicillin. Just in case you were thinking show business is glamorous, think again.

In between all the tours we managed to squeeze in a couple of weeks recording. Mike and Nicky were starting to come apart. On one of the flights, Chapman wrote a song on his own called 'Kids of Tragedy (A and Bs, and in the film *Edgeplay*). We also did 'Tear Me Apart' (Chinn/Chapman), 'Half as Much as Me', 'What's It Like to Be Loved' and 'Close Enough to Rock and Roll' (Quatro/Tuckey). We were in Montreux – great studio, great vibe – having a wonderful time and putting down some seriously good stuff when Mickie Most appeared. He wanted to keep the two of them together, and the session came to a halt as Mickie proceeded to put a guilt trip on Mike. 'Nicky needs you. You're a team. You need each other. You don't write well alone,' and so on. He flew back with a promise from Mike that Chinn/Chapman would continue, and they did. But not for long.

So now it was 1975 – a good year for me. I continued to get awards, accolades, and silver, gold and platinum singles and albums to add to my wall. Due to touring we now had a nice following in America as well, and I made the cover of *Rolling Stone*. Fantastic! Great picture, too. We all have our 'looking good' days, and this was one of mine. I was also Playmate of the Month in *Playboy*, and in American rock magazine *Creem* I was voted third-best bass player after Jack Bruce and Paul McCartney. We were in the circuit – touring, recording, doing media, taking pictures, round and round again. Chapman had moved to Los Angeles to get a different 'buzz'. While there he was influenced by the growing 'funky' sound using clavinet and horns – Stevie Wonder's *Innervisions*, Average White Band – you get the vibe.

Time for album number three: *Your Mamma Won't Like Me!* Mike returned from California and we went back to Audio International, our studio of choice. Doing the engineering was my old friend Pete Coleman, who went on to have great success as a producer in his own right, with Pat Benata. This was the first time we had augmented our sound, using horn section Gonzales together with Sue and Sonny, two well-respected backing singers (Joe Cocker, 'High With A Little Help From My Friends'). Phil Denny (co-writer of 'Rolling Stone') also contributed some string arrangements. It was also the first album that stated: 'Produced by Mike Chapman in association with Nicky Chinn. A Chinnichap production'. A black-and-white live shot was used on the cover, with a reflected image on the back. We had never played so well and the band really cooked – funky as funky can be.

My sister Patty was by this time a permanent member of all-girl California-based group Fanny who were enjoying some success, getting into the top thirty in the USA with 'Butter Boy'. Fanny was on tour with Jethro Tull in England and Europe and, while in London, Patti accepted an invitation to stay in our flat for a few days. She also agreed to sing backing vocals with me on 'Your Mama Won't Like Me'. It's quite easy, for me anyway, to pick her out on the high notes. She had also done some sessions for ELO, and I can hear her loud and clear on their 'It's a Living Thing'. This track, in fact this whole album, has always been Patti's favourite. 'I Bit Off More Than I Could Chew', with Gonzales, also featured Sue and Sonny on backing vocals – true professionals, they had their own sound, which was unusual for backing singers who were supposed to blend into the background. The band was grooving so good when we were laying down this track that Mike let the machines run for ten minutes.

Quatro/Tuckey-wise we were well represented with 'Paralysed', 'Prisoner of Your Imagination', 'Can't Trust Love', 'New Day Woman, 'You Can Make Me Want You' (some of my best lyrics ever) and one of our most special songs, 'Michael'. Everyone agrees that it should have been a single, and Chapman and I have spoken many times about re-recording it some time. Every Michael I knew thought it was about them – Mickie Most, Mike Chapman and my brother Mickey. Hell, it could even have been about my ex-DJ boyfriend, he was called Mike too. Truth is, it's not about any of 'em. (*Aren't you going to tell 'em who you wrote it for? That's not playing fain.*) Whoever said life was fair, Susie?

This was also the year that Len and I bought our first house together, near Romford in Essex. I was twenty-five years old and a homeowner – now that *is* something to be proud of. We ran around all the furnishing stores in Tottenham Court Road, ordering velvet curtains, thick beige carpeting and beautiful furniture including a giant king-size wooden bed from Heal's. We hired a van for the day to move our meagre possessions in three crates, dumped them on the floor of the empty house, then left for a three-and-a-half-month tour of America. This would be the tour to end all tours. We began with ten solo shows in the States and Canada, and then went to Detroit to perform the first of seventy-five dates with my dearest old friend, Alice Cooper, as his special guests on the Welcome to My Nightmare tour. And even though this was the tour that culminated in Alistair's departure, there were lots of magical moments.

(*Before you begin, why not just get that Alice story out of the way? It's followed you around the world for years.*) Okay – here it is. Alice and I go back a long way to our early Detroit days, rehearsing in his band's farmhouse, appearing on stage together and partying – you get the idea. Also, it must be said, we have always been attracted to each other, and one night in 1970 we decided to explore this feeling a little further. We both had partners at the time, but we were young and reckless. Little sister Nancy was going out with drummer Neal and we had both driven out of town to one of Alice's gigs, ending up in the hotel afterwards. I was sitting on the bed with Vinnie (Alice's real name is Vincent Furnier) and we were talking and talking and talking, as we always did. Suddenly the mood changed. We looked at each other, leaned forward and kissed very deeply for several minutes. Then, at the same time, we both pulled back. Long pause . . . nah! We decided then and there that we were better friends than lovers.

Years later, on one of many tours of Australia, my promoter, who had just finished a Cooper tour, said Alice had told him about that kiss, adding; 'It was the defining moment of my life.' Serious stuff. But now, back to that 1975 tour.

The opening Detroit date was at Cobo Hall, which is huge. It was a great experience: there I was in my home town, with lots of old musician friends including Dick Wagner (guitarist extraordinaire, producer and songwriter – 'Only Women Bleed') and Steve Hunter, also on guitar. That night was a resounding success, and 'You Can Make Me Want You' from my new album was *the* big hit. Remember, my albums rather than my singles were the thing in America. Which was nice, as I could do a completely different kind of a show over there – not so trapped in the 'hit single' mode. Next stop, Chicago.

Alice had rented a plane for the entire tour, but it was so packed to the gills with his band, various accountants, groupies, girlfriends and my band that we had to leave most of our luggage at the Quatro house. To say I was nervous was an under-statement: this was a propeller job, and I was petrified. I was sitting in my seat shaking, white as a ghost, when Alice glanced over and decided to take action. 'Come here, Suzi, and sit next to me. These planes are great – even if we lose an engine they can glide to safety.' Gee, Alice, that makes me feel a lot better – thanks! He then proceeded to ply me with Budweiser. As it turned out, the flight was fine. However, the landing was not. It was in the middle of one of the worst snowstorms for years, and as we came in on the final approach we were swaying violently left to right. We landed with a bang and Alice cheerfully remarked, 'See, Suzi? Easy as that!'

That night I made a big decision. We had seventy-five shows to do, and how the hell was I going to stay sane if I was shaking with nerves on every journey? So I made friends with one of the pilots from Air New England, a great guy called Rick, and he helped a lot.

'Suzi, if you're so afraid, why not just sit up here in the jumpseat for take-off, flight and landing? Ask me anything you like, any time you like, and we'll see if we can turn it all around for you.'

I took him up on his offer on the flight down to Tampa in Florida. I had my crossword book, and my bottle of beer (thanks, Alice) as I sat in the cockpit for the very first time. Len was in the poker-playing row, and I remember counting the seats between us so that if I needed to I could run into his arms. Seeing a take-off from the cockpit is a completely different experience. Everything is in front of you and you feel the thrust – scary but thrilling. What I like is that you have the illusion of control. On this first flight though, I had my head buried in my puzzle book because I didn't really want to be there. Once I could feel that were actually up in the air I raised my head. Horror! Both pilot and co-pilot were sleeping, heads leaning against the windows. *Wake up! Wake up!* Oh. I see; it's a joke. Too, too funny!

While Rick was answering my endless questions the stewardess came in and asked, 'What would you like to drink?'

'Another beer for me,' I said.

'Oh, just bring me two large glasses with some ice,' replied Rick.

When she delivered our order Rick reached down the side of his seat and brought out a full bottle of vodka, generously splashing a large measure into both glasses.

'Oh, no, you don't – not with me on the plane.' I grabbed them back. But it turned out to be only water.

'Hey, Suzi,' the incorrigible Rick went on. 'Don't you think it's getting a little hot up here? Let's open a window.'

'Christ, what are you doing!'

I didn't realize you have to be above a certain level before you need the pressure system . . . Green? Oh, yes, I certainly was, and they were having a great time at my expense. The final joke – all pre-arranged, of course – was a large 'joint' which one of Alice's roadies brought in and handed to Rick.

After all this teasing, for the first time I actually started to relax on a plane. I stayed up in the cockpit for all the remaining flights on that tour and did indeed learn a lot, but there were two quite scary incidents.

We were in Denver, Colorado, known as the mile-high city, and the runway wasn't very long. Also we were overloaded – not a good combination. (*Did Alice really need his golf clubs? Or was it all those crates of Budweiser that added to the weight?*) There was a poker game already in session as we rolled down the runway . . . and we rolled and we rolled and we rolled. Conversation dropped away as people started to realize we hadn't lifted off yet. Finally we staggered into the air, little by little, up a bit and down a bit, while we could feel the plane struggling to gain height. No one said a word. Finally, it seemed that we were out of danger and safely into our cruise. One of the pilots, George (a World War II veteran), wiped his forehead and said, 'Phew – that was close.'

On another occasion we were flying from the east coast to the west – a long, long flight in a turbo prop, which needed a fuel stop or two – and we were going over the Rockies. For some stupid reason I was reading *Alive!*, the true story of a football team who crashed in the Andes and had to turn to cannibalism to survive . . . I was just at the part when they were going into the storm that caused them to crash when our own place started to fly through a real hail storm with huge chunks of ice hitting the fuselage. It was terrifying – sitting there, I couldn't understand how the plane wasn't wrecked.

On the personal front, at about this time tiny cracks were beginning to show in the relationship between Len and myself. (*To be fair, Suzi, I think he had a lot of pressures being your husband. Everything was Suzi, Suzi, Suzi – hard to find space as a man in all that.*) Whatever the reason, Len was drinking a lot. This led to many stupid arguments which could have been avoided but were noted by the entire touring party. Many years later Dick Wagner, whom I'd known since the early Detroit band days and who was Alice's lead guitarist on this tour, he told me, 'We could all see what was going on, Suzi.' I was in love with the man, tried to understand him and his pressures in my own way, and attempted to help him however I could. I spent most of our years together treating him like a king, building up his male ego and taking a back seat in our personal lives. I guess I was trying to balance out the product called Suzi Quatro with the private person of that name. Len told me, years later, that he was always aware that I was doing this, and loved me all the more for it. He also told me I had been wrong – he didn't need his ego building. Anyway, whatever the truth of the matter, I was there for the run of the play. I thought we would be together for the rest of our lives, and that any problems were simply things to be sorted out. (*Halt! Time to deviate from the main story for a minute or two and write that open letter to Dick Wagner.*)

'Dear Dick – all these years later, eh? Cast your mind back to 1965. You were in the Frost, a good, popular rock and roll band. You were and still are a great guitarist and songwriter. Very talented – a word I don't use lightly. We were backstage at a gig. I was flitting around, talking to various musicians, and you were standing quietly across the room. Our eyes connected. Now I was only fifteen at the time, and you were quite a bit older. There was something in that look, something I was too young to understand. Sister Nancy happened to notice it. "Susie, do you see that way he's looking at you? Oh, my God!"

'Yes, I did, and I was so embarrassed because what your eyes were saying was, "You are mine. You belong to me." I quickly left the area and never mentioned the incident again until this tour. We spoke on one of those long flights, and you admitted I had read it absolutely right. You were just a little bit in love with me, and I was just too young to take it any further. You were too "serious" – sorry, I wasn't ready yet. And isn't it great that we've reconnected and written a song about it, called "If Only"? Some day soon we *will* record that. Love you, Dick. God bless you always.'

Meanwhile back on the 1975 tour one of our companions was definitely not a musician. Grand Funk Railroad had written and recorded a song about her called 'Sweet Little Connie from Little Rock'. She was a schoolteacher from Arkansas who had a strange hobby – servicing rock and roll musicians on a strictly oral basis, if you get my drift. She had obviously, joined the Welcome to my Nightmare tour for a little light relief, as opposed to self-inflicted hand relief. I just could not get my head (no pun intended) around it, although she didn't seem to have my problems of this sort! She took great pride in this activity, which went against every bone in my body – no self-respect' being the main one. It took women's lib back to the dark ages. I remember telling her one day, in no uncertain terms, 'Come near my man and you're dead.' She didn't. We were also joined by Linda Lovelace (Deep Throat), who was, surprisingly, a very nice shy girl (*interesting segue, Suzi!*), and by Alice's good friend Candice Bergen, who is impossibly beautiful even without a stitch of make-up.

On my twenty-fifth birthday Alice made a very nice gesture: he flew the entire touring party to San Antonio to see the Stones perform. What a great present! (*Yes, Suzi, he treated you real good on this tour. And how did you repay him? By breaking his nose in a dart gun fight.*) Well, we were bored. Hell, we'd been on the road for ever, seemed like a good idea at the time. We took all the mattresses from the beds to use as shields, and went out into the hallway armed with rubber-tipped darts and dart guns. You should have seen the guests trying to get to their rooms while dodging the flying missiles! I could just see Alice's nose peeking out. *Smack*, I got him right between the eyes. Can I help it if I'm a good shot? Sorry, Alice, but thanks for wearing my T-shirt that night on stage. 'Outta respect for Suzi,' you said. I thought you looked kind of cute with that bandage on your nose.

New Orleans is the ultimate party town. You don't sleep, you just go from bar to bar down Bourbon Street and listen to the music – blues, jazz, and rock and roll. There are girls on swings, legs flying out the window at intervals, transvestites, tourists and that great Cajun cuisine that this city is so famous for. We had a ball. One night we found ourselves in one of 'those' bars where the show was a women's extravaganza with a difference – they were men, although it wasn't billed as such. Len, the boys and I then hatched a plan. There was one tour manager, Dave, who was far too full of himself. So we paid one of these 'women' to take him outside and take care of him. Dave jumped at the chance and quickly disappeared. We sat there sipping our Tom Collinses in excitement, waiting for our victim to reappear. 'God, is he going to be mad when he finds out! What do you think he'll do? He's gonna kill us.' Guess what – he never came back which is even funnier than if he had.

The only reason we had agreed to do this never-ending Welcome to My Nightmare tour was to promote our new album, and it was nearing the end when Mickie had a big argument with the record company which resulted in them withdrawing their support. There were ten more dates to go, but we flew back to England. A few days later, I spoke to Alice, who informed me that the day after we left the tour one of the propellers on the chartered plane just stopped. He put it down to me leaving – but I guess he wasn't serious about that!

And so began domesticity. After spending the last four months in hotel rooms, living out of a suitcase, I was so glad to be home. The joy of not having to pack a suitcase, not having to order a wake-up call, not having to get on a plane – though there was a brief moment of confusion on my first morning back home, when I tried to call room service and no one answered.

I walked around the house, taking in every single newly furnished room; then I strolled around the landscaped gardens, marvelling at the forty-foot swimming pool. My very first house, bought and paid for with money I had earned, following my dream: it was a great feeling. I even had a piano, something I had sorely missed.

For the next eighteen months we enjoyed a normal existence for the first time. We had friends over for dinner, we went to the pub, we went shopping in Romford – all new experiences after spending the last three years on the road. (*On the cooking front, it must be said, Lennie could have been a chef. No wonder you never learned how – what was the point?*) I swam, I played squash, I rode my bicycle and I did yoga. All of a sudden we had some free time, but not without reason. Mike Chapman had decided to relocate permanently to California, deserting his songwriting partner Nicky Chinn and all the bands he had worked with. He wouldn't even answer phone calls. Mickie broke the news to us one day at Rak. It was decided that he himself would produce the next contractually due album, aptly titled *Agoraphobia* (fear of open spaces), although he was convinced that Mike would eventually return to take care of future ones. Len and I weren't so sure – it was a scary feeling!

Gered Mankowitz was again shooting the cover photo, this time in an underground car park in central London. Len and I had both permed our hair (God knows why), and I had exchanged my black leather jumpsuit for a beaded beige chamois version complete with Indian necklace and one earring (to have two was very uncool in the seventies). The idea was to look like we were startled and running away from something.

This album was recorded on the Rak mobile at a hotel called the Château du Regard in France. There were four covers: 'Heartbreak Hotel' (Elvis Presley), 'Make Me Smile' (Steve Harley), 'Wake Up Little Susie' (Everly Brothers), and 'Honky Tonk Downstairs' (George Strait). The recording of 'Wake Up Little Susie' was unusual, to say the least. First of all, this is a song from my youth. I had been madly in love with Arlene's husband number one, and used to pretend to be asleep on the couch whenever he came over so that he would sing this song to me. On this latest recording we laid down the vocal outside on the driveway of the hotel, much to the amusement of the other paying guests. Original Quatro/ Tuckey songs on the album were 'Don't Break My Heart', 'Half as Much as Me', 'Close the Door', 'American Lady' and 'What's It Like to Be Loved'. Recalling the ill-fated Montreux session Mickie re-recorded 'Tear Me Apart' and 'Half as Much as Me', but used Mike's production of 'What's It Like to Be Loved'.

After a long day recording we were all having dinner in the sumptuous restaurant at the hotel and a discussion about religion started. Len was very verbal about his dislike of organized religion of any kind; I, of course, stuck up resolutely for my Catholic upbringing: 'It gives you guidelines that you never lose. Right and wrong – can't be beat.' Mickie, more than a little annoyed at Len, told him, 'You should never take away someone's beliefs.' The next day we recorded 'Make Me Smile', and the words took on a whole new meaning for me.

Although Mickie Most is a great producer, with many, many hits to his name, with us it just didn't work. The only reason I can think of is that Mickie's production is too refined, and my band has always been edgy and rough. Nevertheless this third album represented a bridge over troubled waters after. Chapman had deserted the Quatro camp. And on release it did well, riding off the back of our previous successes.

8

MR AND MRS TUCKEY AND HAPPY DAYS

....

In 1976 I was beginning to feel trapped in my image and wanted to spread my creative wings. The year was filled with non-stop tours *again*, playing the hits *again*, wearing the suit *again*, dragging a drunken Len up to bed in the wee small hours *again*. It was in this frame of mind that I said to him one night in bed, 'Exactly what are we waiting for? Let's get married.' We booked the Catholic church in Collier Row, Essex for 12 December, invited a small number of guests, including my parents, arranged the catering and waited for the big day to arrive. I started to go to church regularly again and took my preparation seriously (but stopped short of wearing stones in my shoes for penance). I did go to confession a lot, though, because I wanted to truly cleanse myself of my sins.

There was one blot on the landscape. When I called home and asked Mom and Dad to come over for the wedding, Dad told me he wasn't sure they could afford to do so, which I found difficult to believe. My dad had worked hard all his life and had plenty of money in the bank. What really annoyed me was that I had taken nothing at all from them, and had been earning my own living since the age of fourteen. My sisters and brother, on the other hand, had had weddings paid for (numerous for Arlene) as well as cars and deposits for houses. I know I didn't *need* any of that myself, but that isn't the point. It's a matter of fair play. Dad's favourite saying has always been 'The squeaky wheel gets the oil', so in his assessment I could pay for myself and could and should do so for them too. But that wasn't my way of thinking. I discussed the matter with Mickie, whose reply was quick and to the point.

'Suzi, do you want them there?'

'Yes.'

'Can you afford to fly them over?'

'Yes.'

'Then do it.'

End of discussion. Dad did fly my sister Patti over, as a representative of the family, at his own expense. (*Would have been nicer if he'd flown the whole family over, don't you think?*) I swallowed my hurt and booked the tickets. (*But the pain wasn't over yet, was it?*) Oh, no – there was another dandy to come.

My parents arrived two days before the event to a scene of huge excitement: organizing our house for the reception, the arrival of flowers, food and booze, answering the door as gifts arrived, and getting my wedding outfit (a white silk pants suit) prepared. It seems that for my whole life I have been over-hearing private conversations by mistake. Mom and Dad were in the kitchen on their own looking through all the presents when Dad said, 'Wow, there are a lot of expensive gifts here, Helen. I think we'd better go to the shops tomorrow and buy something ourselves.' Amazing, isn't it? This was an afterthought. So next day they went to Debenham's and purchased a set of silver-plated candlesticks – wowee! I know that sounds bitchy, but it still hurts.

(Well, Suzi, if you're not going to tell it, I will. Years later, in 1988, while you were visiting Mom, Dad, Nancy and her family in Texas, it all came out. Can't even remember what the trigger was. You were sitting in the front room at Nancy's house and all of a sudden you blurted out, 'Do you both know how bad it hurt that not only did I have to fly you to my wedding, but you didn't even have a gift with you? I cried so hard over that – it was so wrong. Do you agree? . . . Do you agree!' To which Dad meekly nodded his head and said, 'Yes, that was wrong of us.' Mom just sat there, quietly crying. Nancy recalls you were screaming and crying so loud that she had to shut all the windows in case someone thought there was a murder going on. Yes, Suzi Quatro – or was it me – I guess that was our 'primal' scream. And scream we did. I think we both felt a little better after that.)

Okay, balance at all times. . . . Their visit wasn't without humour. The day before the wedding we had a rehearsal at the church, as is normal, and Mom and Dad went to confession. Dad went in first but was out in no more than two minutes, which surprised my mom and me who were waiting our turn. Mom looked at me and remarked quite loudly, 'He lied.' Back home I asked my dad how he had managed to be so quick. His reply: 'I just said, "Bless me, father, I've done one of everything. Please forgive me."'

The day itself was magic. Len stayed the night with brother Billy's (the correct way to do things) and we had managed to keep the wedding out of the press. Mickie and Chris arrived at the house early so we could all go to the church together, and because I was really nervous Mickie shared a small whisky with me to calm me down. Quietly in my ear he said, 'Suzi, I'm turning you over now. You are Len's responsibility,' and gave me a big kiss on the cheek. I was touched – he was a surrogate father to me, and that's the reason I loved him.

I rode to the church in our blue Fleetwood Cadillac with Mom and Dad, Mickie following in his Porsche. Dad, always a gentleman in these circumstances, helped me out of the car, took my hand and led me into the church. I walked down that aisle like a little soldier, straight-backed and serious. I felt I was ready to take my vows – vows I meant every word of. When Dad handed me to Len in front of the altar he was in tears. Actually both of us were.

It was over in a flash – then back to the house for the reception. Champagne and laughter flowed all day, but the best part was when Dad and my agent, Dick Katz, did a musical turn together on the piano. Hell, I even dragged out my childhood party piece, 'Five Foot Two' – and this time the door didn't slam in my face!

So I was now a married lady, and it felt good. I was sure that whatever cracks had appeared in our relationship would be papered over now that we were man and wife. We were one in the eyes of God, and I was determined to be a good, loyal wife and make Len happy. Okay, so maybe it *had* been me who had done the proposing. I wonder if he would have asked me had I given him the chance. But that's something I shall never know.

After the reception we drove to the New Forest and stayed in the honeymoon suite at a nice hotel. Once again ghosts appeared, only this time it wasn't me who experienced things that go bump in the night. Len was awake the whole night, aware that he was not alone, while for once I slept. Next morning the staff told us all about the suite's reputation for being haunted. Years later Len's mum and dad stayed at the same hotel in the same room. Mum Tuckey was brushing her hair when she felt something stroke her bottom. 'Oi, stop touching my bum!' she shouted to Dad Tuckey – who was in fact on the other side of the room sound asleep in bed. Don't tell me these things don't exist.

After the fun, it was back to work. On the 1977 tour of Japan we made our only live album, *Live and Kickin'*, recorded at Nakano Sun Plaza Hall in Tokyo on 12 June and at Osaka Kosei-Nenkin Kaikan in Osaka on 15 June. It was a mixture, including our biggest hits and various album tracks through the years. Thank God we had set up more than one recording date, because I developed a serious throat infection of the kind that is often picked up in pressurized cabins on planes. It hit me around song three of the first show, and I could barely croak my way to the end. I was so upset and felt I had let everyone down. A doctor shot me full of penicillin, sprayed my throat and ordered me to bed. By the time of the second recording date I was, thankfully, nearly better. Nothing drives me mad more than not being able to do my show with full voice.

I insisted on this release being a double album so as to represent my entire show, complete with between-song dialogue. For these shows I came out on stage in a kimono – shuffling along, head down, meek and obedient. Then *whoosh*, off flew the kimono to reveal the leather jumpsuit, and away we went. Mickie was supposed to come over to produce to Japan this album, but to Len's and my annoyance never made it. Perhaps it was his fear of flying. At any rate, Len and I did the job ourselves.

This was also the tour on which Len and I married again! Mr Udo, our promoter in Japan, thought it would be a good idea to have a full-blown traditional Japanese ceremony to satisfy our fans. The boys especially, he told us, would be very disappointed at the news that their heroine was no longer available. This was my first foray into traditional Japanese culture, and it's something I shall never forget. We were given the works – I had a hand-painted wedding gown (which I still possess), black wig and white made-up face. The pictures are amazing – I look just like a geisha girl. (*All I can remember is Len cursing you because he had to limp down the aisle in these tight Japanese shoes. 'I do' maybe should have been 'I don't'!*)

As the tour was coming to an end I got a phone call that would change my life yet again. It was Toby Mamis, my American publicist, asking me to fly to Los Angeles to audition for a role in what he said was a very popular American sitcom, *Happy Days*. Two other people were also up for the role: Debbie Harry (who they thought was too old) and Joan Jett (who they thought was too tough). I'd never heard of the show, but Toby assured me it was big news and I trusted his opinion. After the three-week tour was over we flew to back to London for a couple days, then California here I come! I had nothing to lose.

Len and I had done a little research on the show – set in Milwaukee, it featured an all-American family, the Cunninghams, and the 'hoodlum with a heart', Fonzie. I had no idea what kind of role they wanted me for but was excited at this chance to act, something I had always known I could do. So on 12 August 1977 I put on my leather pants, T-shirt and jacket for my visit to Paramount Studios where I met Gary Marshall, Ronnie Hallin (his sister, who did the casting) and Gary Menteer (one of the writers). Gary Marshall started by saying, 'Well, Suzi, it was clever of you to come dressed for the part.' I had no idea what he was talking about until he told me the character was called Leather Tuscadero – destiny again. They then took me to meet the director, Jerry Paris, co-star and director of *Dick Van Dyke* and numerous other big TV shows, and a well-known woman-hater.

'Okay – so act!' Jerry demanded after the most cursory of introductions.

To which I shouted back, 'So what the fuck do you want me to do? Get angry?' I did. 'Laugh?' I did. 'Cry?' I did. 'Come on, Mr Big Time – direct me!' Then I threw the script on the floor. I think he had respect for me from that moment on; I certainly had his interest.

Jerry then took me to meet the Fonz, I guess to see whether we had any chemistry.

'Henry,' he said. 'This is Suzi Quatro. She's a big star in England, and she's here to audition for the part of Leather.'

Henry looked me slowly up and down, then casually walked behind me and stared at my ass. Not to be upstaged, I then strolled around and looked at his. Point made.

By now I had decided I wanted this job really badly but the powers that be just told me to go back to my hotel, where they would give me a call. We drove back to the Riot House (old habits die hard), switched on the TV and waited for the phone to ring. An eternity later (only half an hour by the clock), it did. It was Ronnie Hallin.

'We do want you for the part, Suzi, but there's a problem.' Oh, no! 'We don't just want you for one episode – we want you for fifteen!' And then, before I could take it all in, I saw a newsflash appear on the TV screen: 'Elvis Presley Is Dead'. There I was, in both seventh heaven and hell simultaneously.

Lennie and I just stared at each other, too stunned to speak. Eventually I called home. Mom answered, and before I could say a word she said, 'Susie, did you hear the news about Elvis Presley? I feel like part of the family has died!' We talked a little while longer about this bad news, and finally I told her my good news. Len and I wondered what to do for the rest of the evening. Celebrating seemed inappropiate, so we just went to a small restaurant on the Strip, the Mirabelle, and had a quiet meal together – too many mixed emotions for one day.

As soon as we got the contracts we took them to a lawyer, who negotiated a very good fee per episode, with residuals, plus two first-class tickets every time we travelled from London. I joined the Screen Actors' Guild, which meant I was a bona fide dues-paying actress. The trip to Los Angeles had been successful and the gamble had paid off. Just one more thing to do before we returned home: go and see Mike Chapman.

So early next morning we drove over to Mike's house in Beverly Hills, where he was clearly living the high life. Discussions began. Mike was excited about the possibilities that my appearing in *Happy Days* would open up, and quickly agreed to start working with us again. Hooray! The plan was to fly the band over and record a new album during the evenings while I filmed in the daytime. Everything was turning around again and I was definitely feeling lucky.

One month later, I was on my way. The press had got wind of the news and I was photographed in my blue leather jacket, over skin-tight jeans, boarding my first-ever first-class flight to LA. It is the *only* way to travel, and for once I wasn't in the least bit nervous. Before we touched down, Len said one thing to me, 'Suze, you can't just be good in this – you have to be great!'

On this visit we decided to splash out a little and stay at the Beverly Hills Hotel, which I loved, especially the pool area and the famous Polo Lounge. The rooms are spacious and, most important, quiet – no rock bands running back and forth through the corridors, no screaming and shouting, no wafting of marijuana through the crack in the door. I had a basket of fruit and some champagne from the *Happy Days* office to welcome me. We slept like logs before my first day on the set.

Monday was read-through day – the entire cast, writers, director and creator Gary Marshall sat around a huge table as everyone went through the script together. Everyone was really friendly: it felt like one big happy family, which relaxed me a little. We drank coffee and ate doughnuts. But imagine how I felt when I realized that this was not just a small cameo role – rather the entire script, the pivotal scene being with Henry in the ladies' toilet. I can only imagine how green I sounded reading my lines. I also got a little surprise: one of the writers, Bob Bruen, was from New York and said he used to see me play at Trude Heller's back in the sixties with the Pleasure Seekers. Small world!

Tuesday was on-the-set day. We read from our scripts and worked out the blocking – where to be for each line – with Jerry Paris giving direction at different points. I wanted very much to be part of the team, but was also realistic enough to acknowledge that this was all brand-new to me. So during the coffee break I said to all the regulars – Ronnie Howard, Tom Bosley, Marion Ross, Al Morilano, Scott Baio, Erin Moran,

Donnie Most, Anson Williams and Henry Winkler, 'Listen, guys, I just want to get a couple of things straight. I know you're all aware of my recording success on the other side of the world, but I'm not bringing any kind of ego to this show. I'm new at this, and nervous, and any help you can give me will be greatly appreciated. I'm here to learn!'

My first entrance into Arnold's required me to stand in the doorway, then saunter over, smacking my hand on my pants and pointing (this was to be Leather's bit of 'business', as they say in the trade). We went through this scene a few times, and then I got my first bit of instruction from Ronnie (Richie Cunningham).

'Suzi, you're doing great, you're a natural. The only thing is, bring your voice up a bit – you need to project just a little more.'

Thanks, Ronnie. Such a sweetie, and so goddam professional.

Henry (the Fonz) was next. 'Suzi, do me a favour. Walk across the living room.'

'Why, Henry? Do you want to look at my ass again?'

'No. I just want to see how you move.'

So I did.

'Great – you walk great. So why when we're rehearsing do you walk different? I tell you what. Take some time in this living room, walk around, sit on the couches, until it feels familiar. Then you'll walk naturally.'

Thanks, Henry. A very nice, intelligent, serious person.

By Wednesday we were expected to nearly know all our lines, which I did. Luckily I'm a quick study and have an excellent memory as long as I can put movement and story in my head together. Thursday was blocking for the cameras, in costume. Quite a tedious day, actually – you spend most of your time standing in your spot while the camera man runs a tape measure between the lens and your chin. Friday was D-Day. We rehearsed during the day, the audience arrived in the evening and then the taping began. That first week I was absolutely shitting myself! Would I remember my lines? Would I hit the right spot? Would I be any good?

So there I was, dressed in my own leather pants and jacket (for luck), ready to make my first big entrance into Arnold's. I haven't had many sheer terror moments like this in my career. Bravado usually sees me through.

Henry came over. 'Hey, Suzi, are you ready to kill 'em?' 'Don't worry, you're gonna be great. Hey, that's your cue. Go!'

Leather Tuscadero coolly saunters into Arnold's, looks around totally in charge of the situation, does a mean teenage rebel walk over to the booths ready to speak her first line . . . and then (Jerry Paris) says, 'Excuse me, Ms Quatro. What are you doing out here?'

'Um, that was my cue.'

'No – you have another two pages yet!'

Red-faced, I turned and walked back to a doubled-over Henry, who had sent me out early on purpose! 'There ya go, Suzi. That's the worst that can happen. Now go out and enjoy yourself.' I entered again to thunderous applause, and from that moment on I was home and dry.

This episode was a two-parter, to be continued the following week. Here's the story so far. Leather was a small-time thief who had done time and was now back in town trying to make a name as a singer in a band. She first had to win over Fonzie, who didn't trust her. This all turns around in the ladies' room where Leather is hiding, scared to go out due to harassment from police officer Kirk about hiring ex-cons. This was my acting baptism. I lost myself in the role and forgot all about acting when I confessed to Fonzie, 'I'm scared.' It was a heartfelt moment which felt as natural as can be.

My debut was well received and sister Patti, ex-sister-in-law Lyn (Mickey's first wife) and, most importantly, Mike Chapman were there to witness my triumph. Mike was now definitely back in the team and the very next night, after attending the opening of *Saturday Night Fever*, he and Nicky Chinn went home and wrote 'If You Can't Give Me Love'. With this great song, one of their best, recording was truly ready to begin.

Since we were free that weekend we arranged a little dinner party. Halfway through the meal, I saw that Patti was crying. When I asked her what the problem was she got even more upset.

'Here I am, living in Los Angeles, trying to make it with Fanny, trying to model, trying to get some acting roles. . . . And you just waltz in here and land a part on the biggest sitcom in the country. . . . You always get so fucking lucky, and it's just not fair!'

We were all stunned into silence, and I was embarrassed as hell. I felt really sorry for Patti that night, and didn't know what to say to her. I still don't. It just seems to me, though, that we all have our path to follow, and it doesn't always take us where we think it's going to lead. I guess it would take a lot more years for this anger, resentment and jealousy to end. I just hugged and kissed her, and told her, 'I love you.'

(*Can I just put my two cents in here? That word 'luck' is a double-edged sword for sure, and it's always bothered both of us big time, especially since the family seemed to use it at every available opportunity. 'Oh, Suzi, you got lucky . . . yes, you sure did.' Balls! First of all, 'getting lucky' seems to imply that talent is not required, which is ludicrous. This is the way I see it. You have to work hard and learn your craft. You have to be determined and let nothing and no one stand in your way. You have to set your sights for the finish line. You have to recognize opportunity when it knocks, and indeed open the door and let it in. And the main ingredient you must have is talent. Then and only then can that little thing called luck make an appearance, and then you may or may not have success – which is never guaranteed. And remember this golden rule: to have success is not difficult; to sustain it is the real test.)*

So it was a very busy, demanding time for me, acting in the daytime and recording in the evening. One night during my second week of filming, as I was busy laying down tracks, a bouquet of twelve red roses arrived. Since I was the only girl there, I figured they must be for me. Grabbing the card, I read, 'If you can sing as good as you can act, no wonder you're a star. Love, Henry'. It was a kind gesture that I shall never forget.

By the end of the second week Len and I were getting quite friendly with Gary Menteer and Marty Nadler, two of the writers. It was suggested that we work on a spin-off series about an all-girl rock and roll band that never makes it. Marty adored Len – his sense of humour, his accent and his look. Everything Len said made Marty laugh, whether it was funny or not. In fact the entire company found Len highly amusing. Gary Marshall even asked him if he would consider joining the cast (*which would have made you jealous – you always needed to be number one, didn't you?*). It was also during this second week that I arrived back in my hotel room to discover a gift box from Cartier. It was from Bob Bruen, the old fan of the Pleasure Seekers, and contained a beautiful travelling clock.

We had also had a few dinners with casting director Ronnie Hallin, and it was she who told me how I actually got the audition. Apparently they had been looking for a while for someone to play the part of previous cast member Pinky Tuscadero's sister Leather, and wanted a girl who was tough yet vulnerable and who could act and sing! Ronnie happened to mention this to her older daughter, who dragged her into her bedroom, pointed to the picture of me dressed in my leathers on the cover of *Rolling Stone*, and said, 'Suzi Quatro would be perfect!'

Finally both my first acting experience and the recording were finished. We flew back across the pond again, armed with what Len, Nicky and Mike and I all thought was our next hit single. It would be a month or so before *Happy Days* was aired in the States, and another six months before it hit Europe, so the first business was to go and play Mickie the finished mix of 'If You Can't Give Me Love'. For the first time in all the years I had known him he seemed a little jealous – jealous about my acting role, jealous about the song, and jealous that we had somehow got Mike and Nicky interested again. In fact he took it off halfway through, saying, '*This* is what a hit record sounds like', and played Hot Chocolate's 'Heaven's in the Back Seat of my Cadillac' – which, incidentally, wasn't a big hit. I think he felt threatened, if that's the right word.

Leaving Mickie's office that day, I experienced my first change of attitude towards him. For the first time in our association I felt unappreciated. After all, I'd flown over to LA after buying my own ticket, and with no promise of success. I'd landed the role and made it work. And it was Len and I who had got Mike Chapman back on board – and God knows we needed him. Right or wrong, it felt like Mickie was having a hard time thinking of me in any other way than the 'little girl from Detroit'. I guess I was looking for some respect at this point in my career. Seeds of discontent had been planted in my heart.

Yet deep down I understood Mickie's fear that I would leave him one day – it had happened to him with several artists from the sixties, and as a result he always felt he needed to keep his artists in their place. He placed me with one small label after another in the States preferring me to be big in Europe, Asia and Australia where he felt he had some control. I have often been asked over the years why I didn't enjoy more single success in my homeland, and this, I feel, is the real reason. But I can't and don't allow myself to wallow in it, because without Mickie Most I might never have had any success at all. He discovered me, and I shall be for ever grateful for that. But nobody's perfect.

It was mid-November, time for the first transmission in America of my acting debut on *Happy Days*. My family back in Detroit were beside themselves with anticipation. The *Detroit News* was at the house to photograph and record everyone's reactions. Dad, trying to ensure that nothing would go wrong, hooked up two sets in the TV room and then proceeded to knock one of them on to the floor in his excitement. Since this success was actually on American soil for once I was duly appreciated and applauded by everyone, which made made a nice change. Mom was so very proud – mailman, cleaning lady, shop assistant, waiter, didn't matter who, everyone had to look at my pictures which she kept in her wallet and to hear the story of my success. She even answered my fan mail. Mom never had a problem with anything – she just always loved, believed in and supported me. Nobody understood me like Mom did, and I could never fool her.

We flew back to LA again in December to do the next couple of episodes. It was at this time that Patti announced her engagement, and we were invited to Detroit for the party (paid for Dad, of course) and to spend Christmas at home, which fell in between filming dates. We declined and went to Las Vegas instead, driving all the way and enjoying Christmas Day at Caesar's Palace. I lost $200, my absolute limit – guess I'm not much of a gambler. I'm a great winner, but a really shitty loser. And, the reason we didn't go to Detroit? Well, Len was being protective of me at this point. Through the years he had intercepted many letters from various family members, letters that I never saw. They were full of negativities, criticizing what I was doing and warning me that my career might be over at any time. Yet I was having hit after hit earning lots of money doing what I had learned to do. Since I didn't know about these letters at that time I blamed Len for keeping me away from my family – but who could blame him? He had heard all my stories and had witnessed first-hand how I was treated, and didn't like it one bit.

Once, in the Quatro kitchen, Len heard Dad take a phone call from a journalist. The conversation went something like this. 'Nope. Suzi isn't here right now. Who's calling? . . . Oh, so you're from the newspaper and you want to do an interview. Well, let me tell you about my son Michael – he's the one you should be talking to.' Because of these incidents, there was always more than a little friction between Len and my family. The way I see it now is that he was only trying to protect me because I was unable to protect myself. The more success I enjoyed, the guiltier I felt about leaving the family. It would be many years before I could actually enjoy what I had achieved.

Soon enough 1978 was upon us. I was appearing regularly in *Happy Days*, had a billboard on Sunset Boulevard advertising my new album, *If You Knew Suzi*, and was enjoying living in a rented house with a swimming pool up in the Hollywood Hills. Life was good. When I wasn't filming or gigging we would often go to the 'in' place on Sunset Boulevard, Le Dôme, which Mike had bought shares in. One evening Len and I were there with Nicky Chinn. Also present was Dudley Moore, at one end of the restaurant, and Erik Estrada (star of *Chips*, a popular American television detective series) sitting with a date at the other end. We were somewhere in the middle.

Dudley had seen me come in and shouted out, 'Hi, Suze, how are ya!' We'd never actually met, but that's how it is in showbiz – everyone 'knows' everyone. I went over to say hello, telling him how much I loved the Derek and Clive live album and played it at all my dinner parties. I also explained that this was the one and only time I could ever laugh at the C word, which is actually my least favourite word in the English language. Then I went back to our table and sat down to eat.

Dudley, being Dudley, began to perform the C routine,

right across the restaurant and very loud – to which Erik Estrada, who was trying to impress his date, took great exception. Erik first came over to our table and asked us for a comb, which I found strange, and when we said we didn't have one he returned to his own table and began to comb his hair with his fork! Whatever turns you on. . . . As Dudley went on and on Erik stormed over to our table again, threatening to beat us up. We told him to stop being a silly boy and sit down.

That should have been the end of it, but when we left (I was by now a little tipsy) I stood in front of the plate glass window of the restaurant, stuck my tongue out and gave him the finger. Out he came fuming, hands up ready for a real fight – not just with the guys but with a five-foot-two woman!

Now Randy was our roadie – six foot four inches of mean-looking black ex-marine, ex-Nixon bodyguard – and he just happened to be driving by. He stopped at a red light, saw the commotion, swerved across four lanes and screeched to a halt in front of the restaurant. Then he rose and rose and rose out of the car and went straight up to Erik.

'Excuse me, brother, is there a problem here?'

'No problem,' Erik said meekly, and went back inside.

(*Don't forget the other Le Dôme story, Suzi. Your ego was in full flight that night*.) Okay, okay. You know what, little Susie? Why don't you tell it? You probably think it's funnier than I do.

(*You were high-profile in Hollywood at this time – people were recognizing you from* Happy Days *everywhere you went. So as you approached the restaurant you noticed loads of snappers stationed outside and mentally prepared yourself to be photographed. Which didn't happen. But in you walked anyway. It kind of bothered you all through dinner. You had no idea that Rod Stewart was due there that evening until you ran into him on the staircase on your way to the toilet. When you left to go home (fortified by a few glasses of good red wine, of course) again there were no flashes. But this time you didn't let it slide. You turned around and shouted, 'Do you guys realize who you've just missed taking a picture of?' To which one of them replied, 'Yes, Suzi, we do!')* How mortifying. I guess you could say I asked for it.

Thank you for sharing one of my most humiliating moments, Susie. And just to prove that I have no problem laughing at myself, here's another story. A key phrase with me is 'I know' – doesn't matter what you tell me, 'I know.' Len and I were staying in a particularly beautiful rented home in Beverly Hills with an outdoor pool, sauna and separate guest house. One night, after a long session at the studio, Len rolled up a little 'relaxer', as was his way. Feeling nice and mellow, he gazed up at the wall, noticed a black button on a panel and said, 'I wonder what that is.' Up jumped Miss 'I know', saying, 'You silly boy – that's an intercom system! Look, I'll show you how it works,' and pressed it just as Len shouted 'Nooooooooo!' It was the burglar alarm. Lights came on all over the house, sirens wailed, and after about a minute of this noise we saw helicopters circling the front lawn. Policemen were trying to break down the front door . . . and inside was the unmistakable smell of weed. We panicked and flushed the toilet several times. At the door I managed to convince the police that it was a false alarm. Len was fuming, not only because he had had to get rid of his stash but because I had been being unbelievably stupid. We looked at each other for about five minutes – and then burst into hysterical laughter. It's one of our fondest memories.

If you knew Suzi, released in 1978, was recorded at EMI studios in Cologne in Germany and Los Angeles. Chinn/ Chapman wrote. 'If You Can't Give Me Love', 'Don't Change My Luck' and 'The Race Is On', all of them singles. The covers were 'Tired of Waiting' (Kinks), 'Evie', 'Rock and Roll Hootchie Koo' (Rick Derringer) and 'Breakdown' (from my new favourite rock and roll band, Tom Petty and the Heart-breakers). Quatro/Tuckey originals on this album were. 'Suicide', 'Non-citizen' and a song I wrote based on the way I felt about DC, 'Wiser Than You'.

Wiser Than You

You messed my mind, destroyed my soul
How was I supposed to know about the power of love
You were wiser and older than me

How you touched my heart, then you ripped it apart
You changed an innocent smile and girlish laughter
Into crying eyes overnight

So good luck, I hope you realize what I gave to you
A virgin's love, a child's trust, making love was something new
Oh you found me so young, and taught me all you knew
But I'm leaving a lot wiser than you

I remember when I thought you were my friend
I believed all those lies you said, she doesn't understand
You're the only one for me

Secret rendezvous, stolen nights for two
Then suddenly something happened and I realized
I'd given it all to you

So good luck, I hope you realize what I gave to you
A virgin's love, a child's trust, making love was something new
Oh you found me so young, and taught me all you knew
And I'm leaving a lot wiser than you

(Quatro/Tuckey, 1978)

We toured America and Canada extensively with this album, and one night we played at New York's Bottom Line. Since we didn't have to stick to hit singles the set included lots of album tracks, including 'Breakdown'. The morning after this gig I received a bouquet of roses at my hotel. This time it was from Tom Petty, accompanied by a card that read, 'Dear Suzi, great set, really enjoyed it. Thanks for the plug every night, love, Tom'.

Open letter to Tom Petty. 'Dear Tom, I just want to take this opportunity to thank you in print for that touching gesture and to tell you I was there at the Whiskey-a-Gogo before you broke into the big time. From the moment you and your band took the stage I was riveted. You were, and are, everything a rock and roller should be. You had *attitude*, and it had been a long time since I'd I heard a band I liked that much. When your first album came out I played it so much I wore it out. Why don't you and I do a duet some time? This time, the roses would be on me! Love, Suzi Quatro xxx.'

Happy Days had caught on big time in the UK and I became a bit of a hero as Fonzie's female counterpart. Doing this show was one of the best decisions I ever made: it gave me a new lease of life and extended my career for some years. While it was being shown on TV 'If You Can't Give Me Love' was riding high in the charts. Once again everything was coming up roses. Many fans and DJs have commented that this is their favourite hit of mine – a real 'song' with great melody and lyrics, and sung in my real chest voice. It was on the radio non-stop but, nice as that was, I shall never forget the evening my first episode of *Happy Days* was shown. As soon as it was over the phone started ringing continuously with congratulations. Nicki Caine, daughter of Michael, whom I had become friendly with, told me her dad had said, 'Suzi has what it takes to be a fine actress.' And, after the lull between '76 and '77 it sure felt good to be firmly back in the limelight again.

In early December we flew back to LA again to film two more episodes (*and it was at this point, Suzi, while you were being torn between your exciting new acting career and making more hits, that Len made 'that' statement*). We were sitting in our room at the Beverly Hills hotel as I was reading through my script. Len, sitting on the bed looking very bored and slightly pissed off, suddenly said, 'You know, Suze, if you think I'm going to hang around in California while you act, you've got another think coming.' Quite a bombshell to drop at that stage of our lives together. I distinctly remember thinking that Len could have his way for now but some day I would make another decision. In a way, it was the beginning of the end for us. I realized that Len would never be happy unless I was on stage in my leather jumpsuit and he was standing next to me, playing guitar. To be fair, that's who he fell in love with and it was all he ever wanted – which is kind of sweet. Sweetly claustrophobic!

It was during this time that I filmed my personal favourite *Happy Days* episode, 'Marion Plays Fairy Godmother'. This was the only time I didn't play any music but just acted, and as Jerry, the director, told me, it was important I show 'em what I could do! The storyline was that Ralph Malph (Donny Most) had asked me out on a date to a ball. I would be required to wear a dress and heels – very unLeatherlike, very unSuzilike – and so I took myself off to the Cunningham house to ask Marion's advice. In the pivotal scene I was required to ring the doorbell, then stride across the carpet, all attitude, and say to Marion, 'I have to go on a date. It's with Ralph Malph, and I have to wear a dress!' To which Marion replies, 'Does it have to be leather?' Typical *Happy Days* humour. The problem was that I just couldn't get the walk or the attitude right – it seemed strained and unnatural. We did it over and over again. I couldn't figure out what the hell was going wrong – and then it hit me! I went outside and imagined Joan Jett imitating me. Then I rang the doorbell, strode determinedly to my mark and said my lines. 'Perfect, Suzi.' Thanks, Joan.

At Christmas 1978 we gave in and flew to Detroit. I was determined to put all the emotional baggage behind me. Mom had organized a big party for me with old band members, old friends, relatives and a huge cake. Someone had even set up a stage area so we could all jam. We had a great time and I had the chance to reconnect with lots and lots of old friends. It was really a wonderful homecoming in every way (*except for that party at Nan Ball's house – balance at all times, Ms Quatro*). Okay, here's how it went.

Grosse Pointe is stuck in a time warp. You can go there to this day and see the same shops, the same restaurants, the same fashions – nothing has changed since I left in 1971. So when Nan decided to have a Christmas party with lots of our old school pals I couldn't decide whether or not to wear my extremely expensive mink coat. Something inside said that it would give the wrong impression – that I was showing off. But Len said, 'For God's sake, Suze, wear the damn coat. It's December and it's freezing. What the hell are you ashamed of? You earned it!' As it turned out, my instincts were correct.

As we arrived, every head turned. There was little Susie/Suzi Quatro, blonde-highlighted haircut, slim, wearing leather trousers, white silk shirt and *mink coat*! Who the fuck does she think she is? There were various groups of guys in checked trousers, blue blazers and brown tassel loafers, smoking pipes, and pretty girls in with shiny long hair in black cocktail dresses, elegantly smoking and sipping champagne. Oh, yes, this was a Grosse Pointe soirée all right! I walked on into the lions' den.

Nan's sister Marylou visited me in England the following year and we had many a heartfelt conversation about the good old days sitting outside on the patio drinking a bottle of wine. And of course, this party came up.

'Oh, yeah,' said Marylou, 'we saw you walk in. I was standing in the corner with a couple of friends, and do you know what I said to them? "There's Suzi Quatro – let's ignore her."' And they did.

I had to ask her why.

'Well, basically you'd done everything you'd set out to do, and there I was struggling just to make a living. Will you forgive me, Suzi?'

There were more than a few tears from both of us that night. I totally understood, and harboured no anger over the matter – I'm happy to say we are close friends to this day. It took a lot of courage for Lou to share that with me, and it was appreciated. (*Be honest, Suzi. Didn't it feel good that Marylou, someone you alway tried to imitate, was a little envious of you? What a turnaround!*) Okay, can't deny that. But it was a flash-in-the-pan feeling. To this day, I still need her approval. Must get some more lessons in 'jumping over my shadow'. But first let's get back to the festive season of 1978.

Since this was to be my first Christmas with my family in Detroit since 1970 Len and I splashed out on gifts – after all, we had a lot of years to make up for. We went to my favourite shopping mall and spent lots of money on the entire family, mostly on a silver tea service for my mother. I was happy to do it and glad that I could afford it. Over Christmas Len had been instructed to take lots of snapshots for my publicist Bill Harry. We sisters sang old songs, which ended up in the whole family singing carols around the organ, with Dad and Mickey accompanying us. All in all, this was a special Christmas that I shall always remember.

9

SUZI AND OTHER FOUR-LETTER WORDS

....

Len and I had been married for three years when we began to record what is, without a doubt, my favourite album. I love the front cover because it's actually how I see myself, and I love the songs. Chapman/Chinn wrote the hit 'She's in Love with You' and the title track, 'Four-letter Words'. (*I wish you could reveal who this song was about. Maybe I can. Now let's see, how would a gossip columnist do it? What music industry bigshot is having a secret session with a little lady from somewhere in Texas . . . and this session ain't takin place in the studio!*) That's enough – you'll get us both into trouble.

The single. 'She's in Love with You' took for ever to lay down in the studio. It's like a machine with hardly any movement – up a little in intensity, slowly back down, same riff, same groove, moving without moving and very hard to do. This is the only song I ever had to practise playing and singing at the same time. The bass line is almost mechanical and the vocal lies behind the beat as all good vocals do – they laze around the groove.

I was having a particularly creative writing period and it

was great to have so many originals on this album: 'Mind Demons' (about doing you know what when you ain't getting any; as Woody Allen puts it, 'It's sex with somebody you love'); 'Hollywood' (a song about the ups and downs, and how it can kill you, inspired by a wonderful Len Tuckey chord sequence and one of Andrew Lloyd Webber's favourites); 'Mama's Boy' (about my guitarist at the time, Jamie Crompton and which became a single); 'Starlight Lady' (written for Arlene, who seemed to be searching and searching for Mr Right and still clocking up the marriages – on number four at that time); 'Space Cadets' (a real California lyric – la la land); and 'Love Hurts' (unusually, written on drums). Chapman commented to me, 'I don't know what the hell is happening with your writing, Suzi, but it's great! Keep going.'

The entire album was recorded in Los Angeles. The line-up for the Suzi Quatro band at this time was Franny and Penny backing vocals, Bill Hurd (ex-Rubettes) on piano, Jamie Crompton and Len Tuckey on guitar, me on bass and Dave Neal on drums. Another extensive tour of the States was booked, this time playing lots and lots of big rock and roll clubs to promote the album. It was my biggest travelling unit so far, and for the first time ever I used female vocalists. How wonderful to have that little bit of insurance when I was ill, or if my voice wasn't quite up to par. It just made me relax a little to know that someone could cover if necessary – and of course if you relax things don't go wrong! So, what with recording, taping *Happy Days* and touring we were in my home country at least half of the year. I really enjoyed overdosing on hamburgers and milkshakes, watching the endless repeats of my favourite TV sitcoms (*I Love Lucy*,

Leave it to Beaver, The Andy Griffith Show) and cruising down the huge five-lane expressways in our rented convertible Mustang.

I must have been asked a thousand times how the 'Stumblin' In' duet happened. We were in Cologne doing some recording with Mike Chapman in EMI's studio. There was a huge award ceremony taking place in the Messehalle, and we decided to attend. Loads of other artists were there, including Smokie, Amanda Lear and Bonnie Tyler. Afterwards there was the obligatory party. They had a band on stage and, me being me, I wanted to join in. The first person I tried to drag up was Amanda (dubious-gender disco queen of the seventies). She had just spent half an hour telling me how much like me she was – that she loved rock and roll and Elvis and leather, and had actually gone to see Mickie Most to get a deal (he turned her down).

'So, let's go up and sing some Elvis songs,' I suggested, to which she replied, 'I don't know any of the words.'

Then I asked Bonnie if she would like to join me. 'Nope. I'm not working tonight, Suzi.' Okay.

I turned to Chris Norman (lead singer of Smokie). 'Get your ass off that chair and let's go do some serious jamming.' At last!

While we were singing, Len turned to Chapman. 'Hey, Mike, see how cute they look up there – nearly the same size! And listen to how great they sing together.' Next day in the studio, while I was standing at the piano fooling around, Mike sauntered over with his guitar. 'Suzi, play this. G . . . A . . . D . . . B . . . over and over. Hey, Pete, hook me up to a mike and switch on the machines. Hurry.' Mike began to sing.

'Our Love Is Alive' and so we began foolishly laying our hearts on the table. 'Stumblin' in our love is a flame, burning within, now and then, firelight will catch us stumblin' in.'

'Wow, that's *great*, Mike.'

'Yep. Now I just need to write a verse.'

And that's called talent.

'Stumblin' In' was my first big single hit in America, where it reached one million sales – and in fact it was huge in most of the world. This one and 'If You Can't Give Me Love' have been my most enduring hits of all. England was the only country where 'Stumblin In' didn't chart high – and there's a reason for that. Chris Norman agreed to record the song. We were going to combine the two bands, Smokie and ourselves, but Smokie said no. So it ended up as my band alone. I know Chris was enthusiastic about this duet, but he probably got a hard time from the rest of the boys – he acted nervous throughout, worried about doing this 'solo' project and upsetting the balance in his band. Therefore, whilst he agreed to do a promotional video, he refused to appear on any television shows. This was okay in most of the territories, but in the UK at that time if your record wasn't on *Top of the Pops* it wasn't in the charts. We were at 41 and needed this extra push; Chris, true to his word, declined and wouldn't change his mind even after Chinn, Mickie Most, Len and myself pleaded with him. And that's why we failed to reach a higher position with this record in the UK.

(This seems a good time to mention that letter from Dad. Remember? 'Stumblin In' was riding high in the US charts and just starting to climb everywhere else. This is what your dad wrote to you. 'Dear Susie, I just want to say how disappointed

*I am that you chose to do a duet with this Chris Norman guy –
whoever the hell he is. What were you thinking of? Your
brother is here, struggling to make a name for himself, and
you go and record with a complete stranger. Why didn't you
use Mickey? And while I'm at it, Mickey's son is interested in
learning bass guitar, so if you could send him one over right
away that would be good. Also, Arlene's son Davey is
showing some talent in piano and singing – maybe you could
pay for lessons. By the way, how much money are you
making? How much money do you have do you have in
the bank now?' Etc. etc. etc. I remember wondering whether I
would ever get away from all this.*)

Even though I hadn't finished all my filming commitments
for *Happy Days* it was at this point, with 'Stumblin In'
becoming a million seller in the American charts, that the
decision was made. I would do no more. It was thought by
some (not me!) that playing Leather Tuscadero and being
Suzi Quatro constituted a conflict of interest and made my
rock persona less credible. I wasn't happy about this turn of
events, but that's just how it was. We were now back on the
road, playing our particular brand of rock and roll – just
how Len liked it.

At the end of the seventies Mike Chapman and Nicky
Chinn were still a team. Nicky had married an American girl
and moved to California, buying a house near Mike's. They
decided to set up their own record label. At the same time my
contract with Mickie Most was coming to an end, and it was
time to renegotiate. I started to think, for the very first time,
about the possibility of leaving Mickie and Rak Records. I
still wasn't getting the respect from Mickie that I thought I
deserved, and that feeling had grown (in hindsight, out of all

proportion). Len and I had many conversations with Nicky about the future, and after much soul-searching we came to the conclusion that it was time to sign directly with the team who wrote and produced my hits. Len wasn't as sure as I was, but I can be very persuasive. Nicky would be the one to deliver this news to Mickie – didn't envy him one bit! I wasn't there myself, but after putting together three different versions (Nicky's, Mickie's and Mickie's wife Chris's) of the event this is how I understand it.

Nicky went over to dinner at Chris and Mickie's house and over cocktails he began to talk. He explained how I felt, and that I had decided not to remain with Rak Records but to go to their new label, Dreamland Records. Mickie went absolutely mad – 'Things like this don't happen, Suzi Quatro belongs to me' – there were a few tears and he shut himself in a bedroom. Nicky then started to cry too, and Chris ran from room to room trying to bridge the gap. It was a horrible situation to be in. Both Mickie and Chris were flabbergasted because they had never thought I would leave; Nicky went home feeling like he'd lost his best friends.

When Nicky first relayed this story to me, I went through a lot of mixed emotions. On the one hand I was glad to be with Nicky and Mike directly, which I felt would ensure the realization of my future hit potential. On the other hand I felt terrible about leaving the man who had plucked me from obscurity and taken me all the way to the top. Mickie was very hurt, and rightly so. But the deed was done, and it was too late to turn the clock back. Even so, in the midnight hours I continued to have serious doubts about whether I had done the right thing – I would just have to wait and see.

It felt strange not to be with Rak Records any more, and especially without Mickie Most who had been my father figure, mentor and protector since 1971. I felt a little lost. Things were strained between us, the say the least. We tried to keep things civilized but communications eventually broke down between Mickie and Chris, Len and me, and all dealings were done via the record company.

The band flew back again to Los Angeles to record the next album. Mike had decided to try and re-create the past and brought back on board engineer and by now successful producer Pete Coleman (who had worked with rock singer Pat Benatar). *Rock Hard* was the name of the album, taken from the single of the same name. It was edgy and raw, harking back to the good old days. We laid it down as a band, getting that old drum and guitar sound and double tracking the vocal just like we used to do. Mike was taking no chances on this one and wanted big chart success again in all the territories around the world where we traditionally enjoyed huge record sales.

The Chinn/Chapman compositions were 'Rock Hard' and 'Lipstick'. Cover-wise, we did 'Glad All Over' (Dave Clark Five), 'Love Is Ready', 'Hard Headed' and 'Wish upon Me'. Quatro/Tuckey were well represented with 'State of Mind'/ 'Woman Cry' (an unusual reggae track), 'Ego in the Night' (timely, wouldn't you say?), 'Lay Me Down' and 'Lonely Is the Hardest'. (*Oh, yes. That was written all about your alone time in England before you made it. Mike made you do the vocal at midnight, with all the lights off – he wanted you raw and hurt. One of your better vocals, Suzi Q. Let's put the lyrics in, shall we?*). For the first time there was no keyboard player in the band, so I played organ.

Lonely Is the Hardest

In a rainy city all alone, had no place I could call my own
Small hotel room smokin' cigarettes, nobody knows all the pain
   I felt

Do you believe, when I tell you
That lonely is the hardest
Do you believe, when I tell you
That lonely is the hardest . . . day of all

Wrap my arms around a sleepless night, count the hours till the
   morning light
Pin up photographs on empty walls, writing poems to no one at all

Do you believe, when I tell you
That lonely is the hardest
Do you believe, when I tell you
That lonely is the hardest . . . day of all

Look out the window crowded streets below, seems everybody
   has someplace to go
Look in the mirror, far away eyes, cry in silence for the wasted lives.

Do you believe, when I tell you
That lonely is the hardest
Do you believe, when I tell you
That lonely is the hardest . . . day of all

(Quatro/Tuckey, 1979)

A *Greatest Hits* TV-advertised album was released, with,
on the front, an award-winning painted image of me singing
into a shattered microphone – very effective. But while this

216

album did quite well *Rock Hard* struggled, except in Australia where we enjoyed another hit single. It was starting to look like my decision to change horses hadn't been so great after all.

Around this time, I decided to add some permanent female backing vocalists to my line-up since it had worked so well in America. We had a TV show coming up to promote the single 'Mama's Boy' from the album *Suzi and other Four-letter Words*. This song featured lots of girly vocals, and so the call went out.

One of those who answered it was Gaynor Wild. I remember our first meeting as one of the very few occasions on which I have been dumbfounded by beauty. Gay walked in, classy as hell, perfect face, wonderful figure, and my mouth fell open. I had never before seen, and have never seen since, anyone else manage to roll a big suitcase while wearing high heels and still manage to look elegant! Gay taught me that girls don't 'fart', they 'pop' – well, I guess that's what finishing school teaches you.

She and her husband, actor Jack Wild (well known for his portrayal of the Artful Dodger in *Oliver Twist*), became good friends of ours. They were married for nine years before divorcing, and towards the end of their marriage I received an urgent phone call for help. Jack was fast going down the spiral of alcoholism and needed to go into a clinic urgently. I called Pete Townshend from the Who, who I knew ran a drug dependency clinic, and happily he said yes. A huge thank you to Pete for allowing Jack to go in for treatment immediately at no cost – this saved his life.

But not for long. Jack did beat the booze but unfortunately contracted cancer, having first his voice box removed and

then his tongue before dying in 2006. He was a huge talent –
maybe too huge. Bless you, Jack, you were one of a kind.

Gaynor worked for me from 1979 to 1990 and again from
2001 to 2004, and has remained one of my closest friends to
this day. She has always looked out for me, playing protector
when any asshole tries to get too close. Her sister Lynn joined
me from 1983 to 1984 and again in 2001–4. Lynn, who shared
her sister's ultra-feminine good looks, had an impressive
party piece: ripping telephone books in half. The two of
them together were perfect performance. They used to wear
black PVC catsuits with red belts to match my red B.C. Rich
bass guitar. Silly of me really to allow that, 'cos they looked so
goddam cute and sexy!

10

BABIFICATION

....

In 1980, Len and I moved into a beautiful Elizabethan manor house in Essex which we had seen advertised in *Country Life*. On our first visit we drove up a tiny farm track and then suddenly this huge, absolutely beautiful half-timbered vision came into view. Moated on three sides, with a pond, a huge orchard, three and a half acres of land, a long, poplar tree-lined driveway and a beautiful walled garden – the whole thing was just too fantastic for words I still get the same thrill of excitement every time I drive up the driveway even now, twenty-seven years later. I've never lived as long in any other place. On that first day we were let in by the owner and straightaway I experienced a sense of déjà vu. I *knew* this place, every nook and cranny of it. I could have led the owner around. This was *my* house – I felt it in every bone of my body. I would have my children here, and be buried here too or at least have my ashes scattered in the grounds. My greatest wish is that my children and grandchildren will continue to live here. I have left it to my family in my will. I believe in reincarnation and I'm convinced I lived here in an earlier life – it's just too damn familiar. And of course it's haunted without a doubt. So many things of a paranormal nature have happened – to Len, my kids, my grandchild, various friends and family, even my present husband, Rainer. You are never alone here, but instead of finding it spooky I find it comforting. After all, these feelings, souls, entities or whatever you want to call them have every right to be here – even more than me, in a way.

Let's start at the beginning. The then owner, Mr Seeley, had been living there for over twelve years and shared with us his extensive knowledge of the house's history. Some of the odd happenings were to do with children, and since I was moving in that direction myself I paid attention. On his first night there his family and the bulk of their furniture and possessions had not yet arrived, so he had to spend the night alone on a couch. He woke in the middle of the night from a horrifying nightmare so real that it had haunted him ever since. There were evil demons floating above the pond outside the kitchen door, chanting over and over, 'Beware! The devil dances on her grave. Beware! The devil dances on her grave.' In the local pub he got talking to an old man who had lived in the area for ages and knew all the local gossip. Apparently some twins had once lived here, and one of the children drowned in the pond. Mr Seeley took his dream as a warning which he passed on to us, and I took it seriously. When I had my first baby, Laura, I immediately fenced in the pond, and in due course told all my children that the devil lived there and they shouldn't go near it. While on the subject of Laura, my nanny Michelle, Len and myself all had a surprising coincidental experience. The kitchen used to contain a staircase, now closed off and plastered over, which led up to the first floor. Whenever any of us were in the kitchen holding Laura she would turn to this corner and smile, twisting her head this way and that as if talking to someone. I think the nanny who was in change of the little girl who drowned hanged herself from the banister rail. The spooky stories go on and on . . .

Both my first and second husband are snorers, big time. The first time things got too unbearable in this particular house I ordered Len into the bedroom next to ours, which has since been named the Ghost Room. Indeed, this is where much of the supernatural activity takes place. But after being banished on a couple of occasions Len reappeared, insisting, 'I am *not* sleeping in that room – no way. There's something in there. You'll just have to put up with my snoring.' Some twenty years later Rainer too announced he would not be sleeping in that room any more: 'I don't like the atmosphere.'

While pregnant with Laura in 1982, I had my turn. It was around 3a.m. Len was snoring as usual, and at eight months gone I was heavy and very uncomfortable. So I stumbled into the Ghost Room, desperately in need of some sleep. After a few minutes I felt something, turned on the light, but saw nothing. This sequence of events kept repeating itself for about an hour, until finally I could take no more. I got up and shouted very angrily, 'Look, whoever you are, I'm pregnant, I'm tired and I need some sleep. So *fuck off!* Do your worst, I'm sleeping here tonight.' After that I slept like a log. I have a mental picture of all the ghosts hanging out wherever they hang out, saying, 'Did you hear what she said? What a nerve!'

The bedroom in question has a very high, beamed ceiling with a view over the pond and is situated in the oldest part of the house. It is always a few degrees lower in temperature than any other room. Through the years, Richard (I named him Richard for no particular reason – but read on) bothered many of my friends who slept there while they were visiting us. Shirlie Roden got touched up the bum and awoke with a vision of a man with a beard on top of her. Diana Bailey was stroked all through the night, awaking to a not so nice man staring at her. Corky, a tour manager from Japan, complained that she didn't get a wink of sleep.

It was also the venue, in the 1990s, for a channelling experiment in which one of my guitarists, Robbie Gladwell, turned into a previous resident of the house, with a different voice entirely and walking with a limp. This was witnessed by pianist Reg Webb, who is blind and definitely more in touch with these feelings than the rest of us. I myself was sitting in a chair as Robbie channelled – until I felt someone try to climb into my body. I jumped up and screamed, 'oh, no, you don't!' That is not a trick I want to perform – I'll leave that to Whoopi Goldberg!

My mother, who visited me several times at this house, said she always saw an old man sitting at the dining table. My daughter Laura, who is more than a little psychic, has been frequently visited in her dreams by a soldier (the house was taken over by the army during World War II). I too have had dreams, the most memorable being of a little blonde-haired girl called Belinda, playing in the coat cupboard by the front door.

Now while I didn't mind these 'spirits' being present, I did start to get a little pissed off at them bothering my house guests. So I decided to investigate by gathering every scrap of information I could on the house. I had a feeling that all this activity was happening for a reason, and that I was supposed to do something about it. Digging into things, I discovered that a man named Richard DeFoe had bought the house from James De La Hyde who had built it. I was intrigued to find the name Richard coming up. Then I went to the local church to speak to the vicar, though I feared he might think I was a little crazy. But no. He told me his church was haunted too, and took me inside because, he said, he wanted to show me something. We walked down the nave towards the altar until we came to a burial slab on which I read: 'Here Lies Richard DeFoe, the last surviving member of his family. The line ends here.'

So all he wanted was to be remembered. No problem. I went back home, entered the room and spoke out loud. 'Okay, Richard, you're not forgotten. We remember you. You spirit lives on. Now go to the light and leave us in peace.'

Although the activity lessened, it didn't stop. So in 1995 I had the house feng shuied. The guy who was doing it found a special area where the activity gathered – and just behind it, on my office wall, was a postcard-sized reproduction of an oil painting of Richard which I had come across in the course of my researches. My feng shui adviser got very agitated, ordering me to take the picture outside that very evening and burn it as well as uttering a prayer which would, he hoped, release the spirit's energy. When I did so the picture folded in on itself as it burned, until it looked like a praying figure. Finally it drifted away on the wind, up into the sky.

The activity diminished further, but still hasn't totally disappeared. Recently, Laura was woken by her bed shaking. My granddaughter Amy reported the same thing happening in her room. She actually prefers to sleep in the Ghost Room, now renamed the Princess Room. Her latest dream was a repeat of mine in which she saw a little blonde-haired girl playing, who said, 'Don't worry, Amy. This is a big house, but there are a lot of people watching over you and protecting you.' Far too much for a five-year-old to invent, and on top of that her experience goes hand-in-hand with the rest of the family's sightings.

There's one effect that I demonstrate to every new visitor to the house, especially sensitive people. Under the bedroom in question is our sitting room, with a very heavy pair of wooden doors which are always left open. The reason is that when you close them the atmosphere completely changes: you feel as if you are in a time warp and have been transported back to the olden days. Even the sceptics feel it. This is the only room in the house where I can compose songs. I've tried it everywhere else, to no avail. It is where the creative energy in the house sits – as I do, at my white piano, hands over the keys, pen and paper at the ready, one ear bent to the ceiling, ready to take down dictation from the powers that be as I craft my tunes.

I was very happy in our new house, and we had furnished it beautifully with antique chests, four-poster beds and Chinese carpets. But since moving in I had sensed a shift in our relationship. I don't know if it was because we were in the middle of nowhere, or that Len just needed some space from everything 'Suzi'. Whatever the case, he took up a new hobby: shooting. (*I'd like to admit here and now that I/you/we are exhausting to be around. Everyone says so. We are just this side of hyper with our insatiable need to communicate. Sometimes a partner just needs to get away from it all. Hell, I even exhaust myself!*) He didn't just take it up, he became obsessive about it. We spent hardly any time together any more. I actually kept a diary this year, and on most pages it says something like 'Len out shooting', 'Len out at the pub'. I was alone again. And if you're left alone you eventually learn how to 'be' alone.

I remember many times sitting on the window seat late at night in the front room, gazing out of the window into the walled garden, waiting for hubby to return *again*. I started to withdraw my emotions, which is my way. When things really hurt, I just shut off. I did it when I left Detroit, I did it when I left Mickie, and I was doing it now. The consequences would eventually be disastrous, for I was the glue that held our relationship together. We were slowly coming unstuck.

By 1981 Dreamland had opened up an office in the UK. The *Greatest Hits* album was out on Rak Records and still being promoted, and *Rock Hard* (title of both the album and the single) on Dreamland was released around the world. We made three proper videos, the previous films being nothing more than clips for territories that we would find it difficult to visit and promote live on TV. The videos we recorded were 'Rock Hard', 'Lipstick' and 'Glad All Over'. Dreamland had hired Gary Farrow, now a big mover and shaker in the industry, to run their UK office, and he did a great job booking me on Michael Parkinson's and Russell Harty shows to promote the new album. I was also pleased to be asked to be a guest on Mickie Most's *This Is Your Life*. I've watched it many times and his hug is genuine – there was always a real affection between us. But I wouldn't see Mickie socially till the end of the year.

On the personal front, having decided long ago that I wanted babies at the age of thirty, I had been trying to get pregnant since 1979. But it didn't happen. After many tests, it was discovered that I had low fertility and a tilted womb, considerably reducing my chances of conceiving. Also, my lifestyle didn't help. So in 1981 I was taking a course of fertility drugs to help me along. One month after starting them I was pregnant; my gynaecologist couldn't believe they had worked so quickly. I was ecstatic, having been secretly fearing that I would never have children. I told absolutely everyone the good news – and yes, I do know now that you are supposed to wait till after the three-month danger point.

It was in these early stages of pregnancy that my theatrical agent, Denis Selinger, secured me a role in *Minder*, a TV series which co-starred two excellent actors, George Cole and Dennis Waterman. This was my second acting job. I played Nancy, an American hippy living in a squat, and the episode was called 'Dead Men Do Tell Tales'. My band performed 'Lipstick' and 'Lonely Is the Hardest', and I was lucky enough to kiss Dennis Waterman – although I'm not sure whether he has such happy memories of this occasion. In our first scene together I was massaging half-naked Terry (Dennis) and a smooch was required. Terry leaned over and gave me a really long, passionate kiss. I was really into it when the director yelled, 'Cut!' which startled me, and I'm afraid I laughed, spitting right into Dennis's face. In another scene I had to smoke a huge joint, but the props department really didn't have a clue. So Len (who accompanied me on most of my bookings, whether they were gigs or not) showed them how to roll it properly. Rock and roll training – ain't nothing like it.

I also did a little stint on the Kenny Everett show. I played his magician female helper, dressed in a black corset, high heels and fishnet stockings. My God, he made me laugh! What a wonderful natural comic he was – you could play with the scene and take it anywhere, and Kenny followed. Oh yes, the world lost a good one when he passed on.

Andrew Lloyd Webber asked me to join him on a TV

special he was hosting which showcased one artist from each of several areas of entertainment: dancing (Finola Hughes), opera (Placido Domingo), piano-playing (John Lill) and me doing 'I've Never Been in Love' from *Suzi and Other Four-letter Words*. I also did a jam on bass with a superb husband-and-wife team, John Hiesman (drums) and Barbara Thompson (saxophone and flute). There was a big medley planned for the end which all the guests would join in, and my band was to play the music. But at rehearsals this was changed: since the beginning of the finale was my 'jam' this group of musicians would continue. I was a little worried and asked Andrew if he thought John would be okay doing a little rock and roll. 'Go and ask him, Suzi,' he replied. So I did.

On the way home I told Len about my conversation with John.

'So, do you think you can manage "Oh Boy"?' I innocently enquired of John.

He replied, 'I don't know, Suzi. If you have a copy of the record maybe I can research it.'

'You said *what* to *who*?' he said, aghast. 'Do you know who he is, Suzi? Only one of the best drummers in the world!'

Open mouth, insert foot. I was good at it.

Andrew and I sang 'Oh Boy' as a duet, but unfortunately they cut our special song, 'Hey Paula'. I think that's why I'm still working today! This was also the moment when Andrew told me on air that I should do *Annie Get Your Gun*. I found him a very nice man – with more than a slight naughty streak!

Still only in my second month, I got asked to present an award at the British Rock Awards and another at the annual Australia Rock awards television show, for which Jermaine Jackson would be my partner. We flew out first-class, which was great. Dire Straits were also on tour in Aussie at that time, and Mark Knopfler called me to ask if I wanted to come up and jam with him at his gig. Try and stop me! Now Mark is a perfectionist, so we rehearsed the impromptu jam session for an hour until it was perfect. That night when he called me up I got a wonderful reception. Now up until that point the audience had been sitting down, as you do at a Dire Straits concert. But I screamed at them, 'Get your asses up now! It's time to rock and roll.' Mark and I had a great time: he even did the Chuck Berry duck walk across the stage, and he asked me to come on again the following evening. Those were two of my most treasured moments on stage.

I remember lying in bed in our hotel room in Melbourne feeling sick. Len was talking into my stomach: 'Hello, is anybody in there?' He was thrilled at the prospect of becoming a daddy at last. I also remember being unusually tired, even allowing for the time difference, the TV and the gig. I nearly fell asleep backstage waiting to go on with Dire Straits, which is really strange for me. A horse chomping at the bit is the norm. So, job over, we flew back for Nicky Chinn's wedding to a Californian girl, Jill. Little did I know it would be one wedding and a funeral.

The actual day is vivid in my mind. I was upstairs in my bedroom resting, while Len was mowing the lawn. When I went to the toilet I noticed that I was bleeding, which alarmed me, so I lay back down and tried to relax. I called my doctor, who told me that this sometimes happened. He advised me to take it easy, but to inform him if it got any worse. About an hour later, the contractions started. I ignored them for as long as I could, until finally I shouted out to Len that I needed to go to the hospital immediately. A woman knows when things aren't right – nobody has to tell her. Len was nervous, driving quickly, but kept saying, 'It will be fine, Suze. It will be fine.'

When we arrived the pain was so bad that I collapsed, and Len carried me inside where I was met by my obstetrician, Mr Weekes, who looked as worried as me. Once they had got me into a bed Mr Weekes did a quick examination, then began to cry. 'I'm so sorry, Suzi. You are totally dilated, and the fact that you are having so much pain doesn't look good. You will miscarry. I'm as upset as you – this is my loss too.' Kind words, although at the time they didn't make any difference as I was too distraught. They scheduled me for an immediate D and C, and left me to my sadness. I had failed. I could tour the world and entertain, but produce a healthy baby? Oh, no. As a woman I felt like a no-hoper.

I awoke from the anaesthetic a couple of hours later, feeling empty inside. I wheeled myself to the lounge and sat there drinking coffee, puffing on a rare cigarette, feeling lost and alone. Another lady was wheeled in, and we started to talk. I poured my heart out. She listened patiently, then told me her tale. She had had four pregnancies, never managing to carry to term. I felt like such a pathetic idiot and told her so, to which she replied, 'Don't say that. Your loss is as important to you as mine are to me.' As the old saying goes, there is always somebody worse off than you. Len drove me home later that evening, I went to bed knowing that in the morning I would have to inform family and friends that the long-awaited event would not be happening after all. It would be especially hard for Len's parents, as this would have been their first grand-child. I had never felt like such a failure in my entire life.

The physical recovery was quite easy; the emotional one would take months and months. I drank too much, I cried all the time, I was down down down with no way of getting back up.

Gigs were quickly arranged, as Len thought this would be the best therapy. Mr Weekes assured me that one in three pregnancies miscarried, and it had nothing to do with me. But I wasn't convinced. Had I done too much work? Should I have flown to Australia, especially at that risky early stage before a pregnancy really takes hold? Basically I blamed myself. I was told that after a short rest I could start another course of the fertility drug, but deep inside I felt I would never have a child. And there was more bad news to come.

Late on a cold November evening the phone rang. It was Nicky Chinn, calling from California: Dreamland was folding! We were labelless. So perhaps it had been a mistake leaving Rak after all. Len and talked into the early hours about our dubious future in the music business, and in our shocked state we started to argue with each other. I remember Len being angry with himself for allowing me to talk him into something he hadn't really wanted to do. 'I should have been stronger,' he said. Doubts that I had carried around deep inside started to surface, and I was beginning to feel like an idiot. Whatever my reasons way back, they now seemed childish. I could now see clearly that when I had made the decision to leave Mickie I was very vulnerable and not thinking clearly. This whole situation should have never happened. I needed to apologise – otherwise I would have no peace.

A couple of days later, I swallowed my pride and extended a peace offering in order to clear the air. I phoned Mickie and Chris at home and invited them over to dinner. I wasn't

A favourite photo with fans around the world . . .
By 1980 I had attitude plus a little maturity.

Heeeey! Leather and Fonzie get acquainted.

In 1986 a dream came true. Playing Annie, I swapped my bass for a gun.

HRH Prince Charles
throws me a left curve.

Wrote the music
and starred as
Tallulah Bankhead.
Even my mom
didn't know it was
me in this costume.

A family at last.

Too cute for words . . . I was being a mom, going to work in the theatre. Just another woman juggling her life.

My friend Willie Rushton
did this 40th birthday party
invite for me.

My favourite place to
create, with my angel
on my shoulder.

Doing what I do.

One of those days I
just knew the photos
were going to be
great. In leather, but a
dress! Feminine, moi?

Las Vegas wedding – what a gamble. We hardly knew each other!

Friend, lovers, husband and wife, promoter and artist.

My 50th birthday, the 3rd of June, 2000. 22,000 people sang Happy Birthday.

Looking back on my life . . . I wonder what's around the corner?

hoping that Mickie would sign me up again – I knew I'd blown that chance. What I was hoping was that we could be friends. I missed his friendship, his words of wisdom, his sense of humour and, most important of all, his guidance. I was relieved when they accepted.

Len had done his usual wonderful job of cooking a sumptuous three-course meal, the table was set with our finest crystal and silverware, the candles were lit and there was a roaring fire in the front room – but nothing could warm the atmosphere. I think Chris only came because she was curious. I just don't know why Mickie agreed to come. Maybe it was to hear what I had to say after my painful, unexpected departure from his domain.

Fortified by a few glasses of wine, I began, 'Mick . . . it was like this. Mike and Nicky were always splitting up and getting back together again. We were never sure where we stood. Then this label thing came up and I figured, rightly or wrongly, that I should sign direct with the guys who had always provided my hit singles. It was *not* an easy decision to make. I never meant to hurt you, Mickie. I feel terrible about it.'

Mickie, to his credit, replied, 'Suze, I do understand how you felt at that time. The only mistake you made was leaving Rak completely. You could have signed with Dreamland in the States and stayed with Rak for Europe. That would been have the smart thing to do. Anyway, it's history now. Let's put it behind us. I will always have a special place in my heart for you.'

(*You know, Suzi, be honest, you must have been going through hell. After all, Mickie was having success with another girl singer, Kim Wilde. Maybe if you had stayed with Rak Mickie would have taken the songs and given them to you. It was his policy never to never have two girls on the label at the same time. Methinks you made one big fuck-up.*) Okay, point taken. It bothered me, but what could I do? I was gone, she was there – that's how it crumbles hitwise. And anyway, I would never have wanted to steal someone else's thunder. What's meant to be is meant to be. You make your mistakes and then you must live with them.

I did a lot of thinking over the next couple of weeks, and during that time one of Len's old childhood friends, singer and songwriter Chris Andrews ('Yesterday Man'), happened to call. He had just bought a house down the road from us and had built a recording studio. I managed to convince Len that we could do a new album with Chris and him producing, and started to write songs.

This would be the last album to state 'Quatro/Tuckey'. In truth I was doing it all on my own by now, and only allowed co-authorship to be printed out of respect for our long-standing partnership. I also wrote several songs with Chris, an excellent craftsman who has sold millions of records. The Quatro/Tuckey songs were 'Cheap Shot', 'Remote Control', 'Transparent' and 'Oh Baby', the Quatro/Andrews ones 'Heart of Stone' (which was the single), 'Main Attraction' (another single release), 'Candy Man' and 'Fantasy in Stereo'; and, solo-penned by Chris, 'Two Miles out of Georgia'. On our shared songs Chris wrote the music while I did the lyrics. We were busy in the studio every day from ten in the morning till ten at night. The album, to be called *Main Attraction*, would be released on Polydor. As 1982 approached I looked back on the old year. It had not been a good one, what with my miscarriage and the record company folding. Just to put the icing on the cake, returning home from the studio one night I discovered we had burst pipes: the entire house was flooded. When Len got back later and surveyed the damage he said, 'Suze, you'll make it all better, won't you?' Amidst all this, I was still desperate to get pregnant.

I remember the very night it happened. It was the night of Christmas Day. Someone had told me that if I lay with some pillows under my backside, and didn't move for at least an hour after making love, it would work. So, without telling Len why, I prepared myself in this way. I swear to God I actually felt myself being impregnated. A strange feeling washed over me: *something* had happened.

We were still busy finishing the album as January moved into February. I was off coffee, red meat and wine, and had a strong suspicion my feelings were correct. So I secretly bought a testing kit and it proved positive. I was pregnant again, and this time without the help of fertility drugs. I was beyond excited. I shared this news with Len on the way home from a hard day at the studio. (*Talk about a bad reaction! He screeched the Land Rover to a half and slammed his fist into the steering wheel. 'I suppose you think you're fucking clever, don't you? There's a Suzi Quatro album due out in April – so how the fuck are we supposed to promote it with a baby in your belly?'*) It was very confusing for me. All I wanted was to give him a child, something we had spoken of so often. I guess in hindsight he was just plain worried. We had worked hard as a team, had fallen on bad times and were trying to haul our way out. I was so upset that night that the thought of abortion flitted across my mind. Thankfully it was only a fleeting thought.

The album came out as planned in mid-April. 'Heart of Stone' was the first single. There is a beautiful picture of me on the back: I look so serene, wearing a baggy black sweat-shirt with a baby growing in my belly. We did various TV shows to promote it, getting several plays on BBC 1, especially Simon Bates's show, but it was not to be a hit and sales were only moderate. Obviously I couldn't tour, especially because of my previous miscarriage. In fact I was ordered to take it easy. And so I began nine months of home life – such an unnatural way for me to live that I soon grew bored. I planted a flower garden, grew my own vegetables, bought two green-houses and filled them with tomato plants, even picked some cherries from the orchard and attempted to bake pies. I had many visits to my obstetrician, Mr Weekes, who was taking no chances and monitoring me carefully.

Gradually Len started to look forward to the impending birth. I did promise him that we could go back on the road and earn our living as soon as the baby came. We also decided that we would need permanent live-in help and started to look for a nanny. I insisted from day one that whatever children we were lucky enough to have would travel with us and not be left at home. This might lose us some work, but I didn't care – I was adamant.

I didn't show very early, which pissed me off – I wanted a big belly to show the world that I was a 'normal' woman. Month five was when I started to blossom. The morning sickness had gone and I was blooming – rosy cheeks, healthy-looking hair and slim everywhere except my tummy. I never bought any maternity clothes but just-wore my usual jeans with an extension sewn in and one of Len's Levi's shirts. Even though I was pregant I was desperate to hang on to the image of Suzi Quatro. Somewhere inside I was afraid that this child would change everything – and of course it did.

I was determined to have an easy birth, so I didn't smoke or drink and did yoga well into my eighth month. Len and I attended ante-natal classes together, and I learned how to breathe through the pain. Finally the due day arrived. Mr Weekes had confided to Len that he was not sure I could manage a natural birth due to my small frame, and that there was a very strong chance it would have to be a caesarean. They didn't tell me, though. I thought everything was just fine.

It was the middle of the night when I felt my first contractions. By the time Len and I arrived at the hospital the pains were five minutes apart. Mr Weekes was pleased. 'You're going to have this baby by lunchtime, Suzi, and just to help you along I'm going to put you on this machine.' The machine made the contractions very strong and regular, like the ending of labour. This went on for sixteen hours, with Len beside me the whole time. All the nurses kept popping in to hear the 'rock chick' swear, but even at the worst pains I simply groaned quietly 'oh, shit' and so they went away extremely disappointed!

When Mr Weekes finally reappeared he asked Len to wait outside while he did a quick check to see how far along I was. He didn't look very happy: 'Suzi, you aren't even slightly dilated. This isn't going well.' Then he left the room. As the waves of pain continued to roll over my exhausted body, Len and Mr Weekes came back in, obviously of one mind.

'Suzi, I cannot let this go on any longer. I'm afraid you're going to have to have a caesarean.'

'*Do it now, please!*' They could have told me they were going to chop my legs off – I just wanted it over with.

Len was handed a hospital gown and instructed to hold my

drip feed as they wheeled me to the operating room – this was now an emergency situation. The anaesthetist was ready to give me the knock-out shot and I begged her to hurry.

Poor Len! I don't know how he stayed there during that operation – his emotions must have been in complete turmoil. He shared every moment with me, over and over again. I never got tired of hearing how my daughter came into this world. I was opened up, the baby was delivered and then I was stitched up again all in twenty minutes. Three pints of AB negative blood poured out: in Len's words, 'There was bleedin' claret everywhere.' Laura was way down in my birth canal, trying desperately to get out. Mr Weekes said to Len, 'She's stuck, – I can't get her out.' Then he twisted her legs back and forth, there was a sucking sound, and out she came, screaming her beautiful little black-haired head off. Len held her, cried and fell in love, then looked at me and started worrying. There was his wife, slit open with tubes and blood everywhere. When I asked him why he stayed, he simply said, 'We started this together – we finish it together.' That's what you call 'love'.

The next thing I remember thinking is, 'I must be dead – oh, well, that's the way it goes.' Then I tried to move. *Ouch*. I was alive after all. I opened my eyes with difficulty and saw Len standing over the bed with tears in his eyes. 'We've got a bootiful daughter, Suze, and she looks just like you.' Then I fell back to sleep.

I awoke a few hours later as the nurse plonked Laura down on my stitched-up stomach for me to breast-feed – which was the last thing I wanted to do. I was in shock, and didn't feel this baby belonged to me. In a way, I felt cheated. After all, I hadn't really been there for the birth. I declined to breast-feed and insisted on bottle-feeding her instead. I hated being in hospital, in pain and not able to move, and begged Mr Weekes to let me recuperate at home. But it would be two long weeks before I returned.

The press got news of the birth, and sent photographers to the hospital to take photos of us leaving with our newborn child. The coverage was quite amazing – front pages in the nationals. I guess Suzi Quatro having a baby didn't exactly fit in with the image people had of me. I am proud to say, though, that I wore my own blue jeans to go home. God, doing up that zipper hurt! We drove the twenty-five miles in our silver Rolls-Royce (yes, in 1977 we had purchased the obligatory Roller of every self-respecting hit artist of that time). I felt like I had been let out of prison as I enjoyed the trees, the road, the air on my face. Our nanny Michelle and the baby rode in the back seat. It would take another week before I 'bonded' with my daughter . . .

There she was, having a nap in the cot. I crept in and stared for a long time, and then it hit me. She was mine. She belonged to me. God, I love this little creature, this little bundle of joy! I picked her up, sat down in the rocking chair in the corner, held her tightly and cried like a baby myself for the first time since the birth. Len peeked in and said, 'What's the matter, Suze? Have you just realised you're a mother?' Every time I wrote out a birth announcement card I got such a feeling of accomplishment.

For the christening in November Mom and Dad flew over for it. There was a small competition going on between the two sets of grandparents: for Len's Mum and Dad this was their first grandchild and they wanted all the honour; for mine, it was number eleven. Mom later told me that she couldn't get near Laura in any of the photographs because Mum Tuckey wouldn't put her down, so my mom had to be content with resting an arm on the baby's shawl. Laura had been born with punk hair – thick black sticky-up unmanageable locks. On the day of the christening Mom accused me of purposely doing her hair like that and wetted it to flatten it before putting a white bonnet on her head. One hour later the bonnet came off and *boing*, up went the hair!

That Christmas I designed my first of fifteen years of personal cards depicting children on the front. As Mickie Most said to me, 'You are definitely babified.' Three months later we were back in Australia – band, nanny and baby – rocking and rolling. (*Yeah, it was quite crowded on that tour, what with Suzi Quatro, little Susie, Len, Laura, Michelle. We barely had enough energy to go around. No wonder women are good at multi-tasking – we have to be.*)

It was around this time that I hired as my second guitarist my favourite player of all time, Mo Whitham. I had jammed with him at a pub in Chelmsford, while pregnant with Laura (*kind of difficult to get that bass guitar close enough to play over your stomach!*). I said to Len, 'I want that man in my band', and I got him. He plays in that Scotty Moore, James Burton style, and it added a real classy touch to the band. Mo did several tours with me, along with his wife Kelly who did backing vocals even though she was a fine lead singer herself – they didn't want to be separated. Mo was a very fine musician – praise I don't give lightly.

Because of the success of *Rock Hard*, the tour was sold out. There I was back in the jumpsuit again, but it was quite an adjustment touring with a baby. Usually my off time on tour was spent resting my voice and lazing around until gig time.

Those days were gone, but it sure got me back in shape again. Laura Susan Tuckey, born 23 September 1982, was soon a road veteran. For most of the TV interviews I did my spiky-haired baby came too, dressed in a black-studded waistcoat and Suzi Quatro T-shirt that a fan had sent, all over a blue Babygro – she was so damn cute. (*I, little Susie, was the mum, and sometimes it was hard knowing which person to be – mother or rock and roller. And you know what, Suzi Quatro? If the truth be known, there were many times I wanted to stop being you and just be normal – fire the goddam nanny and be with my baby. I so resented her bathing, feeding and putting my child to bed. Most of the time I fought the urge to snatch Laura out of her arms. I wanted to be Laura's mother, but wasn't allowed to – that's how I felt. Once again I was trapped in the image. I even broached the subject with Len, but he dismissed it immediately. 'We'll always have to tour, and we'll always need a nanny. So just deal with it.'*)

We continued to do Germany, Scandinavia and the UK. But without a record deal there was no chart success on the horizon, so to keep my name in the public eye I asked my theatrical agent, Denis Selinger, to book me as many TVs as he could lay his hands on. *Gas Tank* (hosted by Rick Wakeman), the Leo Sayer show (we did a duet together – 'Baby', a Quatro/Andrews song, and I beat his ass at squash), *Child's Play*, *Give Us a Clue*, and several times *The Krankies*, to name just a few. I was becoming a household name but in reality my career was down the toilet. I was residing in TV gameshow land.

We rolled into 1983 together but separate. The pegging order had changed. Where it used to be career/husband it was now career/baby/husband. (*Speak for yourself, Suzi Quatro.*

For me it was baby/husband/career.) Whatever! I find it difficult to relate to more than one person, maximum two, at any given time. So Laura, Michelle and I did everything together. Len loved Laura to bits but he wasn't then, and isn't now, a hands-on dad. He left everything to me, only enjoying the hugs and kisses at the end of the day. I guess lots of men are like that, but it pissed me off. I was bringing in the money, being, if you like, the mum *and* the dad. Another nail was being driven into the coffin of our marriage. For the first time I started to feel used. Sexually we were off track too – it has to be said, you can't see an operation like that and just fall back into bed. It takes time, on both parts. After trying for so long we finally had our baby, and I wanted more. But Len was still out shooting and pubbing. Whenever he could.

In March we took a rare family trip to Los Angeles and stayed for a couple of weeks at Patti's house. Now here's a strange thing. Patti got pregnant just before me, again after trying for a year or so. She called me one night in tears to say she'd miscarried, and one month later I returned this news. She then fell pregnant again in November, me in December, and we both had girls. Great-Grandpa Quatro was at Patti's and Laura, although only eighteen months old at the time, distinctly remembers meeting him and sitting on his lap. I don't see how this is possible but she is adamant, and has provided details of how he looked and what he was wearing. Mom and Dad were there too to make it a nice family visit. Patti and I enjoyed being first–time mothers together and bonded on that level. Sometimes all it takes is common ground.

Len and I had discussed several times the possibility of having another child. I definitely didn't want to stop at one; in fact I dreamed of four, having come from such a large family myself. Since Arlene had produced my parents' first grand-child when I was only eleven I can't remember a time when there weren't babies around. So Mr Weekes put me back on the fertility drug, but when we had no luck after three months I came back off it. Len said, 'We have to book up some work, Suze. Gotta earn a living. We can try again in a year or so.' I could see the sense of it, and agreed. So we arranged a Scandinavian and Australian tour for April and June 1984.

Christmas 1983 was great because Laura was clearly ex-cited about the presents. Ah, the wonder of seeing things through your child's eyes! I'm not a 'goo-goo-ga-ga' kind of girl, but as soon as kids can talk to me I'm there 300 per cent. The festive season is very special in my house and I always make sure it looks like a Christmas card. I must have over five hundred Christmas CDs which are on constant rotation throughout the holidays. Then we have a huge tree, log fires, presents spilling out of the dining room, lights in every window – it's my favourite time of year and I make the most of it. But, given my talents in that direction, the turkey dinner I always left to Len.

It was early March 1984 when I came down to the kitchen early one morning. Michelle was fixing Laura's breakfast and asked me if I wanted a cup of my favourite coffee. I just snapped her head off: 'No, dammit. Now leave me alone,' to which she replied, 'Suzi, I think you must be pregnant.' I denied the possibility. Len and I had hardly slept together in the last couple of months. But she got me thinking and I started to calculate – which wasn't really a great help, as I have always been irregular. Another problem is my low fertility level. Nevertheless just to humour her I went to the chemist and got a kit. I went up to my bathroom and did the test, never thinking for a minute that it would be positive, but three minutes later I saw the blue line appear. Oh, my God!

Len took the news better this time. Even though we had work booked, it would just have to be postponed – you can't jump around on stage with a baby growing inside. I booked an appointment with Mr Weekes, who confirmed that my next baby was due at the end of October. I felt like the luckiest girl in the world and was determined that this time, although I would still need a caesarean, I would have an epidural rather than a general anaesthetic so that I would be awake. I would not be cheated again.

So instead of touring I began another year of non-stop television shows including *The Cook Show*, where I met Willie Rushton for the first time and immediately fell in love with his wit. Try as I might, I could not outdo him on one-liners – he was brilliant! I think they had me on as comic relief since cooking is most definitely not my forte. I was required to make a fish dish, with a professional chef on hand to help. I honestly did my best, but when she came to taste it she actually gagged! Then there was a fitness programme with Olympic athlete Daley Thompson, in which I tried to teach him yoga; a programme with Jeremy Beadle; *Pop Quiz* a couple of times with Mike Read; a Scottish TV special with the band; a sketch on *tv am* where I pretended to be a secretary; *The Six O'Clock Show* with Michael Aspel; and I even went up to Scotland at the invitation of former racing driver Jackie Stewart to take part in his clay pigeon-shooting competition for charity. I am, by the way, a pretty good shot – just seem to have the eye for it. Among the other celebrity competitors I met Sean Connery (who simply undresses you with his eyes – the sexiest man I have ever met), Barry Gibb (a lovely man with whom I had a long talk about drug addiction – having been there with my brother Mickey and him with his brother Andy gave us common ground), Andrew Ridgley, Michael Parkinson, Prince Andrew, ex-King Constantine of Greece, Princess Anne and Dame Kiri Te Kanawa (who shocked me by using the f-word when she missed a shot – must be a closet rocker!).

Meanwhile in the Quatro house in Detroit, all was not well. All his life Dad had eaten the wrong kind of food and had never exercised. On a trip to Dallas to see Nancy he had collapsed, and was now scheduled for a triple by-pass. I booked a ticket and flew home, baby in my tummy and Laura sitting on it because there was no seat for her – not pleasant, I can tell you! When we arrived Patti was there with her daughter Missy, and Nancy with her two kids, Melissa and Michael. Aside from the worry of Dad's operation, we had some family fun taking our kids to the zoo. Mom was understandably very concerned and said several times that she could not cope alone if Dad were to die; we were all so relieved and grateful that he survived.

Back in London we recorded another album, though without a record company to foot the bill. I had convinced Len that we should go ahead and make it, and then try to place it. We booked Rak Studios for two weeks; I wrote, he produced. Every single track was original except 'Oh Suzi Q' (Dale Hawkins); I wrote one song about Laura, of course, ('Everything I Ever Wanted'). The other songs we recorded were 'Pardon Me', 'There She Goes', 'I'm a Rocker', 'Strange Encounters', 'Comes the Night', 'Starry Night', 'Good Girl

Looking for a Bad Time' (which I wrote for nanny Michelle), 'Secret Hideaway' and 'Just Like Mama' from our first tour with Slade all those years ago. We didn't actually manage to secure a deal for this album, which remained unreleased until 1998 when it came out on the Connoisseur Collection label titled *Unreleased Emotion*. Mickie popped in and out assisting with the mixes, and we decided to do a couple of tracks together. 'Tonight I Could Fall in Love' (Richard Gower) would be the single, coupled with 'She's a Good Girl Looking for a Bad Time' (Quatro/Tuckey).

Towards the end of the year, drummer Dave Neal finally left the band. He had been with me since 1973 and I was so upset that I considered retiring. Bass and drums are a unit. They are the engine that drives the car – everything else is just colour. Dave wanted to put more time into his marriage, and opened up a greengrocer's. Sadly, a couple of years later the marriage failed anyway. Meanwhile I grew bigger and bigger as I awaited the birth date.

This one was a *big* one – my tummy looked like a watermelon. It was a big effort just to move from one chair to another, and I told Mr Weekes in September that I didn't think I could hold on to it any more. I was right. On 23 October Len and I attended his old school reunion, where he proceeded to get plastered. When we got home around 3a.m. Len crawled upstairs while I lay down on the couch. One hour later, still awake, I went to the toilet and discovered blood. The inevitable pains began. This was not good – Mr Weekes had told me I should not go through any labour, and we had booked a caesarean for the following week to make sure. So upstairs I went and shook Len awake. 'Honey, guess what? It's time!'

'You must be fucking joking!' he groaned. We woke

Michelle, got in the Porsche and raced to the hospital as the pains came ever closer. The anaesthetist arrived to give me the epidural as they prepared the operating theatre. But thirty minutes later, she was still trying to inject me. Apparently, after years of carrying a heavy bass on my back there was no space – it's like one long bone. She was sweating and swearing until finally the needle went in. Then I started wondering whether my decision to stay awake had been the right one – I was scared!

After his night out, this time Len was not happy to be there. When I was wheeled into the theatre he pulled up a chair and faced the opposite way, green-faced. The anaesthetist was standing over me, ready to put me out if she had to. They taped my arms down – 'Just in case you panic – could be dangerous.' Jesus! What was I doing to myself? Then, out of the corner of my eye, I saw Mr Weekes approaching with a scalpel in his hand. This was it. There was no backing out now. 'Len, talk to me! Please talk to me!' I urged desperately. So he talked silly nonsense all the way through, to help me. I felt the pressure of the scalpel across my stomach but it didn't hurt – only in my imagination. I kept watching the clock – ten minutes, twenty minutes – remembering how quick Laura had been. Finally, forty-five long minutes later, out came my son, Leonard Richard Tuckey – 7 pounds 11 ounces and 21 inches long. 'Where have you been keeping this?' demanded Mr Weekes. I cried with joy – so lucky to have one of each. He held him up for me to see, then took him away to clean him up and poor Len said, 'Suze, can I go now?'

As I lay there – cut open, baby born and out of the room, Len gone – I started to panic a little, The excitement was over, and I wanted to be outta there. I looked all around the theatre

as Mr Weekes pushed and pulled my stomach area, and finally
I rested my eyes on a shiny light on the ceiling. *What the hell!*
The material the light was made of had the effect of a mirror,
and I was staring at a mirror image of myself opened up, with
clamps holding the skin apart – it looked like spaghetti.
Feeling sick and shocked, I quickly looked away. Then, like
you do at a car accident, I looked again, a little longer this
time – morbid curiosity, I guess. Then I *really* felt sick.
Thankfully they shot me full of Valium, which did the trick.
I was away with the pixies.

This time I was determined to recover more quickly, and I
only had to stay one week in hospital, which was great. But
although I was glad to be home I looked really tired and my
scar got infected – not pleasant. But Patti unexpectedly flew
over to visit and we had lots of chances to talk together,
bonding even deeper. Len, as ever, was still out most of the
time, shooting and pubbing.

I had a different kind of feeling for Richard right from the
start. Laura was Len's little princess, and Richard belonged to
me. Laura is a girl – I understand her and she can't fool me.
Richard, on the other hand, is a mystery, and I was a little in
awe of having created him. Anyway, it's the way nature
intends things. Also, Len found it extremely difficult to be
affectionate with Richard. (*Dad Tuckey said, 'Don't blame
Len. This is the way he was raised. You don't over-kiss and
cuddle boys.' But you know, Len, I just wish you'd touched
your son a little more. It would have made such a difference to
his development. Still, at least he had me. I plastered him with
kisses, bit his bum, chewed on his feet – he was an absolutely
beautiful baby*). Anyway, quite soon I decided that two Lens
in the house was too much and so Leonard Richard became

Richard – well, at least I *think* I decided. Isn't it a coincidence that I named the ghost Richard all those years ago? Maybe he influenced me. After all, he did want to be remembered, and in a way his name now lives on.

Just before the christening I fell sick with 'second child, bad haircut syndrome'. Luckily it wasn't fatal. I went to a hairdresser's in London and emerged with short, dyed black spiky hair – big mistake. Arlene was able to be there for the celebrations – by this time on husband number five. (*Get the glue and the scissors, Dad. Time to paste in another head.*) She had told me over and over how I had it all – success, money, a husband and family, and that if she could just marry a man with money she would be happy. I tried to tell her that this wasn't the case, but she didn't listen and married a millionaire. Did it make it her happy? No, it did not. But, hey, she was wearing an expensive mink coat and a huge rock on her finger, had a wardrobe filled with designer clothes, flew on Concorde and employed two maids at her sumptuous home down South. Problem was, and I quote: 'There's a redhead in my bed.'

My unexpected pregnancy had caused us to delay our Australia tour, but now, with Laura two and Richard six months (and me 108 years old, or that's how I felt!) it was time to catch up on work commitments. Part of me loved being back on stage, while another part of me resented it. A TV documentary at this time was very revealing, showing dark circles under my eyes due to late-night gigs and early morning TV shows, and I looked absolutely exhausted – my smile didn't quite reach my eyes. Most of the interviews centred on the dichotomy of Suzi Quatro and Mum living in the same skin – how was this possible?

'I can't be a twenty-four-hour-a-day mum or I would not be Suzi Quatro. My public gets all of me, and when I'm with my children *they* get all of me.'

Returning from this unbelievably hard tour, I went immediately into filming *Names and Games*, a TV sports competition – good thing I was fit. Actually, you are never fitter than after a tour – tired, yes, but also, dressed in those hot leathers, carrying that heavy bass and jogging across the stage while singing for up to four hours every night, very fit. You get stronger and stronger as the gigs go on, and by the end you're ready to start all over again. I'm often asked how I've stayed so slim and fit through the years, and now you know why. I wouldn't recommend it for everyone, because most people wouldn't last five minutes on the road. We are a breed apart. It either keeps you young or it kills you – nothing in between.

Dempsey and Makepeace, starring Michael Brandon and Glynis Barber, was to be my third acting job. This time I would play a murderer, deluded into thinking there was a romance between Michael and myself, getting crazy with jealousy over Glynis, and trying to kill Michael. Great role, with a lot of scope. I read the script and decided that this character would have to be played totally through the eyes. You know that kind of off-centre look that 'mad' people get? I gazed into my bedroom mirror until I got the light in my eyes to go out. Seeing it back on screen scared the shit out of me and I will never do it again – the light is what makes us 'alive'. I also insisted on doing my own stunt, which required me to fall six storeys from a building. The thing was, I had been doing a real good job interpreting the role. The director said to me, 'I can shoot this scene two different ways. We can use a double and shoot it from across the way, on top of that building over there, or you can do it yourself and I'll shoot it close.' No brainer really. So I was strapped into a harness, holding on to the edge ready to fall. I don't think Michael Brandon has ever forgiven me – he had to hold me as I dangled from the edge, and *he has vertigo*! Sorry, Michael. When I got home that evening I drank quite a large whisky. I was proud of this role, as it was such a departure for me. In fact, it was so realistic that my friends felt uncomfortable watching it. That was the object of the exercise. Tranformation successful.

I also found the time to record a duet with Reg Presley, lead singer of the Troggs. It was a dance version remake of their big hit 'Wild Thing'. Nice that this connection started way back in the Pleasure Seekers, with Nan Ball doing it on her drums in 1964, and then finished by doing it with the man himself. I think I drove Reg a little mad with rehearsal, though – we danced around my front room, with microphones set up to get it just right, and he went out and spent a lot of money on a leather jacket! Love you Reg – you are *my* wild thing.

And so the year passed in touring, TV and raising my kids. And Len? Well, he was shooting and pubbing. No change there! His behaviour was really starting to wear me down. On the work front, however, something really exciting was in the offing. Just before Christmas 1985 I got a call from John Gale, at that time director of the Chichester Festival Theatre. He had been in New York, looking for an American to play the lead role in his forthcoming production of *Annie Get Your Gun*, where he had run into Andrew Lloyd Webber in the lobby of his hotel. Andrew had said to him, 'Why the hell are you looking over here? The girl you want lives in Essex.'

11

ANNIE GET YOUR GUN AND AFTER

....

This stage of my life deserves its own chapter because it truly changed everything. Apart from the kids I had slowly become disenchanted with my life, with Len and with touring. I felt trapped in my image. I was tired of the loud guitar in my ear – volume was a constant source of argument between us – and really needed to find something, *ANYTHING*, different. I needed to spread my wings, mainly creatively (but, it must be said, a little light flirtation wouldn't have gone amiss). This invitation to go to Chichester was a godsend – for me, anyway. Len rightly said, 'I lost you the day rehearsals began', although it would take six more years before I actually did leave. (*In fact, isn't it true that Suzi Quatro was taking a rest, and little Susie from Detroit, who had dreamed of being an 'entertainer' since childhood, was now stepping forward?*) I remember telling Len in no uncertain terms, 'I know we have an Australian tour pencilled in for 1986, but you will have to cancel. I am not turning this chance down!'

The deal was made. We found a really nice house to rent in the suburbs, with enough bedrooms for all of us as well as a garden, and close to a nursery school. The cast would rehearse for one month, then play three months in Chichester and one month in Plymouth, after which we hoped to transfer to the West End. What a role to play, following in the footsteps of Ethel Merman! And this was my first-ever musical, too. But I do love a challenge. To this very day I like being scared – it adds to the performance. Wonderful Irving Berlin score, and such a fun story with plenty of 'heart' moments – I just couldn't wait to get my teeth into it!

On the first day of rehearsals, as always I found myself wondering what I'd let myself in for. Would I be rubbish? The cast consisted of myself (Annie Oakley), Eric Flynn (Frank Butler), Edmund Hockridge (a big star of English musical theatre, via Canada, and playing Buffalo Bill), Matt Zimmerman, Michael G. Jones, Maureen Scott, John Conroy and Berwick Kaler (a great friend to this day, who was playing Chief Sitting Bull – I called him Papa Bull in the show, still call him Papa now, and he still calls me 'my little papoose'). David Gilmore was directing, and Anthony Van Laast doing the choreography. Was it my imagination, or were the rest of the cast looking at me thinking, 'What the hell is this rock and roller doing in our midst?' But I caught Berwick's eye at the read-through and he winked at me, making me feel comfortable instantly.

And so we began the hard preparation required to put on a successful musical. I lost about ten pounds during the next month – not that I needed to. David Gilmore was an excellent director to work with, and clever in his methods. He stripped me of everything Suzi Quatro until I was 'naked' and pliable. I remember him saying, 'The challenge of this part is not in the toughness of the character, but her vulnerability.' Many older theatregoers told me I played Annie similar to Mary Martin.

Various TV shows were booked even before we opened, including BBC breakfast TV with Selina Scott, and Pebble Mill doing 'Anything You Can Do', before we even had our proper costumes. There was also a German TV documentary following my progression from the world of rock and roll into musical theatre. There's one sequence showing me arriving home in our silver Rolls Royce from a hard day's rehearsal, both kids waiting at the front gate; and another as Len, Laura, Richard and I stroll along the beach, lifting the kids into the air – a real family vibe.

I threw myself into the role to the exclusion of virtually everything else, and Len was uncomfortable with the situation. Once one of the male dancers was massaging my back – on stage in front of everyone, mind you, so no funny business – because I had hurt it doing some of the moves. Len came over and said, 'For God's sake, Suze, remember who you are.' I'm still not quite sure what that meant.

That month leading up to opening night was the hardest part. If there are going to be voice problems – something in the wrong key, for instance – this is when they show up, and with luck they can be sorted out before the actual run. It was exhausting and afterwards I needed my sleep – but I didn't get it. First there were the kids needing and deserving my attention, which I tried to provide. And then of course there was Len. One night after an argument he jumped into his Porsche and sped off into the night. Normally I would have thrown myself against the front door and prevented him from leaving. But not this time. I let him go, thinking happily to myself that I didn't care if he came back or not. He did, half an hour later. That night, for the first time, I slept in the spare bedroom. It was absolutely superb – no snoring! (*Suzi, do you remember that recording you made all those years ago? Len kept denying that he snored, which drove you mad. So one day, when the symphony began, you took your cassette recorder, hooked up the microphone and made quite a showreel. And that night at soundcheck you played it at full volume over the PA system. Everyone was doubled over with laughter. But the funniest part was Len saying, 'Sorry, Suze, I just don't see the humour in it.')*

On opening night I was anxiously wondering whether I could pull it off. I put on my little patched dress with the lace-up ankle boots, socks falling over the tops, hair in braids, grabbed my gun and waited in the wings for my entrance. In the small mirror on the wall I gazed as this stranger looked back at me. 'I am Annie Oakley, I am Annie Oakley, I am Annie Oakley.' Then I made my entrance, to huge applause. The opening scene was visual: I had to shoot a rooster weathervane on top of a barn and make it spin. So I cocked the gun, took aim and fired. Click! Nothing happened. No noise. Total silence. The audience laughed. Now in my little green peanut-sized brain I figured that the show could not go on unless the rooster turned round, so I shouted, 'Bang!' The audience laughed louder, which pissed me off. I just didn't understand what was so goddam funny. So I said, 'Bang' again, at which point Berwick Kaler, who was on the floor in fits, came in with his first line and saved me. Choreographer and director were sitting in the audience together. Anthony leaned into David's ear and said, 'Well, it doesn't get much better than this.'

The Chichester run was sold out, which was great news. In the second week the Americans were coming over to see whether they would let us take it to the West End. They were very protective of this show, and nothing was guaranteed. If they didn't like the production, or any of the stars, it would be a resounding no. On the big day, we were halfway through the matinee when I started to feel sick and dizzy and my voice just stopped working. After the show a doctor was called and diagnosed severe throat infection and high fever. Oh God, not tonight of all nights! John Gale came and saw me. 'Suzi, normally I would put on the understudy. But not tonight. You must get through it.' Which I did, croaking my way through. The audience surely realized I was ill and applauded me for my courage (or was it sympathy?)

After the performance we met all the New York people. The lady in charge, in whose hands lay permission to transfer, gave me a letter as she was leaving. It said, 'Tonight I saw a performance unlike any other. You are truly Annie Oakley, and most important, like all great stars, divinely "normal". Good luck in the West End.' I kept this letter for years in my wallet as a kind of good luck symbol, until someone stole my handbag in Rome in 1994.

I was sent home for three days to rest and the understudy was put on. After forty-two years in showbusiness my sick record looks like this: two days in New York, 1967; three days in Chichester, 1986; and one day in 2001. Not bad.

Finally we were off for our run in Plymouth to tweak the show into West End shape. Then there would be another month off while we transferred the entire production to the Aldwych Theatre in London. By this time Berwick Kaler and I were fast friends. I didn't realize it, but we'd actually come across each other in the food bus on the set of *Dempsey and Makepeace* in 1985. He had a part, and was due to do some more filming on the day I spent so long trying to do my own stunt – but because of me he was written out. He shared this story with me on *This Is Your Life*.

One of the first things Berwick told me when we started to get acquainted was, 'I'm very famous in York.' I thought this highly amusing, but it's absolutely true. He has had amazing success playing dame in his original pantomime scripts for over twenty-five years. It's always sold out, and I have taken the kids there regularly every Christmas since 1987. I even contributed a song, which he recorded and released for charity, called. 'The Queen Mother of Rock and Roll'. Berwick has also done Shakespeare, countless West End productions and innumerable TV series, including *Spender* with Jimmy Nail. He is a well-known and respected actor in the business, and always working. I so enjoyed working with him – we really bounced off each other, both of us being 'audience' people. Len once commented, 'You know why you like working with Berwick so much? It's the first time you've worked with someone as talented as you are!' It was because of Berwick that I started to believe that I would have a career outside of 'Can the Can'. He supported me, believed in me and made me believe in myself. Thank you for that, Papa. I love you, and I hope we will always be as close as we are today.

For me, *Annie Get Your Gun* was all about spreading my wings. This was what I had always wanted, right from the beginning. I was excited every night, and always seemed to find something different in the script. This wonderful experience was one of the best, happiest and most rewarding times of my career. Personally, however, it was the opposite. This was not what Lennie wanted – he preferred me to be gigging and I don't blame him for it. We were growing further and further apart. We didn't talk, we didn't see each other. I went to work, came home and went to bed, usually alone. Len had taken to sleeping on whatever couch was available, which at that time was absolutely fine – in fact more than fine, it was preferable. (*Remember when he came unexpectedly into your dressing room after a matinee? He'd had his hair cut, high-lighted and blow-dried, and was dressed to kill. He was so afraid he was losing you.*)

One funny mishap which I must share, occurred in Plymouth. In *Annie* I wore wigs – one with braids and one with long flowing red locks. You put on a skullcap (making you look bald), and then the wig is attached. Berwick and I were on stage singing our duet. 'Doing What Comes Naturally'. At the end of the song, I fall backwards into Berwick's arm's. It was all going so well until I came back up – but my wig didn't, because it was attached to his chest mike. The audience started to laugh and Berwick bowed, oblivious to the problem and thinking he was going down a storm. Finally he noticed. Now my mike was attached to my forehead, so as Berwick pulled me up he shouted straight into the mike, 'Don't worry, Suzi, I'll put it back on.' Well, we could hardly continue! Audiences love mistakes as long as you stay in character. During the next song I had a little bit of dialogue: 'Take those birds back to the kitchen', to which I added 'and bring me some hair clips.' The audience relaxed. Embarassing moment over. We were off to the West End at last.

How great to be living at home and gigging – a rare occurrence in this profession. Rehearsals began in earnest. Sets had to be transported from Chichester, which has a thrust stage, and made to fit on the Aldwych's proscenium stage. I remember looking up at the marquee and seeing my name in lights: 'Annie Get Your Gun, starring Suzi Quatro as sharp-shooting Annie Oakley'. A perfect photographic mo-ment – *snap*!

There was a lot going on in the world at this time. Political unrest in the Gulf and Ireland. A bomb blew up a TWA plane going from Rome to Athens. In Berlin a bomb targeting US soldiers went off in a disco. After the Chernobyl nuclear disaster radioactivity got blown across Europe, including the UK. A Pan Am plane got hijacked. As a result of all this many Americans who would have travelled to England stayed home, which hit the West End – lots of shows suffered. We opened in September anyway, hoping for the best.

Opening night was nerve-wracking, even though I had already done the show for four months. As if this wasn't enough of a strain, we were invited to go on the the Terry Wogan show. Problem was, we had to get there and back in time for curtain up – could we do it? I did two songs from the show, 'Can't get a Man with a Gun' and 'Anything You Can Do I Can Do Better', as a duet with Terry dressed up as a cowboy. Surely this was TV magic. Show over, and rain pouring down, Len said to the taxi driver, 'There's an extra tenner in it for you if you can get us to the Aldwych by seven-thirty.' We flew there, cornering on two wheels, and they held the curtain for fifteen minutes until I arrived. Straight from the car and into the wings to wait for first entrance – phew!

Mom and Dad had flown over, which was wonderful, and there were lots of friends, family and fans too. Princess Margaret made an unofficial visit, which was annoying as we weren't allowed to let the press know – apparently she was a huge huge fan of this particular musical. She sat next to Mom in the balcony and I think Mom must have spent the entire evening staring at her, because afterwards she was able to report every utterance, every laugh, every movement she made. Mom told everyone within earshot, 'That's my daughter Susan up there!' Len, meanwhile, was sipping slowly from his flask throughout the show.

The curtain came down to great applause, and I went to the dressing room to change and greet my guests. First, in came Mom, Dad and Len. (*Don't forget, Suzi, this is the first time Dad said those golden words to you: 'Susie, you were great – I am so proud of you!'*) Music to my ears. Len's parents, his brother Billy and various friends all crowded into my dressing room. One lady friend took me aside and said, 'Suzi, you're a very clever girl and I throughly enjoyed it. But tell me something – how the hell are you going to go back to rock and roll after this?' Damn good question.

After show congrats were over it was time to go home. Although I was emotionally and physically exhausted Len was a little the worse for wear, so I had to drive. Not a nice thing to have to do after the stress of an opening night in the West End. (*It was then that you started to feel like a money machine for the first time – bringing in the cash, but not being looked after properly. It's fair to say, that a little respect was lost that night.*)

Andrew Lloyd Webber came to the opening night, and gave me a rare book on Annie Oakley. It was all because of Andrew that I had even been considered for the part. After the performance he came backstage and said, 'You made me cry, Suzi. It works. The whole thing works.' Thank you, Lord Lloyd Webber. Thank you very much. Maybe we can work together again some day.

Ticket sales were pretty good at the beginning, but as the

weeks progressed it was obvious that the terrorists threats were severely affecting numbers. We performed seven shows a week, and we all prayed. I wanted this so damn bad. Everything in me willed *Annie* to stay open – it was my ticket to freedom. The cast even managed to perform live on Jimmy Tarbuck's *Live at the Piccadilly*, but it was too late – the writing was on the wall. In the second week of December I was called into the producer's office to be given the news that we would close.

On the final evening, which was packed to the rafters, when I sang 'There's No Business Like Show Business' and got to the line. 'The closing when the customers won't come', I cried. It was over. Time to strap on the bass and get back into the jumpsuit. But actually my agent managed to put me into my first pantomime, *Cinderella*, at the Shaw Theatre in London. I didn't stop to think if I actually wanted to do this or not but just grabbed it, so reluctant was I to return to reality.

On a personal level, I was beginning to admit to myself that I was falling out of love. It wasn't just returning to rock and roll that scared me – it was returning to my collapsing marriage on a daily basis. The musical had given me a little respite from the unavoidable decision that was hanging like an axe ready to fall.

Time for the first tour of 1987. Off we went to Ireland, with nanny and kids in tow. After more than forty years on the road it's hard to separate countries, gigs and memories – they all tend to blur into one. In fact it's easier to remember the dressing room than anything else, because that's where you spend most of your time. But Ireland sticks in my mind because of the wonderful Irish logic. We all travelled in a bus with a toilet and a coffee machine. On one journey I tapped the driver on the shoulder and asked him if if was okay if I made myself a cup. 'To be sure,' he replied. So over I went and prepared my cup, then shouted back, 'How will I know when it's boiled?' to which he replied, 'Oh, it will get very hot!' Then I noticed a sign overhead: 'Danger low bridge 9 foot, 12 inches.' Now excuse me, but isn't that 10 feet? Taking rather a long time to arrive at a gig that was only a few miles away, the driver said to me, 'I'm not lost. I just made a wrong turn.' And in restaurants, daring to say you don't want any potatoes is just not done. Of course, I didn't know this. The waitress looked at me long and hard, and when she eventually placed my dinner in front of me, not only were there potatoes but there were three different kinds. Point taken.

All the gigs were very well attended except one, which was confusing. There was only a handful of people there, yet we had been told that all the tickets had sold out weeks before. So, after the show, the boys in the band went to a pub and got talking with some of the locals. They explained, 'A few months ago, Status Quo were booked to appear here. It sold out, but they never showed up. So we bought the Suzi tickets, but nobody went. You see, we didn't want to get ripped off.' Irish logic – ain't it grand!

On the road in Australia again, we did eight weeks with lots of doubles shows (in two different places), lots of flights, lots of TVs appearances, lots of sore throats, lots of hangovers, lots of everything that a good rock and roll tour should have. Watching the videos of the interviews I can definitely detect a subtle change in my demeanour. I was more self-assured, quieter and more reflective – less the rebellious rocker and more the entertainer. I actually said, 'Not entertaining would kill me.' Even so, a lot of the interviewers couldn't get to grips with the idea of me doing musical theatre. (*Just shows you how successful the SQ image was – it sticks to this day.*)

Len and I had returned to our rock 'n' roll lifestyle, but it wasn't the same. Where there used to be closeness on stage and off, there was now distance. He spent most of his time with the boys in the band, while I stayed in my room with the children, only coming out for interviews, soundchecks and the gigs themselves. It started to feel like we were just going through the motions, personally and professionally.

We took a family trip to LA where I met up again with Henry Winkler and discussed the possibility of doing a movie together – maybe this will still happen. We also took a trip to Detroit and, since it was Richard's birthday, gave him a nice party at Chucky Cheese, a restaurant. Lots of my old school friends came with their kids, and it was great.

When I was in Detroit just before Christmas I took a phone call from my agent, Denis Selinger. I was up to host a new ITV chat show in 1988, and got the job. This was good news, as I really wanted to do it. We ran for a year. The show was called *Gas Street*, and was directed by Bob Cousins. Originally I was supposed to co-host with Vince Hill, but after doing just one show together it was decided we would both be better off having our own days. So two days a week, for an entire year, I drove from Essex to Birmingham, stayed overnight at the Holiday Inn and did the show live the next day. Talk about jumping into the fire: autocue, interviews, music . . . and *live*.

I discovered that I enjoy being both interviewee and interviewer. We had lots of guests including Michael Caine, who gave me such a gracious interview, and Lenny Henry, who never stops performing (*Oh yes, he was leaping all over the set singing '48 Crash'. You had no control whatsoever, and he was taking over the show until you asked him, if he knew what the song was all about. When you told him, 'The male menopause', that shut him up! but good*). Then we had Terence Stamp, who is completely gorgeous; Fay Weldon, a very intelligent, deep woman with a strong sense of the male/female dynamic; Rula Lenska and Dennis Waterman, who were then still in love and happily married; Dame Judi Dench, a delightful, fun lady; Imran Khan; Larry Adler; Jackie Collins (whom I had met via Mickie and Chris Most and whose books I love – essential reading when you don't want to think too hard); Nigel Kennedy; Andrew Sachs (Manuel in *Fawlty Towers*, who actually appeared in character for me at the beginning of the show); Clive Barker; Alan Price (*you loved doing a song with him – he gave 300 per cent*); Clare Short; Dame Barbara Cartland; Julie T. Wallace; and Richard Harris (*oh yes, that's the one interview you fucked up by talking too much. But you learned – watching it back you cringed. Keep your mouth shut!*)

I even got to interview Mickie Most, which felt very strange. We were walking out to the set when he said to me, 'So, Suzi, when does this show go to air?'

'Now, Mick. It's live!'

I have never seen anyone turn so white, but after a few minutes he relaxed and we had a nice interview. I was even able to get Mom and Dad, and Len's parents, down to the show. My dad got to do a song with me, one of our old family routines – 'If You Knew Suzi'. It's a piece of film I treasure.

During the year-long run of *Gas Street* I was able to get Michael Jackson's manager, Frank Delio, to do an interview on air. Frank used to be an A & R man and we had worked together in America, so we were old friends. It was great because they were refusing all interviews at this time – but I got him! Michael was on tour and we were invited with the children to see a show, with VIP treatment of course.

We travelled by bus to Wembley Stadium, along with lots of other 'famous' people, and then we were driven out to a special roped off section. I was sitting directly behind Steven Spielberg and I couldn't resist tapping him on the shoulder and saying, 'Steven – call home!' After the show Len, Laura, Richard and I were ushered in to meet the man himself. I remember staring quite rudely at his nose, which looked like a little drop of putty. Len said, 'Hello, mate', Laura shook hands, but Richard got scared and wouldn't say a word, hiding behind my legs. Michael bent down, saying, 'Oh, he's shy.' A photo was taken, and the moment was over . . . or so I thought. All of a sudden my five-year-old son realized he'd blown his chance and started to shout over and over, 'Mummy, can Michael come over to the house and play with us?' Michael, who'd obviously heard all the commotion, turned back, looked at my son, smiled, waved goodbye, then walked out of the door.

Prince Charles requested me to appear on one of his Royal Galas, to be filmed for television at the Mayflower Theatre. They asked me if I could dance. 'Sure,' I said. But on the first day of rehearsal, with Gary Wilmot and Kenny Lynch, I realized I was required to tap. Holy shit! I have never tapped a step in my life. But 'No problem,' I told Ernest Maxim who would be choreographing the entire thing. As soon as I returned home I booked myself on to a crash course for two weeks, and by the time we taped the show I looked like a pro. At the end of the show we were all filmed meeting the man himself. What would I say? Should I curtsey? I had gone through possible questions and responses. Finally, it was my turn. Of course, the ears of the entire cast were on the conversation.

Prince Charles: 'Did you have to do a lot of hard work?'

Suzi Quatro: 'Oh, yes, we worked every single day for three weeks.'

And he moved on. Then, a few steps away, Prince Charles suddenly turned back to me and said in a loud voice, 'And you have the best legs since Tina Turner.' (*Suzi Quatro disappeared in a flutter of eyelashes, giggles and burning cheeks. I felt like I was six years old, getting my first compliment from a man. What an idiot! It never occurred to me to say simply, 'Thank you.'*)

Life in showbusiness was interesting, to say the least, and I was enjoying adding all these strings to my bow. It was around this time that I immersed myself in a completely new venture: I began to write a musical. Just like that – crazy, eh? But I figured that with all my musical training it was possible. The subject was Tallulah Bankhead. I'd been a big fan since seeing her on a TV chat show in the sixties, near the end of her life, and had recently stumbled across a biography. She fascinated me. Such an enigma: ballsy yet soft, hard-drinking, hard-swearing, and bi-sexual, she was a huge theatre star here in England and one of the first women to have female groupies, who were called 'the gallery girls' by the press. I wanted to play the leading role, of course, and I was determined to succeed. I worked on the project all day and every day, writing in the front room on my white piano, researching in books, putting songs down on tape and only stopping to see the kids when they got home from school. It could be argued that I was avoiding reality; but whatever, I was deep into it.

Once I had enough songs together, the search for someone to write the book began. I approached several people who I thought could do the songs justice, until finally, at the suggestion of my theatrical agent Dennis Selinger, I gave Willie Rushton a call. I met up with him at his flat, played him some of the music and we struck a deal. I lived and breathed *Tallulah* until the songs and the book were ready, then handed it all over to Dennis to find someone to put it on, which would take another year or so. Watch this space. . . .

12

YOU NEVER HEARD ME CALL

....

In my personal life, let's just say that the lines of communication were down and neither of us could find the way back. I told Len that by leaving me alone, he'd taught me to *be* alone, but even so, being the one-man dog that I am, I kept yelling, crying, reasoning. But I wasn't heard, and that's the kiss of death in any marriage. Eventually I stopped trying. I was as lonely then as I had been that first year in London. I'd slowly taken over the house, claiming two rooms on the third floor – a music studio and a gym – as my own. And since Len mainly slept downstairs on the couch, the bedroom felt like mine too. I curled in on myself and began writing poetry. It simply had to come out – all the frustration, the lack of affection, the loneliness. If I hadn't been able to write I would probably have killed myself.

But with all those emotions it was hell. Mom had pounded into my head as part of my good Catholic upbringing that you don't divorce. Marriage was supposed to be two horses pulling the carriage together, through thick and thin. Yet every day took Len and me further apart. I was finding *me*, and that was dangerous. Most nights I went to bed angry and alone (*and while you were sleeping, Suzi, I was lying awake desperately trying to come to a decision: stay or go?).* Yet there were some tender moments too. (*Ah yes, this battle between needing to love someone and loving to need someone.*) So, one final poem. Did I write this, or did you? (*We both did.*)

And so, The Curtain Falls

And so, the curtain falls
Applause dies away
Crowds leave the stalls
One bulb lights the stage

One minute more, I stand
Listening to the sound
Of silence once a roar
I feel myself come down

As warmth begins to fade
I turn into the dark
I know what price I've paid
Success has left its mark

And so, the curtain falls
On one more lonely star
You never heard me call
So loud was your guitar.

(Suzi Quatro/ Little Susie from Detroit, 1988)

This was the backdrop of my world when I made a new friend, Rhiannon. She was in a band called Norma Jean, we were both Gemini, and we bonded very quickly – something I hadn't done with anyone since my schooldays. We had first met during the Chichester run of *Annie Get Your Gun*, and later she visited me at home and we decided to try to write some songs together. (*Okay, Suzi, I'll take over now.*)

Rhiannon was younger than me and a Blondie fan. The only hit of mine she knew was 'If You Can't Give Me Love', which was nice because it meant she liked 'me' and not Suzi Quatro – and at that stage of my life this was exactly what I needed. For the past few years I had never been sure 'why' someone liked me at all. Success does that to you – you learn to distrust. I shared with her the ups and downs of my marriage – something I had not done with anyone before – and actually admitted out loud that I was thinking of leaving Len. I found myself pouring out my troubles in huge emotional outbursts, and right up until the divorce she was always on the side of the marriage. 'Work it out' was her frequent advice.

We laughed constantly, something else that was sorely missing from my world, and we wrote songs non-stop. She would play guitar and sing, while I played the piano. She had a fabulous voice, could move like Michael Jackson and was actually very talented. The most important thing, though, was that she was intelligent.

I think that, at first, Len was relieved I had someone to talk to. It took the pressure off him having to spend more time with me, and he encouraged our friendship. What he didn't realize, though, was that by pushing me towards her he was also pushing me away from him. I finally had someone who listened to me and the flood gates were opened. My feelings poured out, never to be contained again. Many of our discussions became the basis of the songs we wrote over the next few years. She was there for me in my time of need, and that's something I will never forget. . . . OK, Suzi Q, back to you now.)

And so as 1989 began I found myself waking early, getting the kids ready for school, stopping at the swimming pool to do a few laps, dropping the kids off, returning home and getting ready for the day's song-writing session. Rhiannon would arrive around noon and we would work until she left at about three, then I would do the school run again, come home, have dinner, open a glass of wine, choose a good movie and go back to 'our' bedroom – *alone*. It was the wonderful world of creativity with Rhiannon that saved me from having to face my life head on. But always floating around in the back of my mind was the big question should I stay, or should I go? I'd been asking myself this since 1986 (*and we were no closer to the answer*).

In the meantime, we had what was to prove the tour to end all tours lined up. Other gigs and tours may blur into each other, but not this one. Since Rhiannon and I were being so productive it was decided that she would take a six-week break from Norma Jean gigs and join me, along with Gaynor, to do backing vocals. That meant I would have two people to talk to on the road, which was great, although I had no idea that this would be Gaynor's last tour. The band line-up was Len, Jamie (second guitar), Ant (drums) and me on bass. Our support group was Blondie (no, not *That* Blondie, but South African singer/guitarist Blondie), Jonathan Mover (an amazing drummer from New York), and Keith on bass. This time taking the kids turned into a huge argument between Len and me because he said the cost of travelling with extra people would cut our profits. But I was adamant: 'Leave my children for six weeks? No fucking way!' I won.

And where we were going on this unforgettable tour? To Russia. Glasnost was then only in its infancy, and things were still not good there. Due to the lack of good food, we supplied our own catering. We were told to pack bathplugs, soft toilet paper, large towels and various canned goods.

First stop, Moscow. We were filmed in the first week, and that video is a great memory jog. It begins with me coming out of customs holding my children's hands – Laura was five and Richard three, and they looked so damn cute! There is one shot of Len looking miserable by my side. He and I had a huge hotel suite in Moscow with two bedrooms (well, I needed the distance), but the rest of the band's accommodation wasn't too good (*and for the first time you travelled with Valium, a supply of port and penicillin – taking no chances with sleep, well-being or illness*).

After checking in we made our way down to soundcheck and discovered that, even though they had stage and back-stage riders, a lot of the equipment we were used to was just not available in Russia and eastern Europe. So we just had to make do. The monitors especially were inadequate – it's a wonder I didn't lose my voice for good, as Len always played so incredibly loud. They were permanently on 11!

On stage we did all the usual hits, plus some new additions that Rhiannon and I had written. There was the obligatory bass solo (no matter how many times I have tried to remove this from the show it's just not possible – people want to see me *play* my bass). It's noticeable in the video that I didn't look at Lennie on stage – there was no connection whatsoever. (*There are a couple of heart-wrenching shots of the kids watching you on stage and looking a little confused. God knows what they made of their mother up there in a black leotard, butterfly belt, leopardskin jacket and boots, belting out rock and roll on her pink guitar.)* Yes – great outfit, I thought, much cooler in temperature than the leather jumpsuit. The BVs were also in black, with studded biker hats – good look.

Now every tour has a hit, and the biggie in Russia was very appropriate. It was based on one of my poems written in the wilderness years of indecision.

Love and War

Love and war . . . who is the enemy,
I lay my body on the bed of Bastille
Ah ah ah
Forgotten refugee, love is the enemy
You use as your shield
Ah ah ah

Was the memory, a peace I knew
Or Just a silent war, behind enemy lines
I was your prisoner, in the cage of your heart
Should've known from the start
It was love and war
Heard it all before

The lines have been drawn,
Beggars and thieves
Will fight to the dawn
You beg for the reasons to believe
Then you steal from them all

You claim you love me ha ha ha
But it's hate that I saw
How many ways can we die
In this act of war
Love and war, love and war

We got to find a way,
Doesn't matter what we say
Words escape the play,
Who dares sins,
In love and war . . . love and war

Who's after love, who comes before
If war is love, and love means war.

(Quatro/Wolfe, 1989)

The applause throughout was tremendous, and finally, as the video recalls, show number one was over. (*Suzi Quatro leaves the stage with two burly bouncers, then in the corridor I spot Richard running towards me, bend down and gather him up in a big bear hug with a huge smile on my face. . . . But there's one bit they didn't put into the video. As you were waiting backstage before the show, you were informed that all the political bigwigs were waiting in the next room to meet you. You weren't quite sure what to expect. In the hospitality suite one VIP walked over to you and the room went silent. 'So, Miss Quatro, do you think glasnost is working?' Pregnant pause. 'So far, so good.' 'Humph,' said Boris or whatever his name was, and walked off. The room volume went back up – obviously that had been the correct answer!*)

Russia was a new experience in so many ways. On every

floor in every hotel we stayed in there was a 'floor lady', usually very heavy-set and very Russian peasant-looking. They were frightening in a way. Their job was to take care of us, bringing tea urns and and slicing rotten bits off fruit that was to be put into our respective rooms. While we were there we were given some Russian money to spend. Trouble was, there was nothing to spend it on. Must be the first time in history that a rock and roll band had dinner, then argued about who would pay the bill. And another thing you would never expect to hear: 'Oh, no. Not champagne and caviar again!' Daytimes were spent hanging out with the kids, walking around the cities, looking in empty shop windows and browsing through food markets where we saw complete sides not of meat as we know it but of fat hanging from hooks. I started to realize how privileged my life was and how much I took for granted. I learned lessons in Russia that I never forgot.

In this new wind of 'freedom' promoters were actually making money, and the authorities didn't always like it. We went to one city, sold out again, then found that the people in charge had cancelled the gig, saying the venue wasn't available after all. So, in desperation, the promoter booked us into a circus tent for four days. Doing my bass solo, and dancing around the ring while dodging elephant shit was certainly a first for me. (*Remember that great joke? Two circus workers are outside doing chores. One guy's job is to sweep up all the elephant shit. 'Hey, Joe, you know I really hate this job,' he complains. Joe says, 'So Harry, why don't you just quit?' 'What!' Harry replies. 'And leave showbusiness!'*)

The most beautiful city of all in Russia is St Petersburg. I have never seen a cathedral like the one they have there. It's stunning, takes your breath away – as did this next incident. The show was over, I had taken my Valium and retired to my bedroom, and Len was sound asleep across the hallway. A sixth sense woke me up. Slightly drugged, I forced my eyes open and saw two men standing by the bed, one tall, one short. I vaguely wondered what Lennie and Ant were doing in my bedroom at this time of night. Then suddenly I was wide awake. Who were these two strangers glaring at me? I jumped out of bed and screamed, 'What the fuck are you doing in here? Get out *now*! They ran out of the door and I went to wake Len up. Fortunately nothing had been stolen, just rifled through, but after that we had a permanent KGB guard on the door.

My fear of flying was reinforced by travelling around Russia and the Baltic states on 'Aeroflop'. Safety did not exist, and I was petrified not only for myself but also for the children, Lennie and the rest of the musicians. On one occasion we were booked on to a small turbo-prop to do a city hop between engagements. But there wasn't enough luggage space, as quite a bit of the stage equipment had to be taken with us. No problem: they simply loaded it into the aisle of the aircraft. Unbelievable, but true. There I was, strapped into my seat, leaning my arm on a huge Marshall amplifier. What would happen if there was turbulence? Just imagine being killed by a flying cabinet! So I jumped out of my seat, ran to the front of the aircraft, sat on the floor and hung my legs out of the luggage compartment; I wasn't moving until they removed the gear from the plane. For my trouble, I received a huge round of applause from the entire travelling party. It worked. The organizers hired another aircraft, and loaded all the equipment on to that. We made the trip safely, disembarked and were making our way to the terminal when I noticed some asshole lighting up a cigarette only a few feet away from the plane. I smacked it out his his hand: '*Nyet, Dummkopf!*'

We had all, especially Laura, lost a lot of weight by the time the tour came to an end. I couldn't wait to return to daily comforts such as hot food, comfortable beds, soft toilet paper, big bath towels and colour – Russia was most definitely black and white. After six weeks playing to over half a million people, coming home was as much of a culture shock as going to Russia had been in the first place.

Around this time I made a quick trip to Detroit to see my mom and dad, who were preparing to move down to Texas to be with Nancy. It was strange walking around this house that was once a home, now filled with packing crates. They knew something was up and left me to my own devices. I went to my old school, the park, the shopping mall and my old house, needing desperately to reconnect. (*You needed me, Suzi, you needed me.*) I sure did – so where were you? (*Sitting on your shoulder the whole time. But you know, you didn't just need me, you needed yourself. The tears had to come, so I left you to it.*)

Throughout this time, Len and I were still working together. Intolerable as things were between us, somehow we managed to stay together and work together, even though 'together' meant living separate lives. I'm sure it had more than a little to do with the fact that we had two children – and truthfully, who wants to go through a divorce if it can be avoided? I often wonder now, looking back, if it was Len who fell out of love first, and if so, why didn't *he* leave *me*? What we did was ignore the issues; what we should have done was talk. The longer this silent symphony continued, the more inevitable our eventual separation became.

In the meantime, though, professional life had to go on and we finally had another record deal. This time it was with Robbie and Ferdi Bolland, two songwriter/producers from Holland who had scored a big hit in America with Falco, the song titled 'Amadeus', inspired by Mozart. Rhiannon and I submitted some of our best songs, along with a number of my own compositions and a couple of covers, to which we added some Bolland Brothers tunes. Then off we went. Len, Rhiannon and me (I was reluctant to be alone with Len at any time), to start recording. The two covers were 'Oh Suzi Q,' and 'Take Me in Your Arms' (Holland, Dozier, Holland). Bolland and Bolland contributed, 'Baby You're a Star,' (a single, released with a video), 'Love Touch', 'The Great Midnight Rock and Roll House Party', 'We Live Forever', 'We Found Love' (a single release) and a song co-written with myself called 'Southern Comfort'. Quatro/Wolfe songs were 'Intimate Strangers', 'Kiss Me Goodbye' (a single release) and 'Elusive Lover' (a duet with Rhiannon). Quatro compositions were 'Victim of Circumstance' and 'The Best Thing in My Life'. (*I remember you writing that, Suzi. You were sitting at the white piano where you always do your best work, feeling bad about how things were going between you, calling up memories of the good times and hoping that you guys could put yourselves back together again.*)

We had some pictures taken, for which I was actually made up by a lady from *Playboy* magazine! I put on my leather suit for some of the shots, and for others a black leather mini-skirt with a black leather jacket trimmed with leopardskin. Then we waited for the release. . . . which came and went. Aside from a few television appearances and radio interviews, no one paid this album much attention – and that included the record-buying public.

On one TV show in Germany I was booked to perform 'We Found Love'. Penny Marshall (Laverne and Shirley) was also on, promoting her directorial debut movie, *Big*. I was standing on the side of the stage waiting to go on and do my bit when this tall guy appeared and said, 'Hi, I'm Tom Hanks and I'm a big fan. I used to go to all your concerts in Los Angeles. You must remember me – I was always in the front row.' Actually I didn't, but of course that's not what I told him. I had no idea who he was at that time, and it wasn't until years later, after awards galore, that the penny dropped and I could return the compliment, telling him in all sincerity that I was a huge fan and never missed a movie.

I was still spending a lot of time with Rhiannon, who, because she was so much younger than me, was rooted in modern rock shows with Madonna-type choreography. Maybe, I thought, I should consider updating my own show. So I added various girls alongside Rhiannon to do dance routines, and sometimes joined in myself. It was great fun, and represented another stretch. (*Actually, you were trying to remove yourself from the band you shared with Len – less volume, less noise, some quiet moments, some dancing, spreading your creative wings. Len hated it.*)

We did two big tours in 1989. First we went for two weeks to Japan, which we hadn't visited since 1978 – our return was long overdue. This was the first time I insisted on separate rooms for Len and myself. I put it down to the snoring, but in truth I wanted to be alone. We were slowly but surely becoing non-lovers – but as it turned out this would be the least of my worries. I took a phone call late one night after a show. It was my sister Patti calling from America to tell me that Mom had stomach cancer and the prognosis wasn't good. I spent the remainder of the dates in deep sorrow. Not my mom. Please God not my mom. She was the 'rock' in my 'roll' and I just couldn't lose her.

And then, after Japan, yet another Australian tour. I seem to have spent more time there over the years than anywhere else, and indeed it does feel like my second home. By now the kids were seven and five and in school proper, so Len's argument about not wanting to take them along because it would disrupt their education made a little sense. The tour would last six weeks, too long for them to be away. So we came to a compromise. I would go away without them for two weeks, after which they would join me for the next two weeks and then return home. I was absolutely devastated by the idea of our first separation since they had been born, but in my heart I knew it was right. The night before I left I went into the small bedroom the kids were sharing at that time, sat on their beds and cried my eyes out. I tried to explain why this was happening, but I'm sure they didn't understand. Richard in particular was almost too close to me, and suffered badly when I was away from him.

Halfway through the second week in Australia I had a vivid dream that I couldn't shake off. I didn't share it with Len because I didn't want to upset him. I was standing in an airport, waiting for Richard, Laura and their nanny to appear and feeling anxious as hell. Finally my precious babies came out of customs and I ran towards them, arms outstretched. I hugged and kissed Laura, then bent to pick up Richard who was still small enough to do that. He was crying non-stop as he said, 'Mummy, you didn't die after all!' Dream over. They were due to join us at the end of that week, and once they had arrived safely the dream wasn't even in my mind any more. But as I tucked Richard into bed that first night he looked at me strangely and said, 'Mummy, I had a dream last night. You were running towards me and I said, "Oh, you didn't die after all."' I *did* nearly die at that point. We had made a psychic connection – the exact same dream, the exact same words. Quite unbelievable.

The new show was now perfected. I loved it and felt it had given all the old hits a new lease of life. I even played one song on the piano, 'Blind Emotions' from the unreleased album we made at Rak in 1983, complete with Temptations-type dance routines. It felt good to go back to my roots, even for a single song.

I was still working on *Tallulah* while waiting for news on its possible production from Denis, writing poetry and songs and of course doing tons of TV shows. This year I got involved in the newly formed Sky channel, being a judge on over sixty programmes of the talent show *Sky Star Search*, hosted by Keith Chegwin. *X Factor*? Been there, done it, got the T-shirt. Acutally, when I watch Simon Cowell on that show I am always amazed that whatever he says closely echoes what I am saying to whoever is sitting with me at the time. We really do think alike.

The funniest moment in my year as judge occurred when a lady who thought herself an opera singer had sung. 'Granada'. Performance over, it was my turn to give my opinion. 'I think you chose a very difficult song, and don't really think you have what it takes. Not in this field, which is very competitive to say the least.' At the end of the show we judges were to go up on stage and shake all the contestants' hands while we were filmed. When I came to the 'opera singer' she whispered in my ear, 'What do you know? You can't sing a fucking note!' But she never stopped smiling, not for a minute. Now *that* impressed me.

Come 1990, emotionally weighed down with my mom's continuing illness, we prepared for yet another Aussie tour. Robbie Gladwell (aka Dr Robert) was a new addition on guitar and would stay for nine years. We became good friends and remain so. I call him an all-rounder – any style, any song, a valuable asset on anyone's stage – even if he is too tall and tries to hog the centre microphone all the time. I know he was a good friend to Len, who bent his ear more than once about our marriage problems. God knows, we both needed someone to talk to – just a shame it wasn't each other.

It was on this tour that I celebrated my fortieth birthday. Imagine my surprise when I walked out on stage on 3 June to find the entire first three rows of the audience, the band and the crew wearing black T-shirts saying 'Suzi is 40'! This was Len's work. I did see the humour, and I did laugh, but inside I was still sad.

This was also the tour on which I moved my bass solo on to a new level, all because of drummer Colin Woolway (Ant). While we were in rehearsals he requested special time with me in order to choreograph the bass with the drums, and it worked. Instead of it just being an opportunity for me to show off it became an orchestral piece; it has remained one of my favourite parts of the show. And, for the first time, I spoke publicly about what we were now calling *Tallullah Who?*. Bill Kenwright had agreed to put it on at the Queen's Theatre in

Hornchurch from 30 August to try it out. I was over the moon and waxed lyrical to anyone who would listen. Hooray! Another escape from reality.

As we gigged nightly, my whole attitude now shifted. Instead of going to bed alone, I started to stay up with the boys and party. I'd never done that very much before, because my main concern was to save my voice for the show and get plenty of sleep. It was surreal picking up the phone to hear Len say, 'When are you coming to bed, Suze?' This kind of conversation usually took place the other way around, and I revelled in it. Rebel *with* a cause. 'I'll come to bed when I'm damn good and ready,' was my reply. Everyone around us could see that Len and I were in deep trouble, but nobody could help.

Once we were back from Australia, without the distraction of the tour our problems hit us smack in the face. I was angry all the time, and one day, while nanny and kids were out, I let rip. 'You've left me alone for the past five years. All you do is shoot and go to the pub. You don't spend enough time with me or the kids. You don't support me in anything other than rock and roll. You're selfish. From now on I want the same amount of money you spend on shooting to do something *I* want to do. It's *my* turn to have some fun. All I do is work work work. I want a life!' Phew – that felt good. I informed Len that I was taking a trip, alone. I would go to LA to visit Patti and Arlene. I had some serious thinking to do. (*Ah yes, but it wasn't you who went to California. It was me.*

I stayed with Patti first. She has always been my conscience. I can cry with her; she understands, and never judges in times of trouble. We talked, shopped, went to restaurants – hell, if I hadn't been so unhappy I would have really enjoyed myself.

But the big decision was hanging over my head like an axe. I went back and forth like a pendulum. I loved Len, without a doubt, but I also knew deep down that I needed to move. I felt trapped and suffocated – I just couldn't breathe with him any more. And yes, it scared the shit out of me that maybe I was making a big mistake. How could I be sure that I wasn't? All the while Patti just held me close, as good sisters should do.

Then I went to Arlene's house. If anyone knows how it feels to leave a marriage, she is the expert – I think it was number six at that time. We didn't actually talk about the situation – didn't need to, because she knew me too well. If I wanted an opinion, I would ask. Len called and we talked for over an hour with Arlene hovering in the background watching my every expression. He wanted me back, he loved me, we would work it out; it was like a broken record, a man pleading for his life. I tried to be tough and keep my stance but it was difficult. We had spent too many years together and there were too many memories to block out. Afterwards I asked Arlene to go for a walk on the beach with me. She let me talk it out until I finally said those golden words, 'What do you think I should do?' This is what she said.

'Okay, Susie. You're feeling pretty raw right now. You feel sorry for him. You want it to be okay. You want to wave that magic wand and go back to the good times. So I'll tell you what you should do. Go back in the house, call him up and tell him everything is fine – that you love him, that you will stay together. And then you'll feel good again, right?' (That was a rhetorical question if I ever heard one.) 'And then,' she continued, 'five minutes later you'll feel shitty. There is no way out of this, Susie. When it's over it's over, and it's gonna hurt until it doesn't.' I returned home with my decision made – or so I thought.

Len met me at the airport looking tired, sad, anxious and glad to see me all at the same time. We hugged. I said, 'I missed you', which I did in a way. 'Good,' he said, and we drove home. I had slept quite a bit on the plane so I wasn't tired, and took my car out for a drive into town. I did a little shopping, not really thinking much about anything at all, then started back. As I turned down our road, it hit me. I began to cry so hard that I had to pull over and stop. I stayed on the side of the road for half an hour, sobbing and slamming my fist on the steering wheel. Finally spent, I went home. I said nothing but just waited for the kids to come home from school, ate dinner with everyone, put the kids to bed, put my pyjamas on and then went downstairs to watch TV with Len for a while. He had been pretty quiet most of the evening, deep in thought. Then he turned to me with tears in his eyes and said, 'You're never gonna love me again, are you?' Jesus Christ – that was so hard to hear and so hard to see. I just didn't have the heart to break his heart. I called him over to the couch, laid his head on my lap and said, 'Don't worry. Everything is going to be fine.' Once again I surrendered.) So in truth, Susie, you lost it in the final moment. Maybe it would have been better if *I* had gone to California? (*So stop with the macho bullshit – we managed to limp along day to day.*)

Tallullah Who? was going to be delayed, because Bill Kenwright wanted to get Shirlie Roden, a talented theatrical composer, and me together to work on some of the songs. He wanted to 'theatre-ize' them. We met, hit it off and began reworking the songs.

Len and I both thought it was about time to start taking real holidays, something we had never done before as all our travelling was associated with work. This may even have been part of the problem – we didn't have any private, family time together. So we rented a house for November in Kissimee near Disneyworld in Florida; Len's parents would come with us. (*It's my turn again. We were having an argument when the phone rang. It was Len's mum, but she was crying too much to speak coherently and handed the phone to Dad Tuckey. He said, 'She just has a feeling that we are never going to make that trip to Florida. She keeps crying. I don't know what's wrong with her – she won't tell me.' I told him to tell her that everything would be fine – covers a multitude of sins, that word and hung up. 'Okay, here's the deal,' I said to Len. 'Let's take this trip – everyone is looking forward to it. Let's just get to Christmas, see how we're doing and re-evaluate the situation. Let's both really try.' I did insist on one thing, though: Len would have to stop drinking. This was not negotiable, and he did. So it was a sober Len, along with his parents, our kids and me, who went to Florida. We enjoyed Disneyland but slept in separate rooms. Christmas came and went with no change. We were just rolling along avoiding each other and avoiding the issues. Happy New Year? Maybe not!*

In fact 1991 marked the beginning of the worst two years of my life. I threw myself even deeper into my song-writing, and it was now that I wrote the first of my collection of songs that would finally be released fifteen years later on the album Back to the Drive. *'Free the Butterfly' is lyrically one of my finest efforts – pain is always the best poet. I put it down on tape, went downstairs, took Len into the front room and played it for him.*)

Free the Butterfly

One kiss for yesterday, one hope for tomorrow
Face to face with sorrow, with nothing left to say
One more love affair, dead and gone,
Two weary contenders, moving on
Will the snake shed its skin, when the truth rushes in

So let the chrysalis begin, free the butterfly within
Spread my wings, I wanna fly
And let my happiness begin, free the butterfly within
Spread my wings, I just got to try
Free the butterfly, free this butterfly

Precious moments we can't forget, a promise for ever
Yes we know that it's over, my heart has no regrets
'Cos the love we shared has flown away
Although I'm beside you every day
We shared the best, now it's time to put this pain to rest

So let the chrysalis begin, free the butterfly within
Spread my wings I wanna fly
And let my happiness begin, free the butterfly within
Spread my wings I just got to try
Free the butterfly . . . free this butterfly

The snake shed his skin, truth rushed in
I start to cry . . . this is goodbye

(Suzi Quatro, 1991)

And what did he say, Susie? (*He said, 'Nice song, Suze.'*)

13
SOMETIMES LOVE IS LETTING GO

....

In January 1991 I went into rehearsal for the opening of *Tallulah Who?* It really was a dream come true – my own musical, my own songs. Just look at little Susie from Detroit now! I had sent tapes to Mom and Dad. Mom in particular absolutely loved it and thought it would be a big success. I often feel her hand from heaven pushing me to get it back on the stage: I will, Mom. I will. She said all the emotion in my lyrics came from her, and she was probably right.

Tallulah lived her life in the fast lane and so we had to have shocking dialogue and often shocking lyrics. Shirlie and I had fine-tuned the songs and written some new ones, while Willie took care of the script. Costumes were prepared and my face was made up – actually all blanked out, with painted-in arched eyebrows and ruby-red lips – so that photos could be taken. I sent one to Mom, who phoned me and asked, 'Why didn't they use you for the picture, Susan?' The image must have been convincing. I threw myself into the role 300 per cent, as was my way, and for a while Tallulah took over my life.

On opening night the audience included Mickie and Chris Most, Denis Selinger, various friends and of course Len, who swigged out of a flask of whisky the entire evening. I think of all my the extracurricular activites (outside of rock and roll, that is) this is the one he hated the most. He couldn't support me, he couldn't applaud, but just made comments like 'The kids are missing you.' So do you think they didn't miss us when we were on tour? We did sell-out business for the entire three-week run. The press wasn't invited because it was only a try-out, but they got in anyway. Here is a review from *Stage* magazine.

Suzi Quatro descends the gilt staircase with the stage presence for which Tallulah was renowned and ploughs headfirst into the role of the hard-drinking, cocaine-addicted nymphomaniac with an acting ability which won her worthy applause. Written by Willie Rushton with music and lyrics by Suzi Quatro and Shirlie Roden, *Tallulah Who?* is arguably the most imaginative and original piece of musical theatre to hit the British stage in recent years.

(*But, Suzi, it didn't fit the spirit of the times – Bill Kenwright's mother expressed horror at some of the content – and this reduced our chances of ever getting to the West End.*) Still, we hoped for the best. Once the run was over the waiting game started. Would or wouldn't *Tallulah* transfer?

After seeing my dream of writing and starring in *Tallulah Who?* realized, I was pleased to get an invitation to appear in concert on TV, live at the Minerva Theatre in Chichester. I was given carte blanche and my imagination took flight. I arranged for Arlene, Patti and Nancy to fly over and re-create the Pleasure Seekers. The show began with my sisters doing back-up vocals on 'She's in Love with You', and then we went into a Motown revue. Nancy sang lead on 'You Really Got a

Hold on Me'. Then Arlene took the spotlight, playing piano and singing 'My Guy' (*I could hardly contain my laughter as she warbled, straight from the heart, 'Nothin' you can say can tear me away from my guy'. Yeah – right!*). Patti on guitar was next, performing 'Dancing in the Streets', then with me 'Take Me in Your Arms'. It was a joyous occasion – finally, after all these years, my sisters were once again beside me, sharing the stage. I was happy as a pig in shit.

Next up were Willie Rushton and myself doing a number from *Tallullah Who?*, 'The Art of Seduction'. For this I actually wore a skin-tight red dress! Shirlie Roden (by now a permanent fixture at the piano in the front room as we continued to work on *Tallulah*), played piano on that song and the next, 'God Bless the Child', my favourite Billie Holiday song. And to finish off we did the single from *Oh Suzi Q*, 'Kiss Me Goodbye'. For the first time I added horns to the line-up – something I had wanted to do all my life, being a Motown girl. The entire evening was magic.

It was also around this time that we began to participate in some 'oldie nights' in Germany, promoted by Rainer Haas. The gigs were big affairs, held in the largest halls in the country, in which acts from the sixties and seventies mingled so that the shows appealed to a wide range of people, making them hugely successful. I didn't like the idea at all, having never done package shows before, and complained loudly to Len, 'What the fuck are we doing here?' I was used to being the star of the show and playing for as long as I wanted. On these gigs I was just another act and had maybe thirty minutes if I was lucky. But it was work, after all, so I shut up.

I had apparently met the promoter years before but couldn't remember the occasion, and I wasn't at all sure about him. He seemed awfully flash to me – and awfully good-looking too! But that was only a fleeting thought. I wondered what he made of the fact that Len and I were married, but booked into separate bedrooms. I would eventually find out everything he thought, in detail.

The year rolled along, Len and I in stalemate. There was no reason to argue any more. Workwise I was busy writing for the hoped for West End transfer of *Tallulah Who?* as well as doing various gigs and TVs; and of course I was also taking care of my family. We were due to be in Aussie again in August and September, and since Shirlie and I now were now so deeply involved in *Tallulah* it was decided that she would join us, playing piano and singing BVs, so that we could complete any changes that had to be made. Here's the line-up for our last tour together (sounds like a song title to me): Len (guitar), Robbie (guitar), Ant (drums), me (bass), Rhiannon (BVs) and Shirlie (BVs and piano). Plus, of course, the kids and Sue, who had by now replaced Michelle as nanny.

As usual, videotapes are my main source of information. Strange what you remember; even stranger what you forget. There's lots of footage of the kids in hotel rooms with Sue and Julie, who ran the fan club at the time. Watching it now, I find myself thinking what an unnatural environment it was for children to grow up in. Laura got chicken pox, Richard got diarrhoea, and we all got knackered. Len was drunk most of the time, even to the point of messing up on stage – something that had never happened before. I would be hanging out with Rhiannon, writing with Shirlie, playing with the kids, doing the gigs or sleeping in my room – none of these activities shared with my husband. Len complained to me, 'I can't get close to you any more, Suze. Somebody's always in the way.' (*So where have you been for the last five years? You had all the warnings, verbal and otherwise, and did nothing. And now it's the final countdown.*) The atmosphere got so bad that Len threatened to quit and fly home in the middle of the tour. If this was meant to scare me, his bluff didn't work. I said it was fine and asked Harley Metcalf, our promoter for many years, to arrange the tickets; Len didn't go. (*Well, while you were working and trying to hold the band together on stage, Suzi, I was buying scented poetry books from The Hill of Content, a wonderful bookstore in Melbourne, and reading aloud from them on long journeys. We were coming to the end of our rainbow, trying to hold on to fading colours.*)

I think when it finally broke, when I finally admitted to myself that there was no way back, was the night Len convinced me to make love. He said it would help. Help who? I thought. But Mom's teachings were always in my head. We were married, I had an obligation as his wife, and so I agreed. It was to be the last time we ever made love. I cried the entire time, and he never knew – that's how far apart we were!

Christmas 1991 would be our last as a proper family. Len filmed it, and the strain leaps out at you from every single frame. We exchanged presents and smiled sad smiles. Early in 1992 I was booked to do a television show in Frankfurt. I spent hours convincing Len that I should go alone and finally he relented. It was the first time in our twenty-year relationship that this had happened. I loved being in the hotel room on my own. I loved standing on stage on my own. I loved being alone.

There I was getting made up when who should walk in but Rainer Haas, who said he had a couple of acts booked on the same show. Later on, wandering around the set, for some unknown reason I grabbed his arm and said. 'I'm alone. You have to take care of me.' Later I relayed all this on the phone to Len, adding, 'He's a very nice man, you know.' Len replied 'He's a bleeding promoter, Suze', whatever that was supposed to mean.

This would be the worst year of all and would wreak havoc in my world. Everything changed – absolutely everything. To say I was ripe for a love affair would be an understatement. I've thought long and hard about how to tell this part of my story and have decided not to name the man or the family involved, for to do so would inflict even more pain.

Early in the year I met a talented actor. Needing desperately to fill in the holes in my heart, I pursued him with vigour – he didn't stand a chance. At first it was quite innocent and we were just going to write some songs together. I drove over to his house one day with my tape recorder, songbook and pen to do just that. We talked, we wrote, we drank coffee and finally we kissed. I'd crossed that line. On the way home, in my little red BMW, I remember looking at my face in the rear-view mirror. Is this who you are? A cheater? God, one more step and you would have been in his bed! (*Yes, both of us really wanted him, but both of us were married and so it didn't happen. But we knew it was just a matter of time, because for the marriage time had run out.*) I cried all the way home, knowing without a shadow of a doubt that it was now the time to go.

My parents were over for the Easter break. The cancer had grown big in Mom's stomach – she looked nine months pregnant, yet skinny as hell. It was her goodbye trip and we both knew it. We managed one last dinner at Mickie and Chris Most's house, though she didn't eat a thing. And we spent hours talking, while taking painfully slow walks down the country lanes by my house. Mom wanted to unload, and I listened. She told me all about her life with Dad, about her mistakes, about her feelings towards me.

'Susan, I have one big regret in my life.'

Did I really want to hear this? 'Yes, Mom, what is it?'

'I let you go too soon. You joined that damn rock and roll band at fourteen. You were still a baby. On the road with all those temptations. I know all about that married man and the trouble you got in.'

This shocked me. 'How did you know that, Mom?'

'Because, Susan, I know everything about my children. Mother's instinct.' She continued, 'Then you went to England and fell in love, and you were really gone. I should never have let you go so young.'

We walked along a little while, both lost in our own thoughts, until I finally asked, 'So Mom, if you felt like that, why did you let me go?'

'Because, Susan, sometimes love *is* letting go!'

That was one of the most poignant things my mother had ever said to me, and it ended up as a song, written by myself and Shirlie Roden, on the 2006 album *Back to the Drive*. I now perform this in my show, dedicated to my mother's memory, on the piano. It's become an audience favourite too, and I can feel everyone walking down their own personal memory lane with me. When I was promoting this album I realized it was a man's love song. Every DJ and every journalist picked it out and commented until I finally asked why. Apparently it expresses lost love in a way that men can understand. Oh yes, sometimes love *is* letting go.

Back to *that* day. I walked into the house, said hi to Mom and Dad who were watching TV, and went upstairs to my third-floor music room. I was hiding. Len eventually came up. 'Suze, how long is this going to go on?'

No more avoiding it, I guess. The words fell out of my mouth. 'Len, I want a divorce. I'll be calling a lawyer tomorrow.' Six years down the road and I'd finally said it!

Len looked long and hard at me and said, 'So then I can make love to whoever I want to. Is that right?'

'Yes, Len, and so can I.'

He left the room and I didn't try to stop him.

I sat there on top of an amplifier for over an hour, feeling shell-shocked. Scared as I was that I'd made a mistake, and scared as I was to face life alone without Lennie, I somehow had to trust my decision. But it wasn't easy. To this day I still wonder if I could have turned it all around somehow. To this day I still feel guilty for all the heartache I caused, and for all the damage done to our children. To this day I still miss the good times we shared.

That evening I told my parents everything. Mom was extremely close to Len and loved him dearly. She began to cry. 'It's a shame you can't turn the clock back. Those two beautiful children – they will suffer. Oh, yes, they will.'

Then Dad broke in. 'For Christ's sake, Helen, can't you see he just doesn't turn her on any more?'

I got myself a lawyer, and the ugly process of divorce began. Anyone who uses the term 'amicable' is lying – it's just not possible. Both sides will feel anger, and both sides will blame the other. It takes years for these feeling to subside, as it did with us. (*As I have said many, many times, and I must say it again now, I was in for the long haul. I loved him totally, he was the father of my children and we had 'grown up' together. If things had been right I would never have left. But that was the dream; this was the reality.*)

I remember telling Rainer at the first opportunity that I was going to get divorced and wanted him to be the first to know. I have no idea why I shared this with him – I just did. (*There's another thing you have no idea about. You were going into the hotel with your two backing vocalists at the time and passed Rainer, who was standing in the lobby talking to some of the other acts. You both said hello. You grabbed your room key, got into the elevator with the girls, and all of a sudden you blurted out, 'Oh, my God. Can you imagine sleeping with him? Yuk – how horrible.' The girls looked on bemused and asked, 'Why did you say that, Suzi?' You had no idea why. What a strange thing to do. You know what I think? Positive or negative, you had a reaction – maybe even a premonition.*)

It would have been better if Len had moved out until things were finalized, because the atmosphere was so awful. So I spent my days at my new boyfriend's house in North London as we now had a 'relationship' going. I just couldn't face Len's or my parents' sorrow. The kids suffered terribly, being too young to understand why Mummy was gone all the time. I was often in tears on the phone when they implored me, 'When are you coming back, Mummy?' (*In this befuddled state I remember being desperate to create a new family for the kids and so, crazy as it seems, I got engaged. As if you could just slide one person out and a new one in! But I was so confused and emotional that the only thing I was sure of was the divorce.*)

I suggested that Len leave the band right away, because to continue working together in our situation would be impossible, and took on a second guitarist. The gigs continued as the lawyers began to thrash things out. One day I drove over to see Mickie, who was swimming in his pool. I sat there on the edge and told him everything. He had no idea that anything was wrong and was very sad about it – he too loved Len very much. I couldn't stand being in my house any more, though maybe if Len had gone I would have felt different. I told Mickie I would sell the place and move closer to London, and he promised me he would start looking for properties the next day. Even now he was still taking care of me – always the father figure. He also suggested a meeting in his office with Len and me; he had a plan, he said.

In due course two weary adversaries arrived at Rak and climbed the stairs to Mickie's office. Len was tough, while I was in tears the entire time. Mickie asked, 'Is there any way you can get back together?' 'No,' we both blurted out together. 'Okay,' be continued. 'Then this is what I suggest. First of all, there are no winners in these situations – only degrees of losing. The last thing you want is for the lawyers to start sending you bills that look like telephone numbers. So why don't you guys agree on a fair settlement? Sign the papers and call it a day – settle out of court. Believe me, it's the only way.' Which in the end is exactly what we did. The decree nisi was arranged, and the decree absolute would come through in September.

Over the following years Mickie and I discussed this meeting many times. He felt that in some way Len thought he had taken my side. But this was not the case, as Mickie's first hope was to reunite us. Once he saw that this was not a possibility, he simply tried to advise us on the most sensible way out of our problems. I know that Mickie felt bad, and would have welcomed an opportunity to talk to Len and put matters straight. But this never happened.

Next step following the meeting in the Rak officers was to tell the children. I didn't want them to hear about our impending break-up from one of their friends' parents, and Len agreed. It was June, and the two of them were running around in the garden, looking so innocent – an innocence that was about to be shattered into a thousand pieces. 'Kids, can you both come in please?' We went up to Laura's room to be in private, something she says damaged her beyond repair. Going to *her* room to be given news like this. I guess I just didn't think – I only wanted a private place away from prying ears, and Laura's room seemed perfect.

It had been decided that I would do the talking. 'Laura, Richard . . . Mummy and Daddy aren't going to be together any more. We keep arguing, and it's better for all of us that we part. You kids will stay with me. Dad will move close by, and you can see him whenever you want. We do love each other, but in a different way. *But we do love you, and always will.*'

Laura was silent, while Richard said, 'Oh, I'm so happy, Mum, I think I'm going to cry', which broke my heart. The poor little thing was so confused, hurt and upset that he just blurted out the first thing that came into his mind, as children do. One thing he was *not* was happy! This was the moment I had been trying to avoid since 1986 – the reality of divorce, telling my children and causing them irreparable hurt. I felt guilty then and I feel guilty now. It's something I will never truly come to terms with.

I continued seeing my by now fiancé, who even got me a

diamond ring – that's how serious I was. And I took him to Florida in place of Len because the family trip had already been booked and paid for. How utterly stupid of me: I just couldn't see beyond my own immediate needs. God only knows what the kids felt during those two weeks. We did sleep in separate bedrooms, though – at least I wasn't *that* stupid. I can hardly bear to think about this time without cringing. I was most definitely unhinged and not myself.

When we returned I figured it was time for Mickie and Chris to meet my intended, so we drove over to their house. As we sat in the kitchen I flashed my diamond ring to Chris, who simply said, 'Oh, aren't you a lucky girl!' Mickie came in – abrupt as hell, looked at him, looked at me and said nothing. But I knew what he was thinking. We played him a couple of tracks we'd laid down in the studio for a new album – oh, yes, we were a creative couple too and had made lots of plans. I guess I was trying to continue as if nothing had happened – 'in denial' seems an appropriate way to put it. As we drove back to my fiancé's place I was deep in thought: something was nagging me at the back of my mind.

Mickie got busy searching for new houses and sending me along to view the likely ones. After one of these property excursions, I ended up back at Rak. Mickie was sitting at his desk, so I asked him if he could drop me off later at my fiance's house, which he would pass on his way home. He just looked at me, then clearly made some kind of mental decision.

'Suzi, I want you to sit there and don't say a word. You must listen very carefully to what I have to say. I took on a responsibility when I brought you over here all those years ago. I made a promise to your parents that you would be safe, and I intend to keep that promise. Now I'm not telling you what to do – you're a grown woman. But I will say this. If you marry this man, the two of you won't be a part of our lives any more – not as a couple. I will always have time for you, Suzi – but only you. Just do me a favour. Take a step back and look at what you're doing. Think carefully. Think long and hard. . . . And now I'll drop you off.'

We drove in silence all the way there. I got out of the car, shut the door and walked inside.

That night I was plagued with nightmares and ended up in the spare room, where I managed a couple of hours of fitful sleep. When I woke up it was 6 a.m. and the sun was just rising. I sat up, feeling as if someone had thrown cold water into my face and I was now back to reality. What was I doing here? This wasn't the man for me. It was all much too soon. As sure as I had been that I wanted to marry him, I was now just as sure that I didn't. (*So, I got up, very quietly, packed my little suitcase, put my bass guitar away and loaded up my car. Ready to go, I ran smack into my intended standing at the top of the stairs. 'Where are you going?' Back to my life, back to the real world, that's what I thought. But what I said was, 'Something's the matter with the kids and I have to go straight back. I'll phone you later.' I walked out of the door and burned rubber getting away. So upset was I that I tried to do a three-point turn in the road and backed straight into a tree, doing a lot of damage to my car in the process. Get me the fuck out of here!*)

A few days later I did the decent thing and drove back to return the ring. I tried to be as gentle as possible, and simply told him the truth. I took all the blame, saying I was mixed up and had no business flinging myself into any relationship so soon after my split from Len. We talked until there was nothing more to say except goodbye.

Now I was back at home with the kids, where I belonged. Len spent most of his time out, trying to get another gig lined up – after all, ours had always been a family business and so he was now out of a job. (*Did you ever stop to think? He lost everything – his home, his wife, his kids and his job. My God, that must have been hard for him.*) We discussed the best way to handle things, and decided that he should actually move while the kids and I were in Japan, which was booked for September. That way, they would be spared the heartache of seeing him leave the family home. (*Remember walking around the house, dividing up the furniture? You weren't there – you left it all to me. Len had a pad and paper, listing all the assets, as we both wandered from room to room, deciding what should stay and what should go. I begged him to leave everything just as it was in both the kids' rooms. Len was quite methodical and I just followed him, crying my eyes out and saying yes to whatever he wanted to take. After all this time, it was Len who emerged as the strong one; I was a lost cause.*

Laura, Richard and I went to Japan as planned, and when I returned, I walked into a half-empty house – probably the saddest moment of all. It had taken me six long years to find the courage to leave, and now, Len had moved out. Once again I was alone.)

Len soon found himself a new partner, an attractive young German girl. I was glad about this because I didn't want to see him lonely and still cared a lot. He had the kids overnight sometimes while we both tried to settle into the new situation. But he was very angry and a lot of further damage was done to them whenever he spoke ill of me, which was often. I went the opposite way and continually told the kids that I loved their dad and always would, but that we just couldn't be together any more. I also invited both of them to express themselves – to scream, cry, whatever – and I would take it on the chin. Richard began to rebel at school, while Laura grew up much too quickly. I felt that all these things were my fault because I was my mother's daughter through and through, and she had always taught me that it's the woman's responsibility to hold the family together. Divorce is not an option. I had done my best, but I guess my best wasn't good enough. Both kids were emotionally damaged. It didn't help that the kids didn't feel comfortable with Len's girlfriend. In their own minds they were rejected everywhere. It's true that it's always the kids who suffer; they are the innocent victims of divorce.

My mother's cancer was growing rapidly, and the decision was made to remove the football-sized tumour which was pressing on her bowel, making every movement painful. I had already flown over to see her a couple of times, and decided to go to Texas while she was undergoing this operation – who knows if she would come out the other side? I had a gig at one of Rainer's oldie festivals that weekend and planned to fly out on the following Wednesday, returning for the following weekend's gigs, again with Rainer. I remember going up to him backstage and saying, 'Excuse me if I seem a little unfriendly, but my mother is dying. Please understand.' (*It was important that he liked you, wasn't it? Mmmmm!*)

Dad picked me up at the airport and we drove straight to the hospital. I hadn't seen Mom since April and was shocked at her deterioration: she looked like a starvation victim. Arlene was there, along with my niece Sherry, Nancy and Patti – all of us standing around Mum's bed in tears. I stood back, wanting to remove myself from the 'drama'. We followed her down the passage as they prepared to wheel her into the theatre for surgery. The trolley stopped at the door, and everyone was sobbing loudly as they said their goodbyes. I crept into a doorway, waiting and watching. Then I saw the vision meant only for me. Mom was lying there, staring up at the ceiling and lost in her own thoughts. Then I saw her hands start to shake a little as she tried to bring them towards her face. I wondered what she was doing as she slowly raised her hands to her cheeks and pinched hard on both sides, then disappeared into the operating theatre. Amazing! Mom had always been a bit vain, and by pinching her cheeks she had caused a nice natural blush to appear. I laughed out loud . . . it was the last time I saw my mother alive.

Arlene had done some assistant work in the theatre before and was allowed in to observe. After the tumour had been removed and the doctors had had a good look around they said it was like someone had taken a can of spray paint and gone to town on Mum – the cancer was all over her body. They gave her three months, and they were right almost to the day. She came out of surgery and Dad said all was fine; he got me to the airport quickly so I could fly back home in time for my gigs. I sobbed like a baby all the way home. I didn't want to see Mom like that again – I couldn't. And I had a beautiful memory to carry with me for the rest of my days.

Christmas was approaching – the first one without Len and his family, so it was going to be very difficult. But I made the usual preparations, trying to make things as normal as possible. We decorated the tree and sang carols, and I shopped and wrapped till the presents spilled out all over the front room. I wrote cards signed with Suzi, Laura and Richard, but every one was difficult. Nancy was on the phone constantly, giving me updates on our mom's health. She wasn't eating any more but just lay in bed, too weak to do anything. Dad had to carry her to the toilet. As the end got closer, the services of a hospice were brought in. All the signs were there: legs turning blue, vomiting and a terrible smell. Cancer was eating her alive. My brother Micky flew in from Detroit; Arlene, Sherry and Patti arrived from California; and me? I stayed put in England. I spoke to my mom many times, trying to explain that I just couldn't bear to see her that way; she always seemed to understand. Ever in mental conflict, I talked to my father-figure Mickie about my decision not to go to Texas again. Was I doing the right thing? Mickie always maintained that I was.

During my daily phone calls in her final days Mom said some important things to me, words that I will carry in my heart for ever. 'Take care of your children, Susan. And whatever Len has done, forgive him – he's a good man. And take care of yourself. Don't go out with any jerks. Behave. And go to church. Don't forget to follow the ten commandments. Stay close to each other, protect each other, and don't ever forget your brother – he is so lost.' And over and over again, like a broken record, 'All that matters is love.' Did she know something the rest of us didn't?

Nancy called me in tears a couple of days before Mom passed. 'It's getting close, Susie, really close. I don't know if I can cope. Do you want me to put the phone to Mom's ear? Is there anything else you need to say?'

'Mom,' I told her, 'I love you. Please forgive me for not being there. Please. I love you I love you I love you.'

Then the phone dropped to the floor. 'Oh, my God, Susie,' Nancy yelled into the phone. 'Did you hear what she just said? "Have a nice life, Susan".'

One day later she was gone. It was five days before Christmas, I was divorced, and my mother was dead.

(*It was 10a.m. and I was sitting in the office when I got the call. It was my brother Mickey. He simply said, 'Susie, the great white spirit has come.' I dropped the phone, went into the front room, sat on the floor in the corner and rocked back and forth for an hour, sobbing like a baby and saying over and over again, 'I want my mama . . . I want my mama. I want my mama.' The kids came in, gave me a hug and left me alone with my grief.*

Hey, Mom, I know you're watching me every step of the way even as I write these words. Can you blame me for not being there? I lived so far away, didn't see you enough anyway, and to have that as my last memory – no. Better my way, I think. I say 'think' because I will never be sure if I did the right thing. A big part of me wishes I'd had the courage to see you again, even under those conditions. I hope you really did understand my reasons. It seems I can't say this enough, Mom: I love you.)

I spoke by phone to Len's parents and to Len himself, and they all offered their condolences. I also had a brief moment to speak privately to Len's mum. 'Why didn't you tell us you were unhappy, Susan? We would have understood. We've always treated you like a daughter – why didn't you come to us?'

'I'm sorry, I just didn't know what to do. And I'm sorry for any pain I've caused. Please forgive me. But I had to move on. I love you both very much, and I will always love your son –

only the way I love him has changed. I hope you will allow me to come and visit you soon, once the dust has settled.'

Thank God for that call, because ten days after my mother passed on Len's mum died too. It was completely unexpected. I wasn't invited to the funeral, but I grieved in my heart.

As I was writing these words, on 20 December 2006, the strangest thing was happening. I couldn't seem to get my timeline together. When did my mother die? I looked at videos and dates, climbed up and down two sets of stairs over and over again trying to make sense of it, had a pounding head-ache all day but just couldn't get anything together. Finally I gave up, switched off my computer and went downstairs to watch TV with my five-year-old granddaughter, Amy Susan, who turned to me and said, 'Grandma, are you thinking about your mummy? Are you missing her?' Then I realized that this was the anniversary of her death. I went to the office to look for the piece that Nancy had written about her passing and lived it all over again, feeling as lost as I had on the morning the news hit me. I cried as I looked at her picture on the wall, and then she spoke to me: 'My Susan, you have a new life in the next room. Take good care of your granddaughter. You have another chance to get it right.' So don't tell me there's not an afterlife. Don't tell me that our loved ones aren't looking on, helping us through. I won't believe you!

14

'48 CRASH' – SECOND TIME AROUND

....

The first thing I did after all the traumas of 1992 was go kinda crazy, dating like a teenage lunatic. After all, apart from my recent short-lived engagement I had been in a monogamous relationship for twenty years and now I wanted to have me some fun. I was a little out of practice and I made a few mistakes, but none of them fatal. Busy doing gigs in Germany, Scandinavia and the UK, and enjoying my new love life, I thought I was happy at last. What I didn't realize was that these 'relationships' (and I use the term lightly) were empty: there was no substance, no love, no depth. (*You were looking for Len's replacement, which didn't exist. Nobody could take his place. You needed to move on and meet someone new, different, with no baggage. You needed to meet someone who didn't need you. Think about it.*)

In the band, I had made a couple of changes. I added a saxophonist/guitarist, something I'd always wanted to do, and the lovely Dee on backing vocals. So for a while the line-up was Robby (guitar), Clive (sax/guitar), Andy Dowding (a recent addition and my third drummer since 1973), me (bass), Rhiannon and Dee (BVs) and Reggie Webb (piano). I found solace in the music, and it kept me from dwelling on the past too much.

In March we toured Australia again, and this time I invited my dad to join us. Nancy had told me that after Mom's death he couldn't get his act together. He wasn't doing gigs any more but was just sitting around, unshaved, in his bathrobe from morning till night. The kids and nanny came too, so it was a real family tour. Before my dates began we were able to attend an Elton John concert in Sydney. Laura, Richard and Dad were seated in the front row. But Dad unfortunately had jetlag and fell fast asleep, snoring loudly through one of Elton's softest songs. Sorry, Elton!

On the road, however, Dad really perked up, sitting up front with our tour publicist, Diana Bailey. Actually he fancied her like mad and kept telling me, 'Susie, if you need someone to look after you, this is the girl. She is organized and professional and a pleasure to be around.' Quite right – in fact she's one of my best friends. He also, surprisingly, fell in love with Dee. I say 'surprisingly' because Dee is black and this was a first for Dad. He had nothing but praise for her, describing her as a real asset and totally professional.

At one venue I remember leading Dad through the kitchen to the dressing rooms, and apologising for the journey. No problem. 'Susie, I have been doing gigs my entire life. Is there any other way to get backstage but through the kitchen?' This was his chance to see what I did for a living, warts and all. One night we were in a steaming hot, sweat-off-the-walls rock club, screaming fans crowding the stage, and Andy started the drumbeat for 'Can the Can'. The place erupted with cheers. Then I spotted my dad standing at the side of the stage, watching the pandemonium in amazement. I called him up and the crowd loved it. Dad simply put out his hands and said, 'Stop.' Andy did. Then 'Unaccustomed as I am to public speaking . . . thank you . . . okay, Susie . . . off you go.' The drums started up again, Dad left the stage and we finished the show. That night when he returned to the hotel, Dad decided he needed to gig. He simply walked over to the pianist, asked him if he would leave and took over. He did this every night at every hotel, and expressed great surprise that his gig sheet wasn't full by the time the tour was up. I think he actually managed to stop grieving for Mom, at least for those few weeks.

I had another odd experience on this tour. Harley Metcalf had been my promoter for several tours. We had known each other since the eighties and he had witnessed my kids growing up and the final throes of my marriage. Both he and his wife Maria I counted, and still do, as friends. One night after the show, around midnight, there was a knock on my bedroom door. Luckily I was still awake, sipping from my bottle of relaxing red wine. It was Harley and Maria, who insisted on coming in. We talked about this and that, and then suddenly Maria changed and her voice and face looked completely different.

'Suzi, what are you doing with your life? This is not the way you were taught to live. You are looking for love in all the wrong places.'

'Okay, okay, I hear you. Who do you think you are? My mother?'

At which point Maria started to sob. 'Yes, I am.'

Spell over, message received loud and clear. None of us could quite believe what had just happened. (*Yes, Mom got through, didn't she? I knew all this, but you were selfish. You wanted fun fun fun, but what you got was shit shit shit. You weren't happy, the kids weren't happy, and it was time to come back home.)*

Shortly after this incident I found myself in Diana's room. We were talking about my mom's death, which I was describing it in tearful detail, when Diana pulled out her runes. These are ancient symbols, on domino-type pieces. You put them in a bag, think about a question and pull one out. Diana had a book which explained their meanings, and she told me they were amazingly accurate. I was game because I loved this kind of stuff. Of course my question was about Mom and where she was, and if there really was an afterlife. I pulled out a blank rune, which meant 'Don't ask the unknowable.' So I did it again, rephrasing the question this time. Again a blank rune. I had a third go, and once more I pulled out a blank rune. Okay, I give up. Guess I'm not going to get any answers to that question. Diana gave me the runes, saying she had had them for some while and it was time to pass them on. They helped me through the next ten years of my life until I gave them to my old Detroit friend Marylou after her sister Nan died. And needless to say, when I returned from Australia I changed a lot of things in my life.

From March till June I hibernated. I went out socially a few times, but mostly I sat alone in my bedroom, only leaving it for gigs and the children. I sat on the floor in the lotus position, candles lit, spiritual music playing, contemplating my navel. I had to find out who I was now that I wasn't a wife any more, and my mother and ex-mother-in-law were gone. I was in the middle of a turbulent ocean in a rowing boat without a paddle. I spent hours thinking about the choices I had made, the men I had met, my children, Len, Mom, Len's mum – everything really. Tears flowed freely, and when I finally emerged I was ready to meet someone . . . because I didn't *need* anyone. I had bonded with myself. (*Bonded, yes, but we were still two different people.*) Yes, that's true, Susie, and the best part was that I rediscovered my enthusiasm for rock and roll. It felt like I'd come back home – to myself and to my art!

Taking Dad's advice, I asked our Australian tour publicist Diana to come to England with the idea of working together. I'd never had a manager before and we gave it a shot, but the timing was wrong.

While she was there, I made my first tentative steps towards Rainer Haas. (*Actually, he had already made a few tentative steps towards you. Remember that box set he gave you – Crosby, Stills and Nash? And remember all those bottles of red wine? Oh, yes, he was making moves way before you!*) Oh, shut up, Susie. I am in control at all times! (*except when you're not!*)

The first time we actually spoke properly was on a gig. My band had been complaining about the lack of catering: we travelled all day sometimes, and needed something warm to fill our bellies. Often we went straight to the venue. So, I asked Rainer to my room to discuss what could be done. I made him a cup of tea, and he promised to fix things.

The next encounter was on a bus journey. We ended up sitting side by side at the front and for the first time we *talked*. To be fair, neither of us liked each other. Rainer found me egotistical and unfriendly, while I thought he was arrogant and flash. The first thing I discussed with him was a raise. After all, Len had negotiated my fee and this was a whole new ballgame. I wanted a fresh start and new conditions, and told him so. Then I told him in detail; about my marriage break-up he reciprocated with news of his love life, having spent the last ten years with a married woman (albeit separated). I told him that if I were to find a permanent man I would want to be seriously wined and dined this time around, and that with me good conversation was the only way forward. He looked at me, taking it all in, and replied, 'You have a perfect bum.' I just stared at him, not knowing how to take that comment. He said nothing more, and just looked out of the window.

We began again. 'I'm going to New York soon to do some recording with Mike Chapman.'

'Oh, I'll come with you. . . . I mean I have some business there anyway.'

Right, okay, I thought. The journey ended.

When we returned to England I sent him a fax – unbelievable that I did this on the strength of that short conversation. I could have ended up looking like the biggest fool, but onward I went, blinded by the possiblities. Sheer instinct led the way.

8 June 1993

Just a quick note to confirm what we discussed in Germany last weekend. To start immediately, any time we travel with less than eight people the extra money is to go to me.

On a more personal note, it was great having the chance to talk privately with you. I think you are a lovely man and there is so much more to you than meets the eye. You're like me and keep a lot hidden. Hope we can get to know each other even better in the future, maybe over a vintage bottle of good red wine. It always loosens the tongue.

Lots of love, Suzi

Rainer now has this framed, along with several photos, on his wall in Hamburg. (*By sending that fax you fell right into his hands – or should I say arms. And although you might not want to hear it, Miss Suzi Quatro, he's just a little bit smarter than you!*) We'll see about *that*.

I went off to New York alone and did a single with Mike called 'Fear of the Unknown' (Mike Chapman/Holly Knight), coupled with my own composition 'And So to Bed', which would be released, on Polydor, in only a few European countries. A photo session was set up in Hamburg, so I called Rainer and told him I would be there. He asked me to dinner with a couple of his friends and picked me up in a Rolls-Royce. Good start! But it was an unusual evening from the start. Conversation was slow, due to me not speaking a word of German. Still don't – put it down to the laziness of English-speaking people. Halfway through dinner I rested my hand on the table and Rainer placed his hand on mine. Oh, my God, what do I do now? I left it there, but wondered exactly what he was expecting of me. Rainer now says, 'Well, you didn't take your hand away, which told me everything I needed to know.' I was a little nervous, though, and when he dropped me off I quickly brushed his cheek with a peck and jumped out of the car like a virgin!

Things were moving along nicely – thrust and parry. The next encounter was in a bar after one of his shows. It was getting late. Rainer was sitting on his own, and I went over and joined him He said he was coming over to London soon to take me out for dinner. 'Fine', I said, then 'I'd better get to bed. It's late.' He grabbed my hand again, saying, 'And what if I don't let you go!' Sexy! I was intrigued by this guy and his style.

We spent the next couple of gigs walking together, holding hands and talking. But we made sure we were away from prying eyes: neither of us was prepared to share our situation with anyone else yet. The outcome was still in the lap of the gods. It was in a town in eastern Germany that we got one step closer. We had left the hotel and gone alone to a restaurant for lunch when I made my move. (*You are so goddam impatient, Suzi – couldn't wait for him to make a move. Off you went in your bull in-a-china-shop manner.*) 'Kiss me,' I blurted out. 'Now!' Rainer looked nervously around to make sure that there were no musicians spying on us, and obliged. It wasn't a very good effort, though, and I wondered if I had made a mistake. After we had eaten we went for a walk along the river and found a beautiful spot with a park bench. He took me in his arms and kissed me properly. I sank into the warmth, breathing heavily and enjoying every moment. That's more like it!

One week later in London, we had our first proper dinner together. I had hired a driver for the evening, and dressed carefully. (*Actually, I, not you, dressed carefully – in a blue mini-dress and high heels, with some tasteful jewellery. Very unlike you, Suzi.*) I arrived at the Dorchester, where he was staying, and called his room. He came straight down, dressed impeccably in a smart suit with a tie and marvellous shoes (I have a thing about men's shoes. If they are wrong, the guy is wrong). Problem was, he didn't have any socks on, which immediately made me suspicious about his expectations. He asked me if I'd like to go to his room for a glass of champagne. Okay, let's see what this guy is really all about, I thought and followed him into the lift, standing as far away as I could. When we arrived I noticed the 'Do Not Disturb' sign on the door – not good. We went inside and, to my horror, the bed was turned down: now I really was worried. I sat primly on the chair and sipped my champagne, anxious as hell to get out of there. This was all happening much too fast for me. As we left, the usual horde of photographers were waiting outside and tried to grab a picture of us, so we ducked quickly into a cab. We went to a three-star restaurant, La Tante Claire, where he ordered the finest wine, a 1945 Château Lafite Rothschild, and the bill came to £850. I was impressed. Over dinner he asked me, 'Would you be prepared to get married again?'

'Yes,' I replied. 'To the right guy.'

'And would you be prepared to have another baby?'

'Oh, yes. I always wanted more.'

We returned to the hotel, where I jumped into my waiting car and went home.

A couple of weeks later he was over in England again, back at the Dorchester. This time I was not so nervous. I was in his room, looking out of the window, when he came up behind and put his arms around me. This was the moment, and it felt so right. As is my way, I made a joke: 'Okay, if you want to sleep with me, sir, you must pay me first.' And as luck would have it, Rainer had my money for the next two gigs all ready in an envelope which he threw on to the bed. Great – Let's go! Every life should have a 'marathon', and this was ours. We made love for six hours non-stop, broke off to attend the opening of *Grease*, came back and continued. If this had been an Olympic event we'd have won the gold for sure. We were now 'together'. It was official.

Next step was to introduce him to Mickie and Chris to get their approval, which always was and still is so important to me. A dinner party was arranged at their home in Totteridge. Mickie and Rainer were like two male lions circling each other: both smart, both arrogant, both intelligent, both stubborn as hell – and both seeing me as 'theirs'. Rainer made quite a few trips out of the room that night due to the amount of liquid going down his throat, which prompted Mickie to say to me, 'Suzi, I think he must be on drugs. Count the number of times he goes to the toilet.' Couldn't have been further from the truth. Chris caught my eye and gestured for me to follow her into the kitchen.

'Why didn't you tell us he was so good-looking, Suzi?'

'Is he?' I slipped back and peeked into the dining room. 'God, Chris, he is! Well, that's lucky, isn't it?' I had fallen for who Rainer was as a person, not what he looked like.

When I spoke to Mickie a few days later he said, 'Don't mess around with this guy. If you make him angry, he won't go down to the pub like Lennie and have a beer. He's a killer.' (*Mickie, you and Rainer could have been great friends had you met earlier in life. Even Chris commented that she never saw you take so much to another man.*)

I'd mentioned to Rainer that I'd always wanted to go to Egypt, having had a love affair with the place from afar since I was a child. It was a coincidence that he too, had always wanted to go. Just like that, a trip was booked. I had already told Mickie that this relationship was serious, but when he heard about this trip he insisted, 'You make sure he books single rooms. Just because he takes you to Egypt he doesn't sleep with Suzi Quatro.' Ever the father figure! (*Hey, Mick, confession time – we didn't book singles!*) Rainer stayed overnight at my house for the first time before we left from Heathrow on this most anticipated journey. We were in my office when the phone rang. It was Dee's mother, and the news wasn't good.

Dee was a great girl, full of ambition backed by tons of talent. She was going places, which is why she had decided to leave my band after the Australia tour in March 1993 and join a new girl group, Divas. I was sorry to lose her, but wished her well. Apparently she had been driving back from a gig late at night when she fell asleep at the wheel. She hit a convoy of army vehicles, which knocked out the locking system on the doors. The car caught fire. The soldiers immediately tried to free the occupants but the fumes overtook Dee and she died. To make it worse, she and her Finnish husband Matti were expecting their first child.

After hearing this news I was in a sombre mood at the start of our trip to Egypt. Nevertheless, it was still a dream come true. I believe in reincarnation, and have so many memories buried inside of me. As we got close to landing I was invited up to sit with the pilots, and gazed out of the cockpit window at the Nile as we did a steep left towards the runway. All of a sudden tears began to run down my face, and I heard myself saying, 'I told you I'd be back.'

Rainer had done everything first-class, which is always his way, and we had an absolutely beautiful hotel suite. First day, we were off to the pyramids. I couldn't believe I was finally standing in front of these beautiful monuments to the ancient Egyptian civilization. While we were walking around an Egyptian guy came up and asked if we would like to see a special pyramid that was closed to the public. I followed him immediately, but Rainer stayed groundside. Bent nearly double, we made our way along a low tunnel, going deeper and deeper, with only a candle to light the way. Finally we entered a tomb containing an empty sarcophagus and I felt as if I somehow belonged there. I climbed down into the hole and let the feeling wash over me. Luckily I had my camera with me, which had a flash, so I have a photograph of this moment.

There was another pyramid I was particularly drawn to. I asked the guide to get behind me with the camera and not to ask any questions, but simply to take the photo when I said so. I walked away from him and Rainer; then, facing the pyramid, with both men behind me, I stretched out my arms towards the sun, looked up to the sky and shouted, 'Now!' A feeling like an electric current was passing through my body, as if I was somehow being reconnected to my true source.

As I walked back towards them, Rainer came to meet me halfway and, quite out of character, grabbed me possessively. He asked the guide to get ready to take another picture, then kissed me deep, long and hard, as if reclaiming me as his own from another time. When we got the photos developed I was surprised to see that in the 'kiss' photo Rainer looked completely different. And the photo of me in front of that special pyramid is mind-blowing: you can almost see some kind of light going through my body. I had it blown up and framed alongside this poem I wrote on my return – my return to 'this' life anyway.

> The bell tolls for no one.
> An empty vessel.
> One woman on her knees,
> Grief pouring from her wounds.
> Yes, she will die for them all
> And leave her power behind.
> Yes, they will descend.

Vultures,
Feeding over scraps of wisdom
That stains the soil
As her blood flows
Into every crack and crevice.
It will permeate centuries to come.
This wisdom will be gorged upon
And then thrown,
Back into divinity, where it belongs.
And the first pyramid will beckon
As an empty vessel,
One woman stands tall,
Arms out to the sun
Claiming her power,
The power is one.

Rainer too had had strong feelings of déjà vu which, although he was a sceptic, he couldn't deny. He found himself purchasing a big painting that he particularly liked – by coincidence, a wedding picture. He then had our names printed on it in Egyptian hieroglyphics, and it hangs on our bedroom wall in England to this day. (*That kiss and that picture – I don't think he was taking any chances with destiny this time, do you? You know, Suzi, you may have been enjoying the ride, but I was looking for commitment. I wanted to be sure Rainer was in love before I said the L-word myself. I was sure he'd fallen, and I can remember the exact moment that I surrendered. We were sitting at a restaurant having dinner. Rainer cracked a joke – not just any joke, but a clever one, and in English, not his first language, which amazed me. His talents are hidden much of the time. He is truly understated in every sense of the*

*word, and you can easily underestimate him – which is what
makes him so damned attractive. I looked at him in aston-
ishment that he could tell, and understand, this kind of joke.
He stared back at me . . . and slowly winked. I fell hook, line
and sinker. It was like going off the edge of a cliff.)*

Our next trip together was to the island of Sylt, off the
coast of northern Germany, and we flew over in a private
plane piloted by a friend of Rainer's. It was a quiet time, full
of private moments and love-making. After one particularly
nice session I turned to Rainer and blurted out, 'Marry me.'
He immediately said, 'Yes, I do.' We were both in shock for a
while: I couldn't believe I'd asked, he couldn't believe he'd
agreed. It would be three months from the first kiss to the
marriage. Rainer was a forty-eight-year-old bachelor and I
was about to clip his wings. Oh, yes, '48 Crash' – you belong
to me!

A couple of weekends later I took Laura, now nine, and
seven-year-old Richard to one of my Rainer gigs in Germany.
They loved seeing Mum work, and I figured it was about time
they met my intended. My kids are very warm, and hugged
him immediately. Soon enough they were in our hotel bedroom and wrestling with Rainer on the bed. Although Rainer,
with no kids of his own, would take a while to adjust to his
new 'instant' family, it was a good start. He has told me many
times since how touched he was by their affection at that first
meeting. They met up a couple times more before the wedding, and I hoped they would build a good relationship
together. Only time would tell.

A couple of weeks before the wedding, Rainer and I were
on a trip to south Germany when we received a call telling us
that there was a huge article in one of the daily newspapers

about an alleged affair between me and Gary Glitter. What! You must be joking!

A few months earlier I had gone to a meeting with Gary and his manager, Jeff Hallin, at their London office to discuss being a special guest on his annual, very successful, Christmas tour. I had agreed all the basics – the fee, the dates, the promotion – and finally sandwiches and tea were brought in. We all sat and ate, and for no reason I started to feel uncomfortable. To break the mood I remarked to Gary, 'You've got food on your mouth', to which he surprisingly replied, 'Lick it off.' I was shocked into silence, which is unusual for me – I've always been a quick retort type of girl. Nobody said anything for a few minutes. Then I said, 'Well, I'd better be going home. The kids are waiting,' and flew out of the office. I relayed the entire thing by mobile to Rainer as soon as I got out of earshot. I have since told many hardcore rock 'n' rollers this story, and not one of them has ever laughed.

So back to that article. There I was, sitting with the man I was about to marry, and splashed all over the British press was an allegation that was completely untrue. Back home, I phoned my lawyer in fury and said I intended to sue. I also cancelled the tour: no way was I going to be on stage with the audience thinking I was only there so that Gary and I could be together. In the end I agreed not to sue but demanded a full retraction, which they gave me: a very nice double-page spread all about my life with Rainer. A year or so later, after many heartfelt apologies from all concerned, I agreed to do the Christmas tour. But I never trusted Gary again, and in the light of what happened in his life I was right.

The wedding date was set for 22 October 1993 in America.

First we went to Thierry Mugler, where Rainer ordered a wonderful black pants suit for me with see-through lace up the side of the legs. Then tickets on Concorde were booked to New York, with two days in Las Vegas (the Joan Collins Special – don't ask!), back to New York and then Concorde home again. Talk about doing things in style! I guess when I told Rainer that I wanted to be seriously wined and dined this time around he believed me. My best friend Berwick and Rainer's best friend Jürgen would accompany us. I flew the kids to Texas, where they would spend a couple of days with their cousins and then accompany my dad to Las Vegas for the ceremony. Arlene came too, with hubby number six and our good friends Marilyn and Charles. I have a wonderful video of a nervous Rainer in the 'Chapel of Love' looking like he's going to a hanging! But soon enough we were married. And here's the best part: on the way home from New York I was invited to sit up in the cockpit for take-off, which on Concorde is something you don't forget.

We didn't have a honeymoon. I was booked on a tour in Japan and Rainer had business in Germany, not to mention taking care of his mother who wasn't mobile any more. I had come from a 24/7 relationship with Len to one in which my new husband and I lived in separate countries. We never discussed 'after' the wedding. I have always said we got married without even knowing each other because it simply felt right, and I guess we both trusted that feeling.

(*We couldn't have been more different. I was one of five, Rainer was an only child. I had to scream to be noticed, Rainer only had to breathe. I felt like the dark horse, Rainer felt like a king. In fact, Rainer was not my 'type' and I guess I wasn't his either. I always went for big-built, tough-looking macho men. Rainer was 'beautiful' and soft-spoken. And the biggest challenge was that he didn't need me! Rainer had always gone for tall, sexy, long-legged blondes, not cute little girl types – great ass or not! and deep inside, I felt I was taking a huge gamble. Maybe I didn't even deserve him. Childhood insecurities came home to roost.)*

Okay, what you say is true. But on the flip side Rainer and Suzi Quatro have a lot in common. We are both intelligent, driven by success, highly opinionated and have the same sense of humour. He tells me that in German he is just as funny (I'll take your word for it, Rainer). And we are both stubborn as hell! (*I remember him saying that he didn't mind being equal at all, as long as he had fifty-one per cent.*)

So our married life began, with Rainer in Germany and me in Essex, flying back and forth to see each other for a couple of days each week. Not the ideal situation, but that's the way it was. Richard began introducing Rainer as his 'new dad' and developed total respect for him; Rainer in turn discovered a real soft spot for his new stepson. Laura's relationship with Rainer was a little more difficult, mainly because he saw me in constant tears over her rebelliousness and it made him angry. And it must be said that only children, as Rainer was, are loners by definition. They think the worlds starts and ends with them and they never have to learn how to share. I, of course, with my own family background was just the opposite. Still, it was all these similarities and differences that made the marriage interesting. After a few years I got used to not seeing him all the time, turned myself around and began to appreciate the benefits of the situation. Rainer is now the one who complains that we don't spend enough time together, and I just love having my own space.

We took our first family holiday together to Majorca when Laura was twelve and Richard ten. This was Laura's time to be *really* angry. We were walking along by the pool one day when she let rip, accusing me of ruining her life by deserting Dad, Richard and her for my new husband. It was a nasty verbal attack and I was shocked because I had never heard her talk like this before. I went back to my bedroom in tears.

In hindsight, some of this reaction was inevitable. She had seemed to cope with it all but of course she hadn't, and it had to come out eventually. And to be fair, I *was* spending a lot of time away from the kids, on gigs and seeing Rainer. Neither of us wanted to move to a foreign country. I was adamant that I would not uproot the children from their home – the divorce had been traumatic enough. And Rainer could not leave his elderly mother. So we did the best we could. If I had it to do again, I would have paid more attention to what was going on in my kids' lives and dealt with it then and there.

(*Mom, I wish I'd handled things better – this is not how you raised me. But in my defence I'm a career girl and you were a full-time mother. It was impossible to wear so many different hats – rock star, wife, mother and substitute father. The two people I didn't want to suffer in any way were the children – and they are the ones who did. But while I take the blame for my part in all of this, it would have helped if Len had played an active role. Many times I begged him to help, telling him Laura was out of control and Richard needed a father, but to no avail. They both grew up without him.*)

The next couple of years were full of European festivals and oldie nights in Germany. (*Slowly but surely you edged your way to the top of those shows, didn't you? Your ego demanded it.*) Bandwise, there were a few changes. I no longer travelled with girl backing singers but went back to my roots – it was now just Suzi and the boys. And in 1994 Ray Beavis, ex-Graham Parker and the Rumours, ex-Shakin' Stevens, joined on saxophone. He is with me to this day and a valuable asset on anyone's stage. What you see is what you get – except if he doesn't get fed!

I played about with various stage outfits, sometimes wearing the jumpsuit, or else cut-off Levi's with fishnet stockings and a leopardskin jacket, or a black leotard with a leather jacket – even a leather mini-skirt made an appearance. We did Australia yet again, and on most of the interviews I talked about how happy I was: 'I am married to a lovely German man, who totally spoils me.' The kids were with me as I announced that Rainer and I were trying for a baby. (*I really wanted to offer him this gift of a child – took fertility drugs which messed with my hormones, got pregnant but lost it. I wanted to continue trying but Rainer said, 'That's it. We stop now. I don't want to play with your health. But thank you for trying, Susie. I don't know any other woman who would have done this for me, and I appreciate it.'*)

In 1995 we brought out a new album, *Latest and Greatest*, on CMC, which we recorded at PUK studios. It was a mixture of re-recorded hits and new stuff. We went from a tour into the studio, flew out for two weekend gigs, then went straight back for another week, and finally on to Rainer's annual Christmas tour around Germany – it was a busy, busy time.

Reg Webb left after this session; John Meany joined me on piano and stayed for several years. And around this time I decided to add a horn section, trumpet and trombone to my line-up – again, something I had always wanted since living in Detroit.

As the years rolled by the gigs continued and Rainer and I visited each other, usually for three days a week, either on the road or in Hamburg or Essex. We also began to take holidays in Miami together. We argued cat and dog sometimes, but always ended up laughing. Richard and Laura began to adjust. We remained 'in love'. (*Oh yes he treated you good – three-star restaurants, diamonds, holidays, the works. And even though money was never a motivation it was nice to be spoiled for a change. Give me a moment here – I want to speak about all things Rainer.*

Open letter to Rainer from little Susie from Detroit. (Yes, you'd better write this letter because it's you that Rainer says he fell in love with, not me.)

Dear Rainer,

It's been one helluva ride, hasn't it? As in all good relationships, we have taught each other many lessons. What you did for me was to hold up a mirror, reflecting the good and the bad. You allowed me to be a woman, putting me in the proper frame. I blossomed under your influence. I'll never forget that one conversation we had, lying in bed in Hamburg. I told you, 'I love the little boy I go to sleep with.' We got talking about Suzi Quatro and you weren't being very kind. 'Please, Rainer, don't ever insult my career. It's all I have,' I said. 'Susie, that's the least of what you have,' you responded. 'We are so connected, at a deep level, that sometimes I don't know where my hand ends and yours begins.'

I am so glad we found each other. I am so glad we followed our instincts. I am so glad I was able to jump over my shadow and take a chance on a good-looking, self-sufficient charmer. I am so glad I allowed myself to fall in love. I didn't see you

coming. You tiptoed in, then hit me over the head with a
hammer.

I love you, baby, xxx)

I have frequently invited Rainer to accompany me to Australia, but he has always refused. Too far away, he said. I also dearly wanted him to see Japan at least once. The opportunity finally came in 1997 when I was booked to appear on a TV show there – one of those bizarre Japanese talent show affairs with loads of impersonators. Two of the actual stars would appear afterwards as a surprise, but their identities would be kept secret until the night. For years I had waxed lyrical about this magical Far Eastern land. Now I was able to show Rainer the Ginza, the main shopping area, and in return he led me, by smell alone, to the red-light district – he was a Hamburg boy, after all!

The other surprise artist on the show was Ben E. King. Now, you haven't lived until you've seen a Japanese man, blacked up, singing 'Stand by Me' – absolutely hilarious. My imitator at least tried to look like me, dressed in a black leather jumpsuit and toting a bass guitar. She was awful. I appeared as she was finishing, much to the audience's delight. Problem was, this was live, and I had forgotten to ask for a bass guitar with both strap and strap locks. The latter are essential for me as I always throw my guitar around – without locks the strap comes off and the bass crashes to the floor, which is exactly what happened. A crew member had to get down on all fours and prop it up until the end of the song – somewhat humiliating. The good thing was that on the way home Rainer said to me, 'That was the best trip I've ever had.' I'll take that as a thank you.

One way or another, mine had always been a family act. In 1997 I got the chance to do the first of two duets with my daughter Laura. We were asked to contribute to the charity fund-raiser *Children in Need* on television, and performed my song 'And So to Bed'.

Fast forward to 1999, one of my busiest years to date and one with a big surprise in it for me. We did fifty-six dates at home, breaking off in the middle for four weeks in Australia, then coming back and doing the second half. The promoter had been after me for years to agree to this British package show tour. I finally said yes because I had spent so many years playing only Europe and Australia that I wanted the UK to see that I was indeed still rockin' and rollin'. I said I would do it just once, and have stuck to that decision. I have never really liked package shows, even when, as in this case, I was headlining. I prefer to do my own thing.

And the surprise? I was the subject of a *This Is Your Life* programme. We were playing the Palladium that night. And before you ask the question, I had no idea whatsoever. If you find out and the TV people get wind of it, your show is cancelled as the surprise element is everything. Anyway, because it was London the tour promoters had asked me to do an encore that night with Alvin Stardust and the Rubettes. I didn't really want to, but agreed, and we worked out an arrangement for 'Sweet Little Rock 'n Roller'. Rainer had been told by my former agent Derek Franks that this show would be taking place, but didn't believe him. How could they possibly do this when I had a gig at the Palladium? Then at halftime, just before my set which would close the programme, Rainer noticed TV cameras being set up and realized it was indeed happening. He went straight to the bar to order two large gin and tonics. It's only when I look back that I realize how nervous he was when he came into my dressing room just before the show. The tour promoter came in too and said, 'Suzi, the news people are here and will film a small segment at the end for tomorrow's broadcast. So after the encore, when you're taking your bows, please aim it stage right, into the box seat section, and then they'll get a good shot of you.' Sounded fine to me.

The show went well, and the boys joined me for the finale. When it ended Alan Williams (the Rubettes' lead singer) and Alvin grabbed my hands and held me tight, which annoyed me. I was trying to take my bow – what were they doing? Suddenly the entire audience rose to their feet. I broke away and went to the front of the stage, ego in full flight, bowing like a ballerina and thinking how wonderful I'd been that night. I had no idea that the real reason for the standing ovation was that presenter Michael Aspel had appeared from behind with the famous red book. When I eventually saw him I went weak at the knees and shouted into the microphone, 'What the fuck are you doing here?' Charming.

As they whisked me off to the studio I was in a daze. Rainer asked, 'Do you know what an honour this is?' Oh, yes, I did. I also wondered who would appear that evening to pay tribute. At 12:30a.m. the show began to tape. The on-stage seats were taken up with friends and various band members, and then the guest roll call began. There was Rainer, with Laura and Richard, my three sisters, my dad, my childhood friend Linda Theuerkorn, Berwick Kaler, Michael Brandon, Nicky Chinn (Chinn/Chapman), Mickie Most, Noddy Holder (Slade), Reg Presley (Troggs), Andy Scott and Mick Tucker (Sweet), Les Grey (Mud), Roy Wood (Wizzard), Chrissie Hynde (The

Pretenders) and finally Nan Ball and Diana Baker from the original Pleasure Seekers. It was a wonderful moment in a long career, and something I will never forget. Afterwards we partied till dawn. Laura had been after Noddy Holder all night to do his famous 'It's Xmas' and he finally performed it right into her ear at 5a.m., standing outside the BBC Television Centre while we were waiting for our cars home. A fitting end to an unforgettable evening.

15
ADDING TO LIFE'S EXPERIENCES

....

The first half of our British tour was over and now we were off to Aussie, where I had a most unusual experience. As usual there were gigs virtually every day – usually six on and one off, which was sometimes a travel day. These trips are exhausting, to say the least. I was asked to do a TV interview with a very popular DJ called John Laws who is known as the Voice of Australia. I didn't want to go, preferring to stay in my room and rest – but it's all part of the game and promotion is always necessary. So I washed my hair, applied the minimum of make-up, dressed in a leather suit, put on my gold Rolex, two diamond rings and earrings (all gifts from Rainer), got in the limo and drove to the studio, where they ushered me into the green room to await my turn. There on the wall was a painting of a distinguished-looking older man with steel in his eyes. I couldn't stop staring at it because I felt I knew this guy – déjà vu for sure. Growing a little bored, I walked outside and wandered around until I found myself standing in front of a huge glass wall. Inside sat 'that man', talking on the telephone. We looked at each other and waved as if we

were old friends. Five minutes later I was being inter-
viewed: 'that man' was John Laws.

The interview is quite amazing to watch. My voice was not
my own, nor were my actions. I was coy, shy, sweet and
giggly. John, who is known as a hard-hitting interviewer,
mixed up his words and stumbled over his questions like a
schoolboy. We talked face to face, as if there was no one else
in the room. On my way back to the hotel afterwards I
wondered what the hell all that had been about. The next day
I put pen to paper and wrote him a song. It's crazy – I'd only
just met this guy and knew nothing about him, so how could I
possibly know what to write about. But I did. Here's the song.

Dancing in the Wind

In this bright society you fly,
You can't face the day, but you don't know why
Down again from an ego, high and mighty
Where illusion plays in between the lies
And I can see the pain in your champagne eyes
It's so damn sad, I just can't help but sympathise
Oh oh oh, ain't life funny

As the critics bite and the cameras flash
The wolves are hungry for you to crash
Picking on every single word you say
They try to put you down, you're still talking free
You won't show your vulnerability
To the paparazzi, circling the prey
Oh oh oh, ain't life funny
How a little too much of truth gets you down

And it's so damn lonely, in a world so phoney
Where the cheaters never know they've sinned
Will your wings keep flying, through the lost horizon
Has your spirit gone dancing in the wind

Ivy suit and tie in a gold disguise
The lion roars as the jungle cries
Fools you've suffered, damn them all to hell
As the game's exposed they can feel your sting.
As the weakest falls to the power king
They just don't understand, they've shown you everything
Oh oh oh, ain't life funny
How reality creeps in without a sound

And it's so damn lonely in a world so phoney
Where the cheaters never know they've sinned
Will your wings keep flying, through the lost horizon
Has your spirit gone dancing in the wind
Yes it's so damn lonely, in a world so empty
Do our chances end where they begin
Come on, share my wings, keep on flying
Into a new horizon
Two spirits go dancing in the wind

(Suzi Quatro, 1999)

Once it was finished I faxed the lyrics over to his office and he called to tell me how much he liked it. The strangest part is that a few months later John *did* get in trouble: he was charged with contravening the Jury Act, and convicted. Every word in this song came true! To this day John has remained one of my strongest supporters, playing old songs as well as music from my current album, *Back to the Drive*. We meet up for radio interviews and lunch whenever I'm in Australia. Thank you, John, for sticking with me – here's to the next time!

This was also the year that I flew Nancy and Patti over to Berlin to join me on stage at the Waldbühne, singing backing vocals. For the first time since the days of the Pleasure Seekers we were able to perform as a family live in front of a huge audience, and I have it all on film. A magical moment for all three of us.

Family life in Essex had altered somewhat. Laura had finished school and was still rebelling big time, hanging around with all the wrong kind of people. I gave her an ultimatum: if she didn't want any more education she would have to get a job. She did, working in a pub twelve hours a day, seven days a week. It was very hard work, but not the best environment. I offered to pay for her to go to stage school, because I believed she would make a fine actress and she also has a marvellous singing voice, but she turned me down. We were butting horns every minute of the day, peaking in a huge fight after which packed her bags and left.

We didn't speak for a few days. When we finally did, I told her she owed me an apology and that if she wanted to remain in my home she would have to follow my rules! It's every parent's obligation to set boundaries. Laura refused, so I went to her bedroom in a fit of anger, threw all her things into black rubbish bags and delivered them to the front doorstep of the friend she was staying with. It was a no-win situation, but I had to put my foot down. I spent the next few months crying every time I went past her bedroom door, but I stood my ground.

Laura didn't move back in until October 2006, when she

brought Amy, her five-year-old-daughter. Part of me loved having my family back together again; the other part was dreading having to face our problems. But everything happens for a reason, and this was our opportunity to talk about it all. It all came out one evening in the kitchen, while Amy was watching cartoons in the TV room. I accepted that I had made some wrong choices, misjudging Laura's maturity, and apologised for that. Laura accepted that she made mistakes too, and was trying to get a fresh start and change her life around. I told her, 'I never did anything to hurt you. My motivation was always love.' A couple of days later, returning from a weekend trip to Germany to do some shows, I found this letter on the table.

To Mum from Laura,

There were times when on the road you wished for a comfy bed, in a small house with a nightlight for comfort. There were times when the noise of a party kept you awake. And there were times when I used to wish for a 'normal' mother. You know, the apron-wearing, cooking, sewing kind of mum. My mother is not a stay-at-home mum. But she gave us more love and care than most kids got. I know the guilt she felt when she had to go away from us. And, even though she is tough on stage, she is soft and gentle and beautiful inside and out. She taught us respect and right from wrong. So no, I didn't get to have an apron-wearing mother, and I don't know what it's like to have a stay-at-home housewife parent. But when I watch her on stage I am filled with pride. When I see how hard she has worked, I want to be like her. And, even though I make mistakes, she is always there for me, So really, even though I didn't have a 'normal' mum, when you look at what she has achieved, and continues to, what better role model could I have?

(*Guess I must have done something right. I do love her to pieces, but I guess we will argue for the rest of our lives. She's a lot more like me than she realizes – too sensitive, too opinionated, too rebellious. She once told me, 'You only want my opinion when it agrees with yours.' How true – and vice versa, Laura!*)

For his part, my son Richard wasn't happy at this time either. For a boy it's so important to have a male role model, especially in and coming up to their teenage years which are difficult even in the best of circumstances. I tried to be both mother and father, and that's impossible. You nurture, then you yell, trying to be tough and soft in equal measure. I could never seem to get the balance right, overdoing both the love and the authority. Here is Richard's contribution to my story, written in 2006 while I was writing this book. In fact I had to bug him and bug him to do it, and he only did so at the eleventh hour!

I am who I am now because of you. All the major lessons that I needed to learn in life were shown to me by you. Obviously from a very young age, watching you, I wanted to be in rock and roll myself, and now I'm doing it the hard way, the way you told me it should be done. Watching both sides of you, I learned that touching people is an amazing thing and so is being a normal mum. I believe that there is no stronger woman around than you. I more than anyone felt what you've been through, and you have come out of it as the woman you are – and I couldn't ask for anything better. But you *still can't cook* – only on the stage!

Richard has matured into a lovely man. He works in a guitar shop, which he loves, and plays guitar in his heavy metal band, FATE (who are excellent and do their own material, and if there's any justice will enjoy huge success). And finally he enjoys a healthy relationship with his father. He lives at home with me and I don't think he'll ever go (he knows he has it good here!).

Rainer at this time was about to experience his worst nightmare. While we were on holiday in Miami in November 1999 he got a phone call telling him his mother had passed away. Because Rainer was an only child, and had grown up without a father, they had an extremely close relationship. He was devastated, and we flew home that day in silence. I've never seen anyone so raw with emotion as he was at the funeral, and my heart went out to him. He said to me, 'As long as your mother is alive, you feel that you are protected.' How true! Even though my own mother has been dead for seven years I still automatically reach for the telephone every time I had a problem. You never get over losing your mother.

This was also the year I began to work on radio, having secured a series with producer Kevin Howlett called *Rockin' with Suzi Q*. I enjoy all kinds of communication, but I did have to get used to not having an audience – no applause, how weird! My radio show has proved extremely popular and at the time of writing we are in our seventeenth series. I was actually nominated for Music Broadcaster of the Year at the Sony radio awards in 2006. Didn't win, but it was an honour anyway. I've also done various special documentaries including *Glam Slam*, *Chinn and Chapman*, *The Mickie Most Story*, *The Janis Joplin story* and one on the making of *Rock around the Clock*. Kevin and I have also done a few series of *Heroes of Rock and Roll*, in which I get to interview all the heroes of my youth including my teenage heartthrob Dion.

This is where I feel I really shine, talking face to face with other artists – we speak the same language. This is a part of my career that I want to expand, on both radio and television. Watch this space!

The next couple of years were very 'spiritual'. I began to delve inside myself, wanting to purge all my mistakes and to help other people do the same. I felt I had come through so many tragedies that I had valuable lessons to share. Shirlie Roden, who is a sound healer, suggested we do workshops at the Festival of Mind, Body and Spirit in England, and we did the same in Australia too. We also recorded a self-help CD, *Free the Butterfly*, with spoken word over music. Another stretch for me. I needed and wanted people to realize that there was more to Suzi Quatro than met the eye. I'd always been an armchair psychologist, and now was the time to go public.

We came up with various workshop ideas and exercises to enable people to get back in touch with their real selves. But I think, in all honesty, that I was helping myself more than anyone else. The workshops were successful but short-lived: I guess I got what I needed very quickly, and didn't wish to repeat this part of my career. I emerged with a better understanding of both Suzi Quatro and little Susie from Detroit. (*So you and I were on a journey to deeper understanding, But the kids hated it and kept saying things like 'God, Mum, stop being so spiritual. This isn't you. Come back to earth!*)

For the children's sake I tried hard at this time to establish some kind of connection between Len and myself – one that we could both be comfortable with. We had had several discussions over the years since our divorce, either at my house or over the phone, when there were problems concerning Laura or Richard. Somehow we managed to establish a basic working friendship, although it would take several more years before we were close again.

During the time between 1991 and 2000 I had written a huge number of songs and wanted desperately to get another recording contract. This version of Suzi Quatro needed to be heard. It was grown up, but still rock and roll, and lyrically I had never been better. I went into the studio with Reg Webb, Andy Dowding and Shirlie to make demos. The search for a company began, and I eventually found someone who would allow me to make another album. Or so I thought!.

There I was, back in the studio recording. Jean Roussel was producing, and for musicians we had my original drummer, Dave Neal, Al Hodge (who has now sadly passed on) on guitar, myself on bass and Jean on keyboards. And, since Len and I were now on reasonable terms, I talked him into contributing. I still trusted his input and opinion as far as my music was concerned – after all, he had been there almost from the beginning. And so we began laying down tracks for this collection of songs that represented my life's journey up to that point. The man who'd given me a contract seemed to love and understand the direction I was going in. He told me all the things my artist's ego needed to hear: the songs were masterpieces, I was wonderful, I would be huge in the charts again, and he would be the 'conductor' of my new success.

One year later, we were still trying to finish. We even recorded a video for one of the songs, 'No Choice'. But all we got were delays and empty promises. Money seemed to be the problem: the studio wouldn't let us in to record until their bill had been paid. Eventually the company went bankrupt, making our agreement null and void. All the work I'd done was for nothing. I was so depressed that I considered giving up. Maybe the music business was finished with me. Maybe I was finished with it. But some need deep inside kept me going: I had to be heard just one more time.

Eventually I picked myself up out of the depression; I had to believe I would get another chance. (*Hope you don't mind me butting in at this point, Suzi, but there's one story that has to be told. You had gone into the studio that day, ready to record 'Shake Hands with Yourself', a very spiritual song. Len was there too, and the idea was to do it very bare with acoustic guitar, bass and vocals. He did his part and left. Then you sat down ready to do your bit. Before you began you started to talk about your mother, and how she died, in graphic detail – strange thing to do at a recording session. Then the mood changed, and you were ready to begin. Bass over, you went out to do your vocal and gave it everything.*

Afterwards you went back into the control room to listen to your performance. As the song began you flew away into the mood, gazing up at the studio wall and enjoying the sound. Then you saw it, like smoke drifting up to the ceiling. Most of you was deep into the mood, but a part of you wondered what the hell it was. At first you thought one of the machines had overheated, but the smoke continued to spiral up until it eventually formed the shape of a face. Hungarian Mom had a very distinctive look with high cheekbones, and damned if it didn't look like her! In your mind you spoke to this vision: 'Okay, Mom, so tell me, have you got wings now?' The smoke immediately bent into two wings, then back again, and the eyes took on a smiling look. At that point you silently began to cry. Then in your head you heard this message: 'And now, my Susan, you don't need me any more.' Then she was gone.

ADDING TO LIFE'S EXPERIENCES

You turned to Jean and said, 'Oh, my God! Did you see that!' You went outside and asked Shirlie to come down to the studio immediately. Did it happen or not? It's not something you could make up, and the environment was totally wrong for just imagining it – you were working. I believe you saw what you saw.

Then, about three weeks later, you were at a gig in Germany. Also appearing were the Rubettes. John Richardson – drummer and friend – is a Hare Krishna, and very spiritual. You told him you had an amazing story to share, and he said he had one for you too. 'No, me first!' You insisted. And so you began. As you got to the word 'mother' John started to gasp and wheeze, and when the story was over he was in tears.

'Suzi, my story was about your mother too. I had a dream a few weeks ago, and in it your mother told me to help you because she couldn't stick around any more. She said she had to come back down, and that her work on earth wasn't finished. She wouldn't be on your shoulder any more. I told my wife I couldn't possibly call Suzi Quatro and tell her that because I'd never even met her mom, so I did nothing. And now all my beliefs are validated.'

Well, Susie, can I just say I don't feel her around any more. My little sister says I needed to see her again. My husband says it was my imagination. Only I know the truth. I saw what I saw.

Mom was right that I still needed help. Laura had been living away from home since 1997, and we were still finding it difficult to communicate. She never knew, but I kept close tabs on her every moment. I tried to give her space, hoping she would be okay, but I believe she was too proud to come back.

I understood this, and in a way applauded her courage, but I missed her so – even the arguments! Finally, thank God, she fell in love. I always felt that all Laura needed was a good man and a good relationship to make her flower.

My first and so far only grandchild, Amy, was born in 2001. Laura wasn't married, though, and I wasn't happy about that. She was only nineteen, and in many ways still a child herself. A few days before the birth I was ill, and went to bed so that I would be all right for Saturday night's gig. But that morning, 15 June, I awoke early, with severe laryngitis. I called my agent and whispered down the phone that I couldn't do the gig. 'This doesn't happen, Suzi! You don't cancel.' Well, I was now. One hour later, I got a phone call to come to the hospital because the birth was imminent. I guess the big guy up in heaven wanted me to be there.

When I arrived, the room was full: ex-nanny Carol, Scott (the father), Scott's mother and a couple of Laura's friends. I really wanted to be there – for her, and for myself having been cheated out of Laura's own birth. She began to scream, and as the volume increased I made a lame joke: 'Oh, Laura, stop being such a drama queen!' Nobody laughed. I stood stroking my daughter's arm as she tried to breathe her way through the pain. Her labour had lasted eighteen hours. Finally Amy's head appeared, her face twisted up to the light, eyes closed. She opened them, looked left to right and slid back inside . . . then *whooosh*, out she came. I whispered into her ear, 'Welcome to the world. You are a very special little girl.'

A few moments later Len and Richard appeared at the door to share the moment. Len gave me a big hug and we were both crying – it was a real family moment which brought us all a little closer together. In the big scheme of things, I feel everything has been evened out. Amy's birth has enabled Laura and me truly to connect for the first time. We were both mothers now, and she began to understand all my fears, hopes and dreams. My mother had always told me, 'You don't understand until you have a child of your own', and she was right! From the moment Amy came into the world Laura and I grew closer and closer, and that truly is a miracle.

In 2003 Rainer and I bought a holiday home in Majorca, and it was here on 31 May that I got an unexpected call from Nicky Chinn. 'I'm afraid I have some bad news. You know that Mickie has been sick for a while? I'm afraid he passed away last night.' I hadn't known he was ill – apparently he didn't want anyone to know – and as a result I was in absolute shock. This man, who had been in my life since I was twenty-one, had gone with no warning, nothing. Rainer was booked to fly out a day before me and I was left alone in the house with my grief. I cried for most of the next two days. Once I'd pulled myself together I phoned Len, but, typically, he was too emotional to discuss it further at that moment. The next day, standing in the departure lounge ready to board my flight back home, I phoned Nicky Chinn back. Right there in front of all those people I broke into great big gulping sobs, and couldn't even speak.

When I got back I called Mickie's widow, Chris, and we talked for over an hour. Mickie had been feeling very tired for some time, she told me. Then one morning he went out on his usual jog with Chris's cousin Frankie, got a few feet down the road and announced, 'I can't do this. I have a tumour in my lungs.' He was right. He went into hospital, where they drained off an immense amount of liquid. Chris was visiting when the doctor came in, and knew what was coming by his actions alone. He shut the door, which was usually left open, pulled up a chair and sat down next to Mickie. Then he told him he had an incurable form of lung cancer.

After he had left, Chris said to Mickie, 'Why you?'

Mickie replied, 'Why *not* me?' He accepted his fate like a man.

As soon as I had finished talking to Chris I phoned Len again, and relayed the entire story. 'Do you think it's okay if I call her, Suze?' he asked tentatively. 'Of course,' I said, and he did. Half an hour later he phoned me back in tears. 'All I could do was cry, Suze. My God, Mickie's gone. Without him, you and I would not have had the life we've had.' Lennie was right!

The next day I had to go to the BBC and add something to my scheduled *Rockin' with Suzi Q*, and that was really hard. I told my producer, Kevin Howlett, 'Get this in one take – I can't do it twice.' We played 'Rolling Stone'. Goodbye, Mickie, and thank you for giving me my chance to be a success. And please keep watching over me. I always needed you, and always will.

Then, on 23 June that year, Rainer's father died, which heralded the rockiest year of our marriage. He was now truly an orphan, and contemplating his own mortality. At the funeral Rainer insisted, 'I won't cry.' He did, of course. As we left the cemetery I asked him, 'Did you say goodbye to your father?' 'No,' he replied, and we made our way to the restaurant with the other mourners. Finally it was time to drive back to the airport, and again I said, 'Rainer, you should have said goodbye.' We got into the car and set the navigation system for the airport, quickest route. Curiously, it did just the opposite, taking us down small lanes and around corners until we ended up right back at the cemetery. Rainer said, 'Guess I'd better go and say goodbye.'

A few months later he made the decision that he did want a baby after all, and suggested we try sperm donation with a surrogate mother. He threw this at me from out of nowhere. I couldn't believe it: I was fifty-three years old, and my husband was considering this step – especially since I had put my health on the line all those years ago when I had tried to give him a child. He wasn't normal for a year and put me through hell, and – there's no other way to say this – he broke my heart. For a while I wasn't even sure we would continue as a couple. But eventually his mood broke, and the talk of a baby ceased. I understand why he went through this process, but I'll never forget that pain.

During this rocky patch in my relationship with Rainer, Len and I truly became friends. He was now breaking up with his German girlfriend and we were able to clear the air and talk, finally, about our own break-up and take on the role of parents together. I was so happy that, after all we'd been through, the love and respect remained. Len has now become a hands-on father, and for the last two years he's cooked Christmas dinner for all of us. I can feel Mom, Len's parents and brother all smiling down. Even little Amy can feel it, and when she was only four years old responded to the family festivities in a most unusual way for such a small child. During dinner she picked up her little glass of milk, said, 'I want to make a toast', and waited for all of us – Lennie, his then girlfriend Bev, Laura, Richard, Rainer and myself – to be quiet. Then she stated solemnly, 'I just want to say Merry Christmas to everyone.' There wasn't a dry eye in the house.

* * *

Many of my gigs at this time were in Europe, often with the band Sweet on the bill. Rainer is a big fan of Andy Scott's, considering him the best rock guitarist of that era, and pushed me gently towards him. Eventually a meeting was arranged to discuss the possibility of Andy, Steve Grant (guitarist, and pianist with Sweet) and me working together on an album. The entire thing could be done at minimal cost because Andy had a studio at home, and to the three of us we only needed to add drums. Perfect.

They arrived with their guitars, and we settled down in the lounge. I went out to make coffee, returning with a big cardboard sign which read: 'Born Making Noise!', held it up to the boys and said, 'This is the first song we are going to write together, before you leave today.' And we did. We listened to the tapes of the recordings I had made with the now bankrupt record company, and I asked the boys to pick out those they felt they could relate to. We went in first with 'No Choice'. One week later we knew it was going to work. I felt comfortable with these guys, who are both talented and creative: I had my team. I guess everything happens for a reason. Without all the tragedy since 1991, I would not have written these songs. Without the disappointment of the previous company folding, I would not now be sitting here with Andy and Steve. And it must be said, that their interpretation of these songs was much more 'Suzi Quatro' than the previous recordings. We came from the same time zone, had shared the same producer/songwriters and had done many gigs together; we were kindred spirits. And so the recording of *Back to the Drive* began.

We worked around the clock, and when we had finished we sat in Andy's kitchen drinking wine and writing songs. It was a fullfilling, creative time and I was in my element, with no doubts that we would get a deal. I remember most of all the recording of 'Sometimes Love Is Letting Go'. I was standing in front of the microphone with my earphones on, waiting for the track to begin. As the title had come from my mother all those years ago, on her final trip to England, I silently said, 'Mom, I'm going to sing this just for you'. I closed my eyes, and gave it every ounce of emotion I had in me. I knew it was good; I could feel it. Song over, I looked up ready to receive my applause from Andy, who was sitting at the console with his head down, and Steve, who was operating the machines with his back to me. No one said a word. Then Andy raised his head, tears streaming down his face: 'That's it. That's the take. Can't be better.' I guess he felt it all the more because at this time his marriage was breaking up, and producing the album may well have given him something else to focus on.

I found time to squeeze in an appearance in Ireland on Phil Coulter's popular television show, *Coulter and Co.*, appearing with his studio band and with Mike Chapman. Mike and I sang 'Stumblin' In' together – it was magic. He also agreed to come on board as executive producer of my new album, giving Steve and Andy lots of tricks and tips along the way.

Every Christmas season Rainer and I take the kids, and now Amy as well, to York to see my best friend Berwick Kaler in his pantomime. But for me the 2004 one was a disaster. Since we were mid-album, Andy and Steve joined us. We walked around the town, had a bite to eat and then attended the performance, which since it was New Year's Eve ended with a cast party in the bar to ring in the New Year. We had brought with us several bottles of good champagne. I drank and danced and had a great time, finally, rather tipsy and argumentative, walking back to the hotel with Rainer around 1 a.m. He then went to the bar for one last drink with Andy, while I took off my make-up, got undressed and went to bed.

About an hour later, I awoke needing a wee. The room was small, and one of my cases was sticking out in the passageway leading to the toilet. Suddenly I was on the floor, but couldn't for the life of me figure out how I'd got there. It felt like someone had pushed me over. I tried to haul myself upright, but my left arm had a mind of its own and I couldn't. So, feeling very confused and disorientated, I used my right arm to get up. I then became aware of a little pain in my left arm, but just went back to bed. When Rainer came in a little later I told him, 'I think I hurt myself.' Oh, boy, did I ever!

I went back to sleep for a while, but woke a little later and couldn't get comfortable. I ended up holding my left arm in position with my right. By the morning, it was swollen up to three times its normal size and I couldn't get my clothes on; something was seriously wrong. On the drive home I dozed fitfully. Once we'd arrived Rainer wanted to take me to hospital, but I felt sick to my stomach and just wanted to sleep. Early next morning, however, I knew something had to be done. I woke him and said, 'Take me now.'

X-rays revealed that the arm was broken. Luckily, though, it was a clean break, so they just gave me painkillers and a sling and told me to rest. Unluckily, I had a sold-out tour in Australia in five weeks' time! The doctor told me there was no way I would be able to play bass guitar by then. I went home depressed as hell, feeling like the stupidest girl in the world.

Rainer then gave me some good advice. 'Suzi, I am a

promoter and the worst thing you can do is to cancel a tour. You must do it. Hire a bass player.' I thought for a minute, and realized he was right. I do pride myself on being professional. I called the boys in the band and let them know what was happening, and found a bass player. He came over and collected all the necessary CDs and tapes, and got to work. We would rehearse in three weeks.

Rainer and I had a trip booked to Miami the following week. I didn't want to go, feeling like I did; but he insisted, saying the sun would help the healing process. He was very supportive at that time, forcing me into the jacuzzi, massaging me, and waking up in the middle of the night to rub on special cream to take out the bruising and swelling. But I was not a happy bunny. I tried not to take the painkillers as they slowed down healing. On a couple of nights' though, I had no choice, because the pain was so bad that I couldn't even lie down. But slowly I started to mend. We flew back home, and rehearsal began in earnest. I had to learn the songs all over again, minus my guitar and minus my jumpsuit. I was naked.

Rainer didn't leave my side, even driving me to the airport to catch my flight to Sydney. After I had checked in I told him, 'You shouldn't have made me do this.' I was that scared. Maybe the audience would want their money back. It didn't help when Laura said, 'God, Mum, it's like going to see Jerry Lee Lewis without his piano!'

On the flight over I sat next to a man who coughed constantly. At first I figured he was a smoker; six hours later I realized he was ill. Two days after I got there, on the night before the first gig, I knew I'd picked up whatever he'd had. A doctor arrived at the hotel and gave me penicillin and a shot of cortisone, the magic drug which always relieved the swelling in my vocal cords. And so it was that on 8 February 2005 I stood on stage with no bass, no leathers, a broken arm, fever and a sore throat, and did the first show of the tour. What more could possibly go wrong?

After the opening two songs I said to the audience, 'It's great to be here on my twenty-second tour of Australia, and this time I wanted to give you something completely different. Be careful what you ask for, eh! You may have noticed I have a bass player on stage – and there's a reason for that. I've broken my arm.' ('*Ahhhhhh*,' went the entire audience.) 'But you know what? I don't give a shit. We are gonna rock and roll tonight!' And off we went. I had told the boys that I would attempt to play a few songs on my bass. They were dead against it, but I insisted – so what if it hurts? When we got to '48 Crash', bass drum pounding away, I went to the microphone and exclaimed, 'Goddam – I can't stand this any more. One mistake that doctor made: never tell Suzi Quatro what she can't do. Give me my bass!' I can't remember ever hearing such a cheer before. After three songs I turned and winced in pain to Andy, the drummer, then handed my guitar back to Glen.

For the first time. I did an unplugged section, talking about my life, playing bongos, doing songs from the Pleasure Seekers, a number from *Annie Get Your Gun* and my tribute to Elvis, 'Singing with Angels', which became the hit of the tour. And, because I had no choice, I rediscovered Suzi Soul, dancing like a stripper all over the stage. I found a whole new me. The show lasted two hours, and the promoter, Aldo Lennard, phoned Rainer three times to tell him it was the best he'd ever seen. As an artist, I had never been more satisfied.

The boys in the band and I have dubbed this one 'The Broken Arm Tour', and it heralded many personal changes. I never went out except for flights, soundchecks and gigs; the rest of the time I stayed in my room and did a lot of thinking. I felt I had broken my arm for a reason, and was desperate to figure out that reason.

There wasn't anything in particular that was wrong – it just wasn't right. First I put the blame on everyone else, but then I began to examine my life in detail. I came to the conclusion that, since remarrying, I had 'fractured' my world into a million pieces – kids in England, husband in Germany, and my career, all in separate boxes – and was trying to please everyone. There just wasn't enough of me to go round any more. I was determined to put the puzzle that was my life back together again, and I did.

I finally worked out that nobody was to blame for anything – I'd made all the choices myself, good and bad. I vowed to bring all the elements together, whatever it took. I was a mother, I was a wife, and I was a performer, and I vowed to be comfortable in my skin from this day forward. To say I came back from Australia a different woman is an understatement. Whatever was broken had now healed, both inside and out.

And now, ladies and gentlemen, after fifteen years please welcome the new album from Suzi Quatro. (*Hooray, hooray! At last!*) *Back to the Drive* was released on EMI worldwide in 2006. I had begun to write it in 1991 and so it represents a decade and a half of my life. Every single song tells a story. This is the album that just had to be heard, or I would die in the attempt. I believe it is my best effort to date.

The title track, 'Back to the Drive', was written and

produced by Mike Chapman. I'd worked with him at various times over the years, and he'd heard all the demos of these songs. 'Hey, Mike, I'm having a dinner party. The menu is all planned but I need an invitation.' Great song – reminded the public of the original Suzi Q and at the same time sounds up-to-date. Although every song on the album is hugely important to me, here are a couple of the highlights.

On 'I'll Walk through the Fire with You' (Quatro/Roden/Tuckey/Scott/Grant) I used Laura, Shirlie, Reg and Kate Webb to do backing vocals. Here's what happened. We had to go up to Leeds, and by the time we got back home it was quite late. Laura and I had had a small tiff, and she went straight up to bed. I sat on the couch with Shirlie, drinking red wine. 'God, doesn't she know? I'll walk through the fire for her.' Shirlie, as always, recognized a good idea and wrote it down. The next morning she, Laura and I sat on the patio with pen, paper and guitar. I said to Laura, 'We are going to write this song together.' It flew out, with hardly any effort whatsoever. As we were playing the song, and discussing the lyrics, Laura got very animated, waved her hands around and exclaimed, 'It's got to stop here' – meaning the song, of course. Then in her agitation she knocked a steaming hot cup of coffee all over my bare legs. I saw it coming, knew it was going to happen and didn't move. Yes, honey, it's got to stop here. These are the words that were in our hearts that day.

I'll Walk through the Fire with You

I'll walk through the fire with you,
I'll dream every dream with you
I'll look in your eyes, I'll tell you no lies
I'll walk through the fire with you

It's being too close that keeps us so far apart
We get burned by each other's light,
But we share the same heart
Too many words, too many fights,
Too many fears and sleepless nights

I'll walk through the fire with you
I'll dream every dream with you
I'll look in your eyes, I'll tell you no lies
I'll live your desire with you
I'll sing every song with you
I'll right every wrong for you
Higher and higher, let's dance on the wire
I'll walk through the fire with you

The truth is too hard, and you don't like the game when I play it
The truth is you hear what you wanna hear,
And I had to hurt you to say it
Are we so different, are we the same?
When push comes to shove
We're both to blame
It took so long to understand
And all you had to do was take my hand
And everything we say makes me walk away
Don't wanna hear it now
But it's gotta be said and how
Let's walk through the fire

The final track, the song that Steve, Andy and I wrote on our
first session together, says it all:

Born Making Noise

I got the toughest little act in this goddamn town
I got the meanest little mouth for miles around
Make no mistake about it, I ain't no shrinking violet
No need to contemplate it, just don't you underrate it
You can't intimidate it, this leather lady loves life

I was born making noise, I may be a girl but I'm one of the boys
I was born making noise, ain't nobody gonna put me down

I got the sweetest little smile in this neighbourhood
Killer eyes that vaporize, I'm bad when I'm good
Don't you debate about it, you want it I got it
No need to criticize it, no need to analyse it
But can you fantasize it . . . this leather lady loves life.

Well I'm the toughest little chick, don't you make me mad
I got the meanest little mouth, I'm good when I'm bad
Make no mistake about it, I ain't no shrinking violet
Don't try to keep me quiet, I'm loud I can't deny it
It's time to start a riot, this leather lady loves life.

I was born making noise, I may be a girl but I'm one of the boys
I was born making noise, ain't nobody, ain't nobody, ain't
      nobody
gonna put me down.

To promote the album I began an extensive media campaign.
It had been so many years since the last time that I'd forgotten
how crazy and tiring it was. After countless interviews, press,
radio and TV, it was finally all over and we went to Miami
for a much-needed rest. I looked 120 years old when I arrived,

but after several days of sun and relaxation I was back to normal. (*Back to 110, eh?*)

Next I was asked to appear on stage as Sonny Jacobs in *Exonerated* at the Riverside Studios in London. The play was based on the true story of six innocent people on Death Row in a Texas Jail. Up until now I had always been adamant that capital punishment was justified in some instances, and after I reading the script I knew I had to do it. Sonny had been put in prison with her husband for a murder they had not committed. Her husband was executed – the process went horribly wrong, and he took over fifteen minutes to die. Most nights I was in tears as I spoke Sonny's words about this terrible miscarriage of justice. It changed the way I feel about things, and I am now anti-capital punishment; I was so proud to have played a part in this production. Strangely enough a few months later I found myself appearing as the murder victim in an episode of the TV series *Midsomer Murders*. I got electrocuted on stage!

Also in 2006 I did my first and last reality show, *Trust Me I'm A Beauty Therapist*. Yes, I've been asked to appear on them all, and have always said no thank you. But this one appealed to me. They said it was a documentary/reality show with the emphasis on documentary. I would spend two weeks living in a house with seven other people, learning how to do the job. What appealed was that I would be out of my comfort zone and – horror of horrors – an employee. I enjoyed the challenge and it was extremely hard work: cameras in your face from 7a.m. until 9p.m. and working all the time. Those two reinforced what I already knew – that I am by nature an entertainer and a boss. And my curiosity about anything mildly related to reality TV is definitely over!

In October Rainer and I took another trip, this time to New York and Miami. We visited Mike Chapman at his home in Connecticut where he'd just spent a small fortune building a state-of-the-art recording studio. 'Our' future was discussed in great detail over a couple of bottles of good white wine. Mike wants to do the next album but – and this is a big but – he wants total control, and that's not something I relinquish easily! He said, 'I would like to take you back to your roots, pure and simple rock and roll, with real musicians in the studio laying down the tracks live. I know exactly what to do with you.'

I told him, 'I trust you, Mike, one hundred per cent, and I surrender to your vision.' Can't wait to get started! But before I wind things up I'd better let Mike have his say, otherwise there will be no album – over to you, oh master!

For more than thirty-five years I have watched the Suzi Quatro story from the inside: a unique perspective on an extraordinary and phenomenal career – a career that has taken her from a wide-eyed kid with a bass and a dream to rock 'n' roll legend and icon. Simply put, Suzi was born to be a star.

Her offbeat, individual style has created a road map for female rock stars of the future, opening the door like Alice in Wonderland for a girl's dream to become reality. As a role model Suzi has no peer. Her drive, enthusiasm and courage are overwhelming and infectious. Her musical integrity is refreshing and her dedication to being the best unquestionable. She is a precious stone in a field of ordinary rocks. Suzi Quatro is the real thing.

So this is my story so far, for it will continue – both professionally and personally – God willing. I still have goals

I want to achieve, and I still have my dreams. (*Don't forget your famous quote, Suzi Q, when that question was put to your all those years ago. 'When will you retire?' they asked. Your answer was, 'When I go on stage, turn my back to the audience and shake my ass, and there's silence . . . then I stop!*) Yes, little Susie from Detroit, and, along the same line of thinking, I sometimes have a fleeting moment of wanting to retire and express this in midnight conversations in bed with my husband of thirteen years. Do you know what always happens then, without fail? I do an unbelievably great gig, and realize it ain't time yet. I hope I will know when that time really does come. I don't want them to have to get the hook and drag me off the stage – but it's a possibility.

I've always been too busy to sit down and write my story, but now, at the age of fifty-seven, I've finally found both the motivation and the time to do so. Since writing this book, my entire focus has changed. Funny thing is, when you examine your life in microscopic detail you see it with different eyes. I had to relive everything, no matter how painful it was, including things I'd locked away in the memory of my heart many years ago. Believe me, it leaves you shaken *and* stirred. I realize now how single-minded I was in my quest for stardom, and the price I paid. The truth is that in every success story something or somebody is always left behind. I realize how difficult it was to try and balance being a successful musician, a mother and a wife, and expect to win on every count – you never can! I've realized I don't need my insecurites any more – I've found my voice at last. But the most amazing thing I've learned is that I don't need my ego. Why on earth have I been running so fast since the day I was born? I don't have anything left to prove to anybody or to myself; I am at peace. And isn't that what we all search for in this world – a little peace? I want to remain exactly as I am at this moment in time and enjoy the rest of whatever is left for me on this planet. I will take whatever comes my way, trust in destiny and, as we Americans say, *enjoy*! And now, just before I sign off . . .

While writing this book, I mentioned to Rainer that I had the perfect ending: I would have little Susie from Detroit and Suzi Quatro become one person. To which he replied, 'No, Suzi, that would be fiction!' Amen.